HERE ARE TH[...]
TO ALMOST A[...]
YOU CAN ASK ABOUT CATS.

Every aspect is covered. You'll find chapters on history, kitten care, health, nutrition, grooming, travel, protection, behavior, training, and much, much more.

You'll meet the twenty-eight pure-breed cats, learn their origins, their personality traits, and find information on each breed's conformation and recognized colors from the official Cat Fanciers' Association show standards.

If you're interested in learning all you can about cats, you'll find the facts. If you're thinking about choosing a cat, you'll find help in making an intelligent choice. This is an invaluable aid and reference guide cat owners will always want to keep handy.

SHIRLEE A. KALSTONE and her husband are members of the Empire Cat Club and have owned cats for many years. She writes for a number of magazines on cat and dog care and teaches at several animal academies. She is the author of *Dogs: Breeds, Care, and Training* as well as *The Complete Poodle Clipping and Grooming Book* and *The Kalstone Guide to Grooming Toy Dogs.*

By Shirlee A. Kalstone

The Complete Poodle Clipping and Grooming Book
The Kalstone Guide to Grooming Toy Dogs
First Aid for Dogs (with Walter McNamara)
The Art of Handling Show Dogs (with Frank Sabella)
Dogs: Breeds, Care, and Training

CATS:
Breeds, Care, and Behavior

Shirlee A. Kalstone

Illustrations by
Judith Tillinger Docherty

A DELL BOOK

Published by
Dell Publishing Co., Inc.
1 Dag Hammarskjold Plaza
New York, New York 10017

Dell ® TM 681510, Dell Publishing Co., Inc.

ISBN: 0-440-11218-4

Printed in the United States of America

First printing—December 1983

To the memory of Yum-Yum, and to Katie . . .

Yum-Yum, our beloved champion Burmese, died at two years of age of feline leukemia virus. My husband and I were desolate and believed we would never replace her softness and sweetness. No matter how many animals one owns in a lifetime, it's heartbreaking to have to put a young and precious one to sleep. Then along came Katie, an Abyssinian-American Shorthair-Siamese-Egyptian Mau (we think!) stray that I didn't want because it was too soon. It's a miracle that this bedraggled little creature survived. But she did. She's strong and healthy, and she's made a wonderful new place in our lives.

Contents

ACKNOWLEDGMENTS

I wish to express my everlasting gratitude to the many individuals and organizations who gave freely of their time and expertise during the writing of this book, especially to the Cat Fanciers' Association; *Cat Fancy* magazine (and Norman Ridker, its publisher); *Cats Magazine*; Jerry Benisatto of Felines of Distinction in New York; Mark Morris, Jr., DVM; T. D. Philips, DVM; Lon D. Lewis, DVM; F. J. Alberson, DVM; Edward A. Hoover, DVM; Valerie Matthews, DVM; Dr. William Hardy, Jr., Head of Veterinary Oncology of Memorial/Sloan Kettering cancer center in New York; William Campbell; the Morris Animal Foundation; Ellen Yanow and the Tree House Animal Foundation; the Animal Medical Center of New York; the A.S.P.C.A. of New York; the U.S. Department of Agriculture; the National Research Council of the National Academy of Sciences; Hill's; Gaines Professional Services; Gaines Dog Research Center; the Carnation Company; *DVM,* the Magazine of Veterinary Medicine; Dagmar Swanson of the National Dog Registry; I.D. Pet; Frani Lauda of the Niki Singer Agency; the Shorthair Cat Club of Southern New England (for letting me paraphrase some material on how cats are judged from their "Cats—Plain and Fancy" show catalog); and to all the cats whose photographs appear herein, especially John Nash's Arlo, Loretta Vogt's Mona, and Darrell Smith's Ptolemy.

My special thanks go to Judy Tillinger Docherty for her lovely illustrations and her enthusiasm about the project, and to Cynthia Vartan and Joan Raines.

Introduction

An enormous number of Americans have become enchanted with cats. According to a recent article in *Pets/Supplies/Marketing* magazine, 24 percent of all the households in the United States own a cat. Furthermore, 75 percent of all pet cats live in multiple-cat homes. Projecting these figures throughout the country, it means a total cat population of around 36 million! Americans spent close to $2 billion last year to buy cats and cat products, and feline adoptions from humane shelters increased more than 20 percent.

Tremendous changes have occurred in the feline world in the past three decades, and one could say that cats have become big business. As recently as the 1950s they were eating canned fish with no supplements or additives, and dry meal that had changed relatively little since the late nineteenth century. Manufacturers of pet foods, encouraged by the demands of cat breeders and owners, began to show an interest in feline nutritional requirements. The result was palatable and more nutritious food that not only enhanced the cat's satisfaction but also improved the cat's health and longevity. The pet food industry is immense today. Americans spent more than $1.4 billion, according to the John C. Maxwell report, for over one million tons of cat food last year.

Cats were sent outside to relieve themselves, prior to the mid-1940s, or they used shredded newspapers or sand in trays. The development of commercial litter products to absorb moisture and, in many instances, to release a deodorant to eliminate unpleasant odors has elevated the quality of sanitation for cats and their owners. Retail sales of all brands of cat litter, according to *P/S/M,* totaled more than $185 million last year.

The increased attention to pure-breed cats has been phenomenal. *Cats* magazine reports that a total of fifty cat shows were held throughout the United States in the early 1950s. Only seven breeds—Abyssinians, Burmese, "Domestics," Manx, Persians, Russian Blues, and Siamese—were eligible for showing at the time. Today there are hundreds of shows held in every part of North America, and more than thirty breeds are eligible for exhibition in one or more cat associations. The Cat Fanciers' Association, largest of the registering bodies, with around six hundred affiliate member clubs in the United States, Canada, and Japan, expects to sponsor three hundred shows throughout the country this coming year. Other groups constituting the North American Fancy will sponsor hundreds more (see "Cat Fancy Organizations" in Chapter XVI).

The most important advances, beyond question, have come in the field of health care and veterinary medicine. A few decades ago most small-animal practitioners directed 10 percent to 20 percent of their practices to felines, but today they are devoting 50 percent to cats. Diseases that were once considered incurable can be ministered to. Veterinary medicine has become highly advanced, and today's practitioners are armed with sophisticated procedures and drugs to treat many feline illnesses and injuries. Along with the improved procedures, the development of vaccines against feline panleukopenia (also called feline infectious enteritis) and other respiratory viruses has protected and lengthened the lives of millions of cats over the years.

The growing list of cat products and services prove that today's cats are more than just pets. Boutiques such as Felines of Distinction in New York City, The Legal Cat House in Swampscott, Massachusetts, the Feline Inn of Chicago, and the Cat House in Santa Monica, California, cater exclusively to cats, selling basic supplies and such specialized items as real fur mice; mechanical mice and spiders; cat Christmas stockings; three-story houses, pedestals, pyramids, or cat trees—some eight feet tall—covered with carpeting; the Tunnel of Love, a yard-long denim tunnel complete with catnip mouse at one end for kitty to play or hide in; velveteen hammocks; zippered kitty bags for trimming nails; the Gommelgrabber, a plastic container and Ping-Pong ball; and kits for plant-nibbling cats, complete with soil and seeds, that convert to a planter. Other stores specialize in cat items for people: engravings, prints, wall hangings, porcelains, teapots and cozies shaped like cats, mugs, T-shirts, tote bags, notepapers, and so forth. *Time* magazine reports: "There is a pet motel in Prairie View, Illinois, that offers apartments, roomettes and imperial suites to guest cats for up to $6.50 a day; letters sent by the vacationing owners are read to the animals. California, as always a seismographic chart of late-breaking obsessions, now has a cat resort, a cat department store, a cat rest home, a rent-a-cat agency, a cat dating service, cat psychics, cat acting coaches, and a special annual contest to judge cats' meows."

Advertising is probably the most visual proof of the cat's importance in modern society. On Madison Avenue the cat is a salesman par excellence of both feline and nonfeline products. The blasé Morris, the world's most famous celebrity cat, is cherished by millions of television viewers as ambassador for 9-Lives cat food. Chessie, the sleepy kitten, has been the symbol of the Chesapeake & Ohio Railway since 1933. Domestic and wild cats have symbolized elegance, beauty, charm, cleanliness, lissomeness, playfulness, mystery, and ferocity, and have advertised such products as perfume, automobiles, tires, breakfast cereals, beverages, liquor, and shoe soles.

Cats have become the darlings of the media. *Time* magazine put one on the cover of its December 7, 1981, issue, and devoted eight pages of its "Living" section to cats as well, declaring them a national mania. Seven of the top fifteen trade paperback best sellers early in 1982 were books about cats. The world's No. 1 "best-selling" feline is Garfield, a ravenous comic-strip character that prefers Italian cuisine to cat food. Millions of volumes about Garfield's escapades have been sold, and his creator, cartoonist Jim Davis, is the only author to have several books on the best-seller list at one time.

Cats are the aristocrats of pets, exotic creatures with natural style and elegance. They are quite friendly and devoted; nevertheless they remain mysterious and remote. Even playful kittens have a certain standoffishness that you will never find in puppies of the same age. Cats prefer to choose their friends—you have to win a cat's confidence and affection—yet there is still a certain aloofness. They love being stroked, but behind that purring demonstration of affection dwells a cool and shrewd mind that knows all the angles.

I The History of the Cat

Although at the present time the cat undoubtedly occupies a fairly important position, it is equally true that no other animal has experienced more varied changes in the estimation of mankind. The cat is now pampered and petted, exhibited, painted, and caricatured; it is provided with its own Burke and Debrett, and has its Clubs and shows, its boarding establishments and hospitals. This happy state has succeeded to a period of suspicion and ill-treatment, the latter having followed still earlier ages, when puss flourished—an object frequently of reverent homage.

—Anne Marks,
The Cat in History, Legend, and Art

The domestic cat, *Felis catus**, belongs to a family known as the *Felidae*, of the order *Carnivora* (or flesh-eating mammals), of the class *Mammalia*. Authorities differ in opinion as to how many species of cats

---

*Felis catus, a name given to the domestic cat by the Swedish botanist Linnaeus in 1758, is the scientific classification recognized by most zoologists, though others use *Felis domestica*.

inhabit the earth's land areas, but most place the number at between thirty-six and forty, including the domestic cat. Some other members of the *Felidae* include the lion, tiger, leopard, snow leopard, jaguar, puma, cheetah, lynx, serval, bobcat, African wildcat, European wildcat, margay, ocelot, and jaguarundi. In the past the cat family was divided into several genera, with the big roaring cats grouped in the genus *Panthera* and the smaller cats in the genus *Felis*. Today, however, most zoologists classify both small and large cats in the genus *Felis* with one exception, the cheetah, which is placed in its own separate genus, *Acinonyx*, because it differs from all other cats in several respects, most notably in that its claws do not fully retract.

Although the cat family members vary considerably in size and have adapted to diversified climates and environments, there is very little difference, with few exceptions, between the wild and domestic forms. The savage jungle predators and the feral domestics, along with the purring creature curled up in your lap, share many of the same physical characteristics and behavior patterns:

- A large, rounded head with a short face, permitting great force to be exerted on the teeth to break the neck of their prey.
- Large ears, pointed at the top, with open funnel-like bases to give them an acute sense of hearing. Cats can detect the slightest of sounds as well as ultrasonic frequencies much higher in pitch than can be determined by the human ear. The upper ranges of human hearing ability reaches 18 to 20 kilohertz (kHz) or 18,000 to 20,000 cycles per second. It is known that a cat's hearing ranges

The pupils of a cat's eyes react to the amount of brightness and, like a camera lens, they can expand and contract tremendously from (a) full circles in dim light to (b) narrow slits in bright light. (c) The third eyelid (the nictating membrane, or haw) is normally concealed by the lower lid. Its prominent appearance for long periods usually indicates that something is wrong, and that a veterinary examination is necessary to determine the cause of the illness.

from 20 to 60 kHz, or 20,000 to 60,000 cycles per second, and perhaps higher, the latter figure being several octaves above the limit of our hearing. To amplify this extensive range, the muscles of the *pinnae,* or external flaps, permit the ears to move backward, forward, and downward in a rotating manner to locate every sound.

● The largest and most highly developed eyes of all the carnivores. A cat's eyes are huge, set wide apart and forward on the head to give it an extremely broad field of vision. In many mammals the sense of smell is of primary importance in locating prey or perceiving danger, but cats depend principally on their eyes.* The pupils react to the amount of brightness and, like the aperture of a camera lens, they can adjust tremendously from narrow slits in bright light to a

*The sense of smell is highly developed, however. Although cats do not track prey by scent, smell is important in sexual determination, territory marking, and food identification.

full circle in dim light. A cat's eyes appear to glow at night when light shines on them because of an iridescent layer called the *tapetum lucidum,* located behind the retina, which reflects and amplifies the light to increase vision in semidarkness. Contrary to popular belief, cats cannot see in total darkness.

- The jaws and teeth of a fierce predator. A cat's powerful jaws help it to clutch prey in an unyielding grip. Adult cats have thirty teeth— sixteen in the upper jaw and fourteen in the lower—that act as devastating weapons. Six small incisors make up the center of the upper jaw, flanked by one dagger-like canine, three premolars, and one small molar on each side. Six small incisors are also located in the center of the lower jaw, followed by a large canine, two premolars, and one molar on each side. The carnassials—the last huge premolars of the upper jaw and the lower molars—intersect to perform a special shearing action. They operate like scissor blades, cutting the flesh into large pieces. Cats do not chew or crush their food but swallow it in chunks. Once the food has been swallowed, strong digestive juices thoroughly dissolve it and it is absorbed into the system.

- A tongue covered with barb-like backward projecting papillae that help to clean flesh from the bones of the prey. The raspy tongue projections also help a cat to keep its coat clean: to wash and comb the fur, to remove dirt and dead hair, and to smooth the fur when it becomes disheveled.

- Antennae-like whiskers, or vibrissae, that fan out sideways on the upper lip and stick out over the eyes. These act as sensory organs and relate the animal's almost imperceptible contact with an object to the roots implanted in the skin. When a cat creeps through small spaces or moves in darkness, the whiskers supply details on the surrounding environment and help the cat to determine if an opening is large enough for its body to pass through.

- Long and curved sharp claws on the forepaws to stun and grasp prey, to use in self-defense, or to climb to good ambush positions. The hind claws are not as curved or as tapered as the foreclaws, but they, too, are strong and efficient combat instruments. All cats except the cheetah can retract their claws into sheaths. The claws do not show on the footprints because they are retracted when not in use, but they can be extended instantaneously for grasping, tearing, fighting, or climbing. The clawing behavior of cats is a healthy and normal inherited trait, one that is especially vital to the survival of wild felines. Cats sharpen the claws of their forepaws on trees and other rough surfaces primarily to pull off the worn-out shells and make way for sharper ones. They remove the outer claws on their hind paws with their teeth.

- Digitigrade posture, which means that all cats walk on their toes on thick, cushiony footpads. Normally there are five toes on each forepaw and four on each hind paw, with pads (sensitive to touch and pressure) at the base of each toe plus a larger pad in the center of each paw.

- An expressive tail, with few exceptions, that possibly serves as a balance for running and climbing but definitely expresses variable moods and intense feelings.

- A lithe and agile body with a powerful and highly developed muscle system to enhance the cat's hunting proficiency. The extremely flexible skeleton permits a cat to bend and arch its back easily into a variety of positions. The collarbone is small; in some cats, in fact, it is completely absent. This frees the shoulder blade and lets the forelegs turn freely in almost any direction to enhance the cat's flexibility. There is great muscle power in the lower back and hind legs (enabling a cat to spring and pounce smoothly) as well as in the neck and shoulders. With the exception of the cheetah, cats are not very good runners.* Although they are agile and fast in short sprints, they cannot maintain high speeds for very long. Instead, they prefer to stalk their prey, crouching low, with head, body, and tail held more or less even, gliding gently forward to pounce suddenly on their prey rather than run to catch it.

These common characteristics lead zoologists to believe that all felines descend from a common ancestor and, since cats have not been as genetically altered by man as have dogs, that their behavior is influenced by patterns that developed centuries ago.

---

*The cheetah, the fastest four-legged animal in the world, is the least feline member of the cat family. It does not roar or purr but makes doglike howling or barking sounds. Cheetahs do not pounce on prey but depend almost entirely on speed to overtake it. They can accelerate to forty miles per hour within two seconds and quickly reach speeds of over sixty-five miles per hour.

The Cat's Prehistoric Ancestors

Theories abound regarding the evolution of the cat family, and probably we will never really know its origins, which have been the subject of speculation over a long period of time. But although the exact beginnings of the *Felidae* are obscure, all living carnivores can be traced back to the middle of the Eocene epoch, some forty-five to fifty million years ago, to a primitive ancestor known as *Miacis*. A small arboreal ferret- or weasel-like creature, *Miacis* had a long, slim torso with short, flexible legs and a tail as long as its body. Its feet had catlike retractile claws that made tree climbing very easy. At the close of the Eocene period the *Miacidae* greatly diversified and gave rise to the ancestors of the various carnivores known today, including cats, civets, dogs, bears, raccoons, hyenas, and others.

At the dawn of the Oligocene epoch, about forty million years ago, the descendants of *Miacis* became gradually less arboreal and more adapted to life on earth. During the Oligocene period it is believed that two distinct types of early cats with short limbs and specialized teeth and skulls, but with more primitive skeletons than in true cats, descended through *Miacis*. The first, *Hoplophoneus*, became the progenitor of a family branch that eventually produced *Smilodon*, the powerful saber-toothed tiger. *Smilodon* was a hulking, lion-like ferocious beast that inhabited North America, Europe, Asia, and, eventually, South America. The term "saber-toothed" is derived from its extremely long and saber-like upper canine teeth, which struck downward with the mouth wide open in a stabbing or slicing action. As its fangs grew progressively larger during the Miocene epoch (twenty-five to ten million years ago), the saber-toothed tiger became the most abundant and important member of the *Felidae*, feeding on huge thick-skinned and slow-moving herbivores such as giant pigs, rhinoceroses, and elephants. Saber-toothed tigers began to decline during the Pliocene epoch, which began about ten million years ago, and finally became extinct about 13,000 B.C. It is believed that as the mammoth land creatures came to an end, so did the saber-toothed tiger when he could not adjust to catching and killing the smaller and faster-moving prey.

The second descendant of the *Miacidae, Dinictis,* is believed to be the progenitor of all modern cats. The various species of *Dinictis* were predatory animals: smaller, faster, more intelligent and agile than the saber-toothed tiger, with smaller but more efficient teeth for killing and eating. *Dinictis* also had longer and more flexible legs to run swiftly after victims, which were abundant at the time due to the development of grass over a great part of the world, and its claws were fully retractile for better grasping and tearing of prey.

The descendants of *Dinictis* subdivided into many different species over the next several million years, and all are probably related to modern cats. But the infinite missing links make it impossible to ascertain any distinct line of evolution. Although archeological excavations throughout the world have yielded evidence of primitive man's relationship with dogs, horses, goats, sheep, pigs, and cattle, no cats appear on Paleolithic cave paintings or in rock carvings. Their fossilized remains have been uncovered near prehistoric settlements alongside those of other wild carnivores, but it is impossible to determine whether these animals were killed for food or, more likely, for their pelts. There is a mysterious void surrounding the spread of *Dinictis* and the time from extinction of *Smilodon* to the appearance of the cat as man's companion and house pet in Egypt some five thousand years ago.

The Domestication of the Cat

There is no documentary evidence regarding the exact origins of the domestic cat, but we do know that cats were domesticated long after dogs, goats, sheep, and cattle. It is assumed that domestication first occurred in Egypt about five thousand years ago and involved the African wildcat (*Felis libyca*), a yellowish or buff-colored animal (with pale markings similar to today's domestic tabby), and possibly a larger jungle cat, *Felis chaus*. Indeed, the majority of Egyptian cat mummies preserved in museums throughout the world, and cat skulls from ancient Egyptian cemeteries and from tombs at Gizeh, are of the *F. libyca* type while a few resemble *F. chaus*.

Domestication could have taken place in many ways, but it is likely that it did not happen overnight and instead developed over myriad years. The first friendships between cat and man may have begun possibly when hunters killed small jungle cats and brought home their orphaned kittens as "pets." As time passed a primitive type of selective breeding must have occurred, with a preference for those animals that could survive in a human community, grow to be an adult, and breed successfully in confinement. By the time of the Middle Kingdom (2181-1567 B.C.) cats are depicted in wall paintings as pampered house pets.

When the Romans introduced these tame Egyptian

cats to the European continent, it is believed that they interbred with the native European wildcat (*Felis silvestris*), a slightly larger and sturdier and more whiskery animal with tabby-like markings, and that the resulting offspring became the progenitors of present-day cats. There is no doubt that both *F. libyca* and *F. silvestris* will breed freely with each other as well as with domestic cats. Many authorities consider these two wildcats as different geographical races of the same (instead of separate) species, and subdivide them as *Felis silvestris silvestris* and *Felis silvestris libyca*.

In *Domesticated Animals from Early Times,* Juliet Clutton-Brock, a principal scientific officer in the Department of Zoology at the British Museum, writes that in 1907 the taxonomist R. I. Pocock studied the probable origins of the English domestic cat and based his views on features of skull shape and pelage. His work still stands as an accurate account, and although much work has been done in recent years on the genetics of coat color and pattern, no new results have emerged to deny Pocock's conclusions that all present-day breeds of domestic cats are descended from the European wildcat, *F. s. silvestris,* and the African wildcat, *F. s. libyca.* Clutton-Brock adds that Pocock supposed it was the latter species that was domesticated first and that interbreeding then took place with the northern wildcats. This theory is supported by Pocock's assertion that when *F. s. silvestris* is interbred with *F. s. libyca,* the offspring resemble the domestic striped tabby in their hair patterns more than they resemble either parent.

The Domestic Cat Through the Centuries

At the dawn of history, while some areas of the world were in primitive stages of development, the

Middle East—particularly Egypt—abounded with activity. As organized society began to emerge the domesticated cat quickly became an important part of Egyptian life. In fact, the time of the pharaohs was truly the Golden Age of the cat because the reverence and attention bestowed on it has never been equaled.

The cat was adored and treated with great affection in Egypt, where it was called "mau." Wall paintings from the tombs of the pharaohs as well as bronze sculptures depict a sleek, leggy, short-haired creature very similar in type to present-day Abyssinians. Paintings from various periods show cats inside the house, sitting on their master's or mistress's lap or under chairs, eating delicacies, or wearing fancy collars, golden earrings, and necklaces. Wealthy Egyptian men were passionate sportsmen and took along packs of cats when they went wildfowling, training them to flush marsh birds from the reeds. Plutarch tells us how carefully Egyptians planned the breedings of their cats, making sure that male and female were compatible. Herodotus wrote that when a cat died, all the family members shaved off their eyebrows as a gesture of mourning and refused to touch food present in the household at the time of the cat's death. Elaborate plans were made for embalming the cat, and the body was preserved by the same method that was used for humans. The preservation took many days, and each step was governed by strict religious ritual. Once prepared, the body was wrapped with strips of linen (sometimes twenty or more layers), with resin applied between every few layers as a binding agent. Sometimes the body would be placed into an elaborate wooden coffin decorated with a likeness of the deceased, or a mask depicting the dead cat would be placed over the mummy's head. It was then buried in a special ceremony together with its favorite toys and a few mice for afterlife enjoyment. Close to a century ago archeologists discovered the remains of more than 300,000 mummified cats buried in subterranean tiers on the site of the Temple of Beni Hassan, dating from the Twelfth Dynasty of the Middle Kingdom, or about 1900 B.C.

In parts of Egypt from around 1570 B.C. the cat was regarded as sacred to the goddess Bastet (or Bast or Pasht, a name thought to be the origin of the word *puss*), the spiritual ruler of Bubastis, a city east of the Nile delta. Bast, who represented fertility and maternity, is usually depicted with a cat's head on the body of a woman, carrying a mystical instrument called a sistrum adorned with the heads or figures of cats.

Sacred cats were worshiped in Bast's temples and safeguarded by priests twenty-four hours a day. On Bast's feast days, which according to Herodotus were the most lavish in Egypt, cats were adorned with garlands and paraded through towns. The Egyptians believed that Bast was the representative of the moon and, as such, the Sun God's eyes during the darkness. They thought a cat's eyes glowed in the dark because, like Bast's eyes, they absorbed the sunlight during the day and discharged it at night. The mysterious waxing and waning of the cat's eyes, like the phases of the moon, also signified the animal's close relationship to that heavenly body.

At the height of the cat's prestige, to kill one deliberately was a crime punishable by death. King Cambyses, the son of Cyrus the Great of Persia, capitalized on the Egyptian reverence for cats in 525 B.C. when he invaded the walled city of Pelusium.

Legend has it that he ordered each of his soldiers to carry a live cat as a shield before him as the army advanced upon the town. When Cambyses threatened to throw all the cats over the wall, the Egyptians surrendered because they feared the beloved animals would be killed.

It is probable that domestic cats were household pets in India around 2000 B.C., for they are mentioned in Sanskrit writing of the period. Legends and fables about cats are found in several compendiums, among them the *Mahabharata,* the *Ramayana,* and the *Panchatantra.* The cats were called "mouse eaters," and their cunning rat-catching qualities were extolled.

Cats probably arrived in China at about the same time as in India. Chinese legend has it that they originated from a cross of the lion and the monkey. They were called "mau" or "mao," the name the Egyptians gave to the cat, and were cherished by Chinese ladies. Although they were highly prized for their rat-catching abilities, there was also a saying that "The coming of a cat to a household is an omen of approaching poverty." The Chinese often used the eyes of the cat as a clock and believed that one could accurately tell time with the changing of the size of the pupils. One author wrote that "the pupil of the cat's eye marks the time: at midnight, noon, sunrise, and sunset, it is like a thread; at 4 o'clock and 10 o'clock, morning and evening, it is round like a full moon; while at 2 o'clock and 8 o'clock, morning or evening, it is elliptical like the kernel of a date."

It is believed that cats arrived in Japan at a much later date, possibly about the same time as Buddhism, early in the sixth century A.D. It was the custom to keep two cats in every Buddhist temple to protect the religious scrolls from damage by vermin, and to employ them in the silk industry for the same reasons. Cats were so cherished in Japan that they were kept on leads until well into the seventeenth century, when the government decreed that they should be free.

Although the cats of Egypt were considered sacred and jealously guarded by the Egyptians, Roman soldiers are credited with carrying cats to Greece and Rome. The ancient Greeks do not appear to have been too interested in the cat as a pet, but they were associated with certain goddesses. The Greeks believed that during the creation of the world, the sun and the moon caused all animals to exist. The moon, they thought, spawned the cat, and as such the animal is associated with the Greek moon goddess, Artemis (with whom Bast is also identified). It was believed that Artemis assumed the shape of a cat when the gods fled to Egypt to escape the monster Thyphon. Black cats were linked with Hecate, the ruler of Hades, and considered to be an omen of death. The cat (with a rat) is also identified with Demeter, the Greek goddess of grain.

The Roman counterpart of Artemis, the goddess Diana, is closely connected with cats. The poet Ovid (43 B.C.–17 A.D.), in his book *Metamorphoses,* writes that Diana assumed the shape of a cat when the gods had to flee from the giants. The cat was regarded as the spirit of liberty in ancient Rome, perhaps because of its unrestrained ways and independent attitude. When Tiberius Gracchus (163–133 B.C.) built the Temple of Liberty, he included a statue of the Goddess of Liberty with a cat beneath her feet. Pliny the Elder (A.D. 23–79) defined the cat's physical attributes in his work *Natural History*. Although no remains of cats have been uncovered at either Pompeii or Herculaneum, several mosaics bear witness to their presence, notably one of a spotted tabby with gleaming eyes firmly holding a bird down with one paw, and another of an ornery housecat hungrily eyeing two parrots and a pigeon perched on the rim of a birdbath, both artifacts now in the collection of the Museo Nationale in Naples.

Roman soldiers and Phoenician traders took cats to Europe and Britain to protect their ships and granaries from rats and mice. It is believed that before the Roman invasion of Britain in 55 B.C., only wildcats lived there, which were hunted for their skins. Even though Julius Caesar feared cats intensely, skeletal remains of house cats have been discovered in Roman villas throughout Britain. Remains of domestic cats have also been unearthed at Roman fortresses and trading stations in Holland and Switzerland.

At a later date European explorers, traders, and colonists would carry the cat to every part of the world. Thanks to the exploratory and commercial instincts of man, the waters would become busy thoroughfares for cats. As soon as man ventured out to sea and mastered the art of navigation, cats took up residence on ships to keep them free of vermin. As fast as man spread, the cat went with him.

During the early Middle Ages many saints were associated with cats. Saint Agatha was called "Santo Gato" ("Saint Cat") in the old province of Languedoc because she was said to appear as an angry cat when she wished to punish women who worked on her feast day. The wise Saint Jerome, the chief preparer of the

Vulgate version of the Bible, who lived between A.D.
340 and 420, is frequently shown with his domestic
cat as well as his lion. Saint Gertrude of Nivelles, the
patron saint of cats, widows, and travelers, is usually
depicted with a cat and was known to be invoked by
those who were infested with mice. Saint Yves of
Treguier, the patron saint of lawyers, is depicted with
or characterized as a cat, possibly to represent a
symbol of liberty. Saint Francis of Assisi declared that
men were "the brothers of all living creatures." In one
Italian legend, when a plague of mice sent by the
Devil begin to gnaw at Saint Francis's robes and chew
at his feet, a cat magically springs from his loose
sleeve to save the beloved saint. The cat must have
been highly esteemed by Celtic monks, too, for there
are beautiful illustrations of them in both the Lindis-
farne Gospels (seventh century) and the Book of Kells
(eighth century), the latter called the greatest achieve-
ment in Irish manuscript illumination.

Persuasive evidence of the value of the cat is found
in remarkable laws and decrees organized by the
courts of kings about a thousand years ago. In the
famous Welsh laws codified in 914 by King Hywel
Dda (Howel the Good), animals were divided into
beasts, dogs, and birds, and a value of worth ranging
from one to four pence was placed on cats, based on
the services they rendered and the rank of their
owners. Howel the Good's laws stated:

> The worth of a cat and her *tiethi* (qualities) is this:
> 1. The worth of a kitten from the night it is
>   kittened until it shall open its eyes is a legal
>   penny.
> 2. And from that time, until it shall kill mice, two
>   legal pence.

3. And after it shall kill mice, four legal pence; and so it always remains.

King Henry I (1068-1135), the son of William the Conqueror, ruled that anyone who killed a cat would be fined fifty bushels of corn, the value of the animal in relation to the grain it protected from vermin.

The cat's value was greatly enhanced between the eleventh and fourteenth centuries when Christian knights returned home from the Crusades in the Holy Land. The Crusaders are believed to have brought with them from the East the first long-haired cats to be seen in Europe. They also carried back the dreaded Black Death, for in the holds of their ships lurked the formidable Asiatic black rat that bore in its blood a form of the bubonic plague that spread over Europe in the fourteenth century and is estimated to have killed a quarter of the population. The rats eventually diminished in number, but despite the cat's vigilance they did not totally disappear. It has been argued, however, that cats saved European culture from destruction!

The cat's good fortunes came to an abrupt end in the late Middle Ages. It was not fated to be highly regarded in Christian Europe because the Church, in its renouncement of paganism, succeeded in lowering the status of this once venerated animal to that of a devil. Pope Clement V suppressed the order of the Knights Templars with the help of King Philippe IV of France early in the fourteenth century, and many of the Templars confessed under torture that they rejected the orthodox Catholic Church, denied the validity of all clerical hierarchies, and worshiped the Devil in the shape of a black cat.

The cat's torment heightened about the middle of

the fourteenth century with the revival in Germany of a pagan fertility cult immortalizing the Norse goddess of love and fertility, Freya, or Freyja, whose chariot was said to be drawn by two black cats. (Freya is frequently identified with the Greek goddess Artemis and her Roman counterpart, Diana.) Cats played an important part in cult rites, which also included orgies and bacchanals among the participants. The Church decreed that these pagan rites demoralized its foundations and, in addition to persecuting the devotees of Freya, accused the cat of being a disciple of Satan and took shocking action that involved torture, witch hunts, and burnings throughout Europe.

When the persecution of witches was sanctioned by Pope Innocent VII, a considerable number of guiltless people were tortured and went to the gallows, or were burned alive at the stake, simply because they owned cats and were thought to be witches. Witches and their cats were blamed for everything: floods, fires, illness, deaths, shipwrecks, crop failures, foul weather, and any other misfortune. People believed that witches and even Satan could appear in the form of a cat, and that every follower of Satan owned a cat. Grueling tests were concocted for "witches" and their cats that were impossible to pass. Witch trials were conducted in England and in Europe, and the judges inevitably passed down death sentences. The victim in 1566 of one of the first trials of English witches was Elizabeth Francis and her white, spotted cat named Sathan. Sathan supposedly fed on the blood of his mistress and then performed evil deeds.

Because cats were thought to be the Devil's creatures, they were tortured and massacred in every

European country in the name of religion. They became a favorite sacrificial victim on holy days in ceremonies presided over by priests. Sacks of cats were burned alive in hilltop bonfires during the Festival of Saint Jean in France. It was customary in that country to roast cats alive to drive away evil spirits on Shrove Tuesday and Easter in bonfire ceremonies. Cats were thrown off the tops of cathedral towers in Belgium during Lent. Nothing was too horrible for the creature that had been worshiped in ancient Egypt, and the hellfire, damnation, and killing continued for several centuries. The madness subsided eventually, but it would be a long time before the cat would regain its former status. Even well into the eighteenth century black cats were still tortured and burned alive in parts of Scotland in a grisly ceremony, *Taigheirin,* to secure from the gods the gift of second sight.

Domestic cats first came to North America on the Mayflower with the Pilgrims. And as new settlers arrived with their pets over the succeeding years, the feline population gradually increased. The cat clearly established its worth as a killer of vermin early on, but it became associated with witchcraft, evil, and superstition too in New England. People believed that when a cat jumped over a body that had been laid out for burial, the dead person would turn into a vampire. Increase Mather, the famous New England Puritan clergyman, observed in the late seventeenth century: "There are some who, if a cat accidentally comes into a room, though they neither see it nor are told of it, will presently be in a sweat and ready to die away." The cat's fortunes in the New World changed abruptly in 1749, however, when the colonies were plagued with black rats and they came to the rescue to save precious supplies of grain. By the mid-eighteenth century the cat was back in favor in most parts of the world, and was highly regarded by writers, poets, painters, and sculptors.

The discoveries of French chemist and bacteriologist Louis Pasteur (1822-95) in the nineteenth century helped to strengthen the cat's position in a suddenly hygiene-conscious Europe. People began to believe that most animals were dirty and carriers of disease-producing bacteria, and they avoided touching them. The cat—unsociable to other animals and a paragon of meticulous grooming—became the exception. The general public opened its doors, and, at last, the cat was emancipated. It is recorded that cats were imported from Europe at exorbitant prices during the California Gold Rush. The nineteenth century also heralded the establishment of the pedigreed cat, or the mating of two selected animals to produce offspring superior to their parents. The first Siamese cats arrived in the Western world around the middle of the nineteenth century. The origins of the Siamese are shrouded in mystery, because for generations they had been vigilantly protected by the royal household in Bangkok. Siamese kings believed that their cats were sacred and that they immortalized the spirit of the dead. When a king or royal prince was buried, his favorite cat would be consigned live to the tomb along with the body. If the cat made its way through a small opening in the roof of the mausoleum, it was assumed that the dead man's soul had entered into the cat's body.

Although cats were informally exhibited at many agricultural expositions in the 1860s, the first organized show took place at the Crystal Palace in London in 1871, the conception of Mr. Harrison Weir, an artist and a cat lover. The 160 short-haired and long-haired feline competitors created such a sensation that other shows followed in rapid succession. Cat shows and the breeding of pedigreed cats became fashionable in English society. The wealthy, accompanied by a staff of servants, exhibited prizewinning cats at shows all over the country. The cat's popularity was enhanced by Queen Victoria, who owned a pair of blue Persians, when she attended cat shows regularly and often presented trophies and prizes. Although early cat shows and the matings of pedigreed cats were largely diversions for the wealthy, cats quickly captured the imagination of people from all walks of life. The first British cat club was organized by 1887, laying the groundwork for present-day cat fancy organizations devoted to registering and showing cats. By the turn of the century splendid British pedigreed cats were being exported to many other countries.

In the United States the breeding and exhibition of pedigreed cats became popular after the first professionally organized show was held in New York in 1895 at Madison Square Garden. The American Cat Association (ACA), the first club in the United States, was founded in 1904, followed by the formation of the Cat Fanciers' Association (CFA) in 1906. Today the CFA is the largest cat fancy association, with around six hundred member clubs in the United States, Canada, and Japan.

The fortunes of the cat may have fluctuated throughout history, but the fundamental animal has changed very little. Edward Topsell, an English author, captured the quintessential cat in his zoological work of 1607: "It is needless to spend any time about her loving nature to man, how she flattereth by rubbing her skin against one's legs, how she whurleth her voice, having as many tunes as turnes . . . how she beggeth, playeth, leapeth, looketh, catcheth, tosseth with her foot, riseth up to strings held over her head."

II Choosing Your Cat:
A Guide to the Breeds

*Cats, as a class, have never completely got over the
snootiness caused by the fact that in ancient Egypt they
were worshipped as gods. This makes them prone to set
themselves up as critics and censors of the frail and
erring human beings whose lot they share.*

—P. G. Wodehouse

Recent studies indicate that cat ownership is on the
increase. That's not extraordinary, because cats make
ideal pets for several reasons: They are clean and
fastidious; they are affectionate; they demand little
from their owners; they don't have to be walked (cats
can live long and happy lives without ever going
outside); and they are easily trained to use a litter box.
Most dogs, conversely, need regular outdoor exercise,
forcing a rigid schedule on their owners or a guilty
conscience. And a cat's litter cleanup seems comparatively simple when one considers the stringent canine
scoop laws imposed on many urban Americans.

Cats come in a variety of colors and coat patterns.
These variations, however, are limited when one con-

siders size and dissimilar physical features. Through the centuries dogs, from the tall Irish Wolfhound to the tiny Chihuahua, have been selectively bred by human beings to be hunters, herders, guards, war dogs, and companions, while the cat's principal occupation has been to hunt and control vermin. Although cats have been associated with humans for thousands of years, they have rarely been intentionally bred for specific purposes, and their conformation and natural hunting tendencies remain basically unchanged.

Choosing a cat is like adding a new member to your family, one that you will be living with for perhaps the next *fifteen to twenty years*. You will experience much enjoyment, companionship, and endless devotion if you select your cat carefully and wisely.

Although there are many purebreds and mixed breeds to choose from, anyone can find the right cat with careful consideration. Every kitten is adorable, so how do you find the right one for you? Here are some questions and answers to help you decide the kind of cat that's best for your life-style, some suggestions about where to acquire it, and how to ensure that it will be healthy.

Can You Afford a Cat?

Owning any pet can be costly. The expense of raising a purebred or a mixed breed are the same; only the purchase price is different. And the initial cost of a cat is insignificant compared to what you will spend for its upkeep during the animal's lifetime. The consumer price index has risen dramatically in recent years, and everyone, including pet owners, has been affected by increased costs. In these inflated times you will spend the most on veterinary care and food, but supplies, accessories, toys, treats, the cost of neutering, and boarding fees (while you are on vacation) must be considered also.

Purebred or Mixed Breed?

A pure-breed cat is one whose sire and dam belong to the same breed. The advantage of choosing a purebred is that you can reasonably predict the cat's size, type, personality, conformation, coat, and markings. Purebreds are more expensive than mixed breeds, but if you want to breed or show, then you must buy a purebred of breeding or show quality.

A mixed-breed or random-bred cat is one whose ancestors are of mixed-breed origin or unknown. If you just want an affectionate pet and have no desire to breed or show, you may be willing to settle for a kitten or cat without a pedigree. Some random-bred cats do look very similar to certain purebreds. It may be hard to imagine how others will look when they mature, but it's possible to end up with an exotic, "wild-looking" creature that possesses the attributes of several breeds. Cats whose type and coloring do not conform to any existing breed standard, incidentally, can be exhibited at cat shows in the Household Pet class. (See Chapter X for more information about cat shows.)

Male or Female?

The choice of male or female is a matter of personal preference if you plan to have your cat neutered, for both make excellent pets. Unaltered males or toms, however, are generally more energetic, more territorially aggressive, and more inclined to roam the neighborhood. When toms reach maturity, around eight to nine months of age, they become possessive about their home or territory and begin to

spray urine to mark it out. Owning an unspayed
female or queen can be a nuisance to some people,
because she will start coming into heat at around six
to eight months of age. Each cycle lasts about three
weeks, during which time the queen emits noisy
courtship cries and becomes quite restless. Unless she
is bred or spayed, the heat periods will recur frequently at certain times of the year. If a male or
female is not intended for breeding, neutering will
solve these annoyances as well as the problems of
accidental matings and unwanted litters.

Shorthair or Longhair?

Cat breeds generally are divided into two groups:
longhairs and shorthairs. Although all cats need
regular grooming to keep their coats in good condition, longhairs must be combed and brushed *every day*
to prevent tangles from forming and dead hair from
accumulating. Shorthairs require less frequent attention, and the grooming procedure is much easier. If
you don't have much time to devote to grooming, do
your potential new friend a favor and choose a short-
haired breed.

Kitten or Adult?

Kittens adapt quickly to new homes, children, and
other pets, and it's charming to watch them grow up.
But a tiny kitten, like a baby, requires observant care,
for you will be responsible for its training, social
experiences, and other requirements that will affect
its health and behavior as an adult cat. If you decide
on a kitten, it should be at least eight weeks of age
before it moves into your home. Kittens need maternal nursing and cleaning, and play patterns with
littermates, and the best time for separation from the
nest is between six to eight weeks of age.

If you do not want the responsibility of raising a rambunctious kitten, consider an adult cat. The adjustment period takes a bit longer, but you know what you are getting in terms of looks and temperament. Older cats do adjust nicely to new life-styles, especially when the new owner is loving and tender, and tries to understand the cat's emotions and previous experiences.

How Much Will a Kitten or Cat Cost?

It is impossible to say exactly how much you will pay for a kitten or an adult cat. The price depends on the cat's age, conformation, and breeding or show potential, and the expenses involved in raising the litter. You should be able to buy a fine-quality pet within the $150-$250 range, depending on the breed. A "pet" means just that—you are not buying breeding or show quality.

Breeding and show quality cats start at $350. The finer the quality, the higher the price (sometimes in the thousands), especially if a cat has placed well in shows. The cost may be greater, but so too is the pleasure of showing or breeding from a superb specimen.

If price is the object, consider adopting a cat. Millions of cats of all ages (some purebreds) in animal shelters all over the country are longing for homes. They cost very little and make wonderful and affectionate pets.

The Responsibilities of Cat Ownership

Ownership of any living creature is a very responsible job. Just as parents are responsible for the actions of their children, cat owners have certain responsibilities to both their cats and their communities. The cat is entitled to love, attention, nutritious food, clean living quarters, training, discipline, regular grooming, immunity from certain infectious diseases, and regular veterinary care.

Cats should remain indoors; but if they do go out, they should be kept under control and not permitted to become the neighborhood nuisances or to interfere with the rights of others. Allowing a cat to roam free to damage the neighbor's garden, to raid garbage cans, kill birds, fight with other animals, scratch or bite children, to create disturbances at night, or to breed indiscriminately, is thoughtless. Because of irresponsible cat owners many communities have solved these and other perplexing problems by passing strict laws regarding the control of cats as well as dogs. Many cities throughout the United States now require cats to be licensed and to have rabies shots. Other ordinances limit ownership to a small number of cats and dogs, or any combination of the two.

Special Considerations
Cats and Children

Cats make jolly companions for children, and they encourage healthy emotional development and socialization as well. Pet ownership stimulates a child to develop humane instincts and the compassion for other living creatures. More importantly, it teaches a youngster that giving love and being loved involve responsibility and sharing.

As soon as a kitten arrives in the home, the parents must assume the responsibility of teaching all the children in the household how to handle and care for it properly and of supervising interaction between feline and youngsters. The children, especially tod-

dlers, should learn kindness, basic handling, and that
a cat is a living creature with distinct emotions.
Toddlers often look upon pets as stuffed toys and
don't understand that when abused, cats often scratch
or bite in self-defense. Every child in the family
should learn to do the following:

- To treat the cat gently. Cats may be stroked or
  patted, but they must never be teased, pulled, or
  handled roughly.
- To talk quietly to the cat. Loud, impatient
  children usually frighten animals.
- To move carefully, especially around a little
  kitten. An uncontrollable, running child may
  accidentally step or fall on a kitten and injure it.
- To lift and hold a cat properly (see Chapter III).
  Not to lift a kitten by its front legs or tail, nor to
  pull or twist these parts, or drop the kitten, or
  cause it pain.
- Not to antagonize the cat while it is eating or
  sleeping.
- Not to overtire the pet, especially a kitten. Young
  animals need plenty of sleep.
- Not to hold the cat close to the face.

As children grow older they become able to handle
more serious responsibilities and, with parental guidance, can learn to feed, water, groom, and train the
cat, and take care of litter-box duties. When there is
more than one child, these responsibilities can be
shared; the oldest, of course, in charge of more
serious duties. When children care for pets, according to Dr. Boris Levinson in *Pet-Oriented Child
Psychotherapy** it gives them a sense of purpose and

---

*Boris M. Levinson. *Pet-Oriented Child Psychotherapy*, Springfield,
Illinois; Charles C. Thomas, 1969.

responsibility, something tangible to care for and protect.

A section on children and cats is not complete, unfortunately, without mentioning the child who abuses animals. Inhumane treatment that is the result of a child's ignorance or curiosity must be discouraged immediately. Often a lecture on humane treatment is all that is necessary to make the child feel compassion. Serious and repeated abuse, however, is a symptom of serious emotional problems and requires professional help. Then there is the "bully," the youngster who is intimidated or treated brutishly and takes out his frustration on animals. Dr. Michael Fox, world famous animal behaviorist, reports in his "Understanding Your Pet" column for *McCall's* magazine: "If parents are authoritarian or frequently strike their children, they should not be surprised if they see their child ordering a pet around or even beating it. Whenever a child does abuse a pet, parents should neither scold the child nor ignore the matter, but rather find out why the child is acting that way."

Cats and the Elderly and Lonely

The medical and psychiatric professions are discovering that cats have a therapeutic effect on the elderly, the convalescing, the lonely, the isolated, the troubled, and the ill. Recent studies have shown that people who own pets have a better mental outlook, are more active, and usually live longer. At the first International Conference of Human/Companion Animal Bond held recently in Philadelphia, Pennsylvania, Dr. Aaron Katcher, associate professor of psychiatry at the University of Pennsylvania, commented that while animals are not substitutes for human contact, they make ideal companions, are a stimulus for exercise, and are warm living creatures that a person can care for and be entertained by. "When these needs are satisfied," added Dr. Katcher, "people are less likely to be anxious or depressed, which increases their chances for good physical health." At the same conference Dr. Leo Bustad, dean of the College of Veterinary Medicine at Washington State University, indicated that heart attack victims who are pet owners had a higher survival rate than those who did not own pets. Dr. Bustad also spoke of the success of pet-facilitated therapy efforts in treating the handicapped, and of the pet's role in helping the elderly to defer senescence. Many nursing and convalescent homes already recognize that pets are wonderful therapy for the elderly and convalescing, and allow residents to own and care for pet cats. The simple routine activities of feeding, watering, and grooming give an elderly person a reason for being, a feeling of being loved and needed at a time when perhaps no other human cares.

Other programs, such as C.A.T.S. (Children and Animals Together for Seniors) in New York, receive funding from humane or civic groups from which senior citizens may have their cats neutered, immunized, tested for worms, or receive veterinary care free of charge. Boy Scouts receive merit badges in the C.A.T.S. program, for helping the elderly with their pets.

Cats and Allergies

Sensitivity to animals, according to the Asthma and Allergy Foundation of America, is among the most common allergies. The sensitivity manifests itself usually by allergic rhinitis (sneezing, nasal discharge or stuffiness, and itching), or by bronchial asthma (cough, shortness of breath, and wheezing). It isn't the cat's hair that causes the sensitivity, but its dander, or skin flakes. The dander accumulates on carpets, furniture, and other household surfaces and creates problems for allergic individuals. Generally breeds with little or no shedding are less troublesome to allergy sufferers.

If you already own a cat and are troubled with sensitivity, don't panic. Some allergic individuals and cats can coexist when proper steps are taken to gain relief, such as installing an air-filtration system in the house or apartment; "desensitizing" your surroundings—a fancy way of saying to keep everything clean and free of dust, animal dander, and dead hair; grooming the cat regularly to reduce shedding; feeding the cat a balanced diet that includes some natural oil to make the skin more supple; and avoiding undue stress. Tree House Animal Foundation, one of the most progressive of the humane groups, publishes a brochure entitled *Allergic? You Can Have a Pet*. (To order, see Chapter XVI under "Free and Low-cost Literature About Cats.")

Think positively and consult an allergist. New developments are constantly taking place in the field of immunology, and allergy problems often have a happy ending. For instance, a new method of treatment was recently patented by two physicians for the Foundation of the Study of Asthma and Related Diseases in Boston, Massachusetts. The patient is given injections of cat-dandruff extract for a period of three to four months. Studies have shown significant reductions in the bronchial sensitivity of people who suffer an asthmatic reaction to cats.

The Multipet Family

Many individuals and families frequently decide to own more than one pet. Two animals generally are no more trouble than one; as they become more involved with each other, they become less demanding of your time and attention. Single-pet owners who live in apartments or who work all day often find it difficult to provide sufficient excitement or exercise for a solitary animal. Moreover, a lonely pet frequently becomes bored or destructive simply because there is nothing interesting to do. Providing a companion animal is a practical solution. There are decided advantages to owning two pets:

- If you work, you'll feel less guilty about leaving a lonely animal at home all day.
- If you travel, pets that are boarded in pairs provide a great deal of comfort to each other.
- While cats adore human attention, the companionship of their own kind is stimulating and healthy; having a member of the same species to play with, sleep with, or to groom can give a bored pet a new lease on life.

If you're planning to own more than one cat, or a cat and a dog (surprisingly, they can become closer companions than two cats), the ideal pair would be two youngsters of approximately the same age but of the opposite sex.* When two young animals arrive in a new home at the same time, they hit it off from the start and form a friendship quickly. An adult cat or

---

*If two kittens are not intended for breeding, have them neutered as soon as they mature. Two unaltered cats of the same sex are more likely to fight when they become adults. Combining an unaltered male and female is an invitation to unwanted pregnancy.

dog usually is more hospitable to a young kitten or puppy than to another full-grown cat or dog. The toughest combination is bringing together two adult cats, but even that can be mastered with some discipline and common sense.

Before bringing the new animal home, be sure it is immunized and checked thoroughly by a veterinarian so you don't expose your present pet to a disease or parasites the new animal may be carrying. The best way to introduce a new pet to an old one is to supervise their first encounter. Pay generous attention to the older pet at first, to avoid jealousy or potential fighting. When a new arrival gets all the attention, "pet number one" may refuse to eat, may become destructive, or may forget that it is litter box-trained or housebroken. If the older pet is a dog, keep it leashed and under control at all times, to keep it from frightening or chasing a new cat. Introducing two cats, particularly adults, can be troublesome. They may spit and hiss at each other at first, and it can take weeks—even months—for them to settle down together. Ideally it's best to keep them in separate rooms for a few days and let them become acquainted with each other's odors before they actually meet. If that's not possible, confine the new arrival in a cage so that both cats can meet face-to-face without being able to fight. Don't be too alarmed by a little power struggle at first. An adult cat that hisses or swats at a newcomer may just be stating who's boss.

Give each pet its own food dish, water bowl, and litter box in different areas of the house. Point out these areas to the new pet, and watch for competition over food, toys, or attention. Do not give catnip during the adjustment period; it stimulates some cats

into temporary aggressiveness. Keep both pets separated when you go out or when they are unsupervised, until you know they get along.

Most animals will adapt in time, but a few "loners"
really become upset when a stranger invades their
territory. An effective way to deal with this situation is
to keep a spray bottle filled with water close by when
the two pets are together. When one spits or hisses, or
if a fight erupts, immediately spray the water at the
offender (the animal must associate this action with its
offensive behavior), and discipline it by saying "No"
in a firm voice. This action probably will have to be
repeated many times to be effective, and after each
disciplinary spray, allow fifteen to twenty minutes to
pass, then make up with the aggressor.

Making Your Choice

Now you are ready to choose. And in the case of a
pedigreed cat, choosing means advance preparation.
Study the "Breeds in Brief" section of this chapter to
meet and learn about the purebreds. Few people,
though, choose a breed by reading about it. Their
choice will almost certainly be influenced by seeing
photographs and drawings or observing living cats.
The best way to see a variety of different breeds
together is at a cat show. Shows are held almost every
weekend in most parts of the United States, and they
can be enjoyable excursions for the family. Information about local shows usually appears in your newspaper's calendar of sporting events, and especially in
CATS and *Cat Fancy* magazines (see "Cat Fancy
Magazines" in Chapter XVI). You can also write to
the cat fancy organizations listed at the end of this

book and request the dates and locations of shows in your area, or you could call local breeders and ask.

Go early and purchase a catalog as soon as you arrive at the show site. The catalog lists the judging times and ring locations for the various breeds, as well as the names of all the cats entered along with their owners' names and addresses. Stroll around the caging area, study the exhibits, and talk to the breeders and exhibitors. Most cat people are pleased to give advice to a novice. Some, however, do not like to be bothered while they are preparing for judging, so wait until they are relaxed and have time to "talk cats" with you. Pick up any available breed-literature. Keep the show catalog for future reference; it can help you locate area breeders. If what you have observed makes you decide on a certain breed, you may find such kittens for sale at the show.

Where to Choose Your Cat

When you have some idea of the breed you want to own, the next important consideration is where to get it. Kittens and adult cats can be obtained from pet stores, private breeders or catteries, and humane societies and animal shelters. A great many kittens are sold every year through pet stores. Generally the stores are middlemen, buying kittens from local catteries or offering a referral service through local breeders. Often, however, they buy litters produced in assembly-line fashion from large commercial breeding establishments. It is possible to get a good quality healthy kitten from many pet stores, but if a shop buys from establishments that mass-produce and ship very young kittens (often under traumatic travel conditions), the quality of the animals may be dubious. The shop owner probably has no idea of the physical characteristics, temperament, or the health of the kitten's littermates or parents.

The best source of kittens is the private breeder or cattery. Some who fall into this category, however, may be as inconsistent as the assembly-line establishments. You want to make every effort to buy your kitten or adult cat from a reputable, dedicated person who tries to improve the breed with each generation by breeding kittens that are better than their parents. Quality animals have seldom just happened. They are planned in advance, and after they are born, they receive the best possible health care. A dedicated breeder spends years accumulating knowledge about genetics, breeding and whelping, nutrition, and kitten pediatrics, and evaluating prospective owners— not for monetary reasons but to ensure that the kitten's temperament matches that of the new owner. The best way to locate private breeders/catteries is through cat shows (and catalogs), from newspaper advertisements, from advertisements in the "Breeders Directory" of the magazines listed in Chapter XVI, or by referrals from other people who own quality cats.

Remember too that humane shelters or adoption agencies have cats of all ages and breeds waiting to be adopted for a small fee or voluntary contribution. Most of these are mixed breeds, but purebreds are sometimes available. If you want to adopt a cat, visit a humane society or shelter and look around. If you are serious about adopting, you will be screened to determine that you will be a conscientious cat owner, then you will be asked to read and sign an adoption form. Keep in mind that a shelter atmosphere influences almost every cat's personality. But almost every one will be more contented and adaptable after a few weeks in a new home, especially if there is plenty of love and understanding. Most shelter cats are so grateful to be rescued that from day one they become devoted to you. More than eight million abandoned and unwanted cats end up in animal shelters each year. Fewer than 20 percent are adopted. The rest are euthanized for lack of a home. It would be a lovely and humane gesture to adopt a shelter cat, because undoubtedly you will be saving a life.

Guidelines for Choosing a Kitten

1. Visit as many private breeders and catteries as possible before making your decision. Observe the condition of the cattery or the breeder's home. Is the place clean? Are there unpleasant odors? Look at the adult cats. Do they seem healthy and content? Are they friendly toward the breeder?

2. While there are many elements to consider in selecting a kitten—age, sex, purebred or random-bred, coat length, grooming—none is as important as temperament, because you will be living with the cat for a long time. Ask to see the entire litter all together if possible. Watch how the kittens interact with each other. Observe which are friendly and lively and which may be timid. The kitten that is interested in you, its littermates, and surroundings, one that doesn't cringe when you approach or become aggressive, is the one to consider.

3. Ask to see the kittens' mother (and father, if he is available). You can learn a great deal by seeing

one or both parents and watching the kittens with either or both. If the parents are timid, hostile, or aggressive, go elsewhere.

4. When you see a kitten you like, ask the breeder if you may give him or her a close examination. Pick up the kitten. If it purrs, seems content, and is easy to handle, that's a good sign. Look the kitten over carefully for the following signs of good health or illness:

- Good overall condition: the kitten should be in good flesh, neither obese nor underweight. Even in the oriental breeds the body should be slender, not emaciated. The abdomen should be firm; a very distended belly may indicate the presence of internal parasites.
- Glossy, unbroken fur with no bare patches.
- Clean, healthy-looking skin with no indication of skin disease or external parasites.
- Clear, bright eyes.
- Moist (but not sniffly) nose with no mucus discharge.
- Clean, pleasant-smelling ears.
- White baby teeth.
- Pleasant-smelling breath.
- Pink and firm gums.
- Smooth and effortless movement.
- The kitten should be alert, playful, curious, and interested in its littermates, surroundings, and you.

Signs of a sick kitten include:

- Mucus discharge from the eyes, nose, or other body openings.
- Dull, dry coat or bare patches on the skin.

- Constant scratching (may indicate external parasites or skin irritation).
- Diarrhea.
- Foul odor from the ears or the presence of waxy brown or gray matter inside (may indicate ear mites).
- Excessive head shaking or ear scratching.
- Distended abdomen or pot belly.
- Pale pink or whitish gums (may indicate anemia, which can be caused by a heavy worm-infestation).
- Listlessness or brooding.
- Difficulty in moving.

5. If the kitten does not satisfy you in all respects, continue your search. If, however, you decide to buy the kitten, the seller should provide the following:

- The kitten's pedigree (if the kitten is a result of a planned mating between two pedigreed animals). A pedigree is a genealogical record or family tree that lists the kitten's sire, dam, maternal and paternal grandparents, great-grandparents, and so on and proves that the ancestors have been purebred for several generations. If the kitten is registered with a cat fancy organization, the name of such registering body and the registration number. A registration number is no guarantee of quality, but it is proof that a kitten is of purebred stock. While the breeder takes care of the initial registration, it's up to you to register the change of ownership in your name. If the

breeder promises but does not provide the
pedigree or registration, get a signed written statement or bill of sale listing the cat's
breed, sex, color, date of birth, the names
and registration numbers of its sire and
dam, and the name of the registering governing body, along with the breeder's name
and address. Don't accept a promise of later
identification.

- A history of temporary or permanent immunization against certain infectious diseases, such as panleukopenia (feline infectious enteritis), three feline viral diseases—
rhinotracheitis, calicivirus, and pneumonitis—and rabies (depending on the cat's
age), plus the dates when future inoculations or boosters are due. It is also suggested
that you request a test for feline leukemia
virus.
- Health record, specifying wormings, if any.
- Diet sheet, listing the amounts and kinds of
food the kitten has been eating, plus a
schedule of feedings.
- Health guarantee. A reliable breeder, cattery, or pet store should furnish a written
guarantee that a kitten may be returned or
replaced within a specific time period if it
shows signs of illness or is found to possess
inherited defects. Determine if the guarantee specifies a cash refund, replacement, or
a discount. Some establishments will refund
monies; others do not but will replace the
kitten or offer a discount on another. The

latter means is often used when a severe congenital defect manifests itself at some later date.

Once you buy a kitten or adult cat, it is your responsibility to have it examined by a veterinarian as soon as possible. If for any reason the cat is unsatisfactory after examination, return it immediately. Do your homework and learn as much about cat health problems as possible before you buy, especially if you want a cat for show or breeding purposes. Of all domestic animals, cats have the lowest risk of congenital defects; nevertheless they can experience genetic or environmentally induced defects of the eyes and ears; of the musculoskeletal, circulatory, digestive, urinary, reproductive, and integumentary systems; congenital hernias; and metabolic defects. Some disorders are rare, while others occur more frequently. For instance, polydactyly, or the presence of extra toes (usually on the forepaws), is quite common. Persians may experience inverted eyelids and other ocular problems. The short-nosed breeds often suffer from breathing difficulties. Deafness is associated with white cats with blue eyes. Strabismus, or squint (one eye turns inward while the other is fixed on an object, making the cat look cross-eyed), and kinked tails may occur in Siamese. There can be no guarantee that any kitten or cat is totally free from all possible congenital disorders, but you can lessen the chances of a life-threatening condition or excessive medical bills by being better informed, discussing potential problems with a veterinarian before you buy, and dealing with reputable and knowledgeable breeders. Don't be afraid to question breeders, especially when you are looking to buy show or breeding stock: Does the line have any problems you should know about? Have the sire and dam experienced any recurring health problems? What were they and how were they solved? Did the dam deliver her kittens normally? What was the survival rate of her litter? Any breeder who is truly interested in producing and perpetuating a line of healthy cats should answer these and other questions honestly.

The Breeds in Brief: All About Pure-breed Cats

In this section you will meet twenty-eight pure-breed cats, officially recognized for registration and championship competition by The Cat Fanciers' Association, Inc. (CFA), the largest registration body in the world. The CFA, organized in 1906, registers more cats and sponsors more shows than any other organization. CFA has no individual members; breeders and exhibitors join local clubs that are affiliated with the association. Club memberships in 1982 totaled approximately six hundred in the United States, Canada, and Japan. The addresses of the CFA and other cat fancy associations in the United States, Canada, Great Britain, and Europe are listed in Chapter XVI, "Reference Material."

All of the breeds recognized by the CFA appear on the next pages and are accompanied by the following information:

1. Illustration of the breed.
2. Information about the breed's origin.
3. The author's comments about each breed's personality traits. These were obtained from interviews with breeders. Comments about personali-

ty and temperament, of course, can only be generalizations. It is impossible to categorize any breed's personality in a few words. Every cat is an individual. Within each breed some cats may be demanding while others are reserved; some may be aggressive while others are peaceful; some can be talkative while others are quiet. The best way to ensure good temperament is to deal with knowledgeable breeders. Early in each kitten's development a concerned breeder sees certain traits beginning to emerge, and can assure the greatest potential by directing a kitten to the right home environment.

4. Comments on grooming and coat care.

5. Highlights of the breed's conformation and recognized colors from the official CFA show standard. Every breed eligible for registration with a cat fancy organization has an official standard or written description by which it is judged. The standard describes the ideal specimen of each breed, point by point, and is composed of sections defining a cat's general appearance, its head, neck, nose, muzzle, chin, eyes, ears, body, legs, paws, tail, coat, and coloring. Each of these sections is assigned a certain point value, the total being 100. By putting the sections together, one can develop a word picture of each breed. No written standard, though, can exactly describe a cat, because each one is an individual that must be observed as such. Should you wish to read the entire show standards for the various breeds, you can obtain a copy from the CFA at a nominal charge. (The address of

the Cat Fanciers' Association is listed under "Cat Fancy Associations" in Chapter XVI.)

At the end of this section you will also find some information about rare breeds plus additional breeds that are recognized or accepted for championship competition by organizations other than the CFA.

ABYSSINIAN

- Easy to groom
- Friendly with children
- Intelligent
- Active and playful
- Good companion
- Quiet

The Abyssinian presumably originated in Ethiopia (formerly Abyssinia) or Egypt long before the birth of Christ. Its ancestors are thought to be the wild Caffre cats that roamed North Africa. Present-day Abyssinians closely resemble the sacred cats depicted in ancient Egyptian sculptures and wall paintings. The breed first appeared in England in the late 1860s when, it is believed, a cat named Zula was brought to Great Britain at the end of the Abyssinian War. It was also called the "Bunny" or "Hare" cat because of its similarity in coloring to the British wild rabbit. The first Abyssinians were brought to the United States around 1909.

Elegant and graceful, Abyssinians are people-oriented cats that are intensely interested in their surroundings. They are extremely active (particularly as kittens) and love being where the action is. Abys can be terribly affectionate and demanding cats. They will persistently help you do everything from preparing meals to bed making, and frequently interrupt the work to give you a big kiss! Abys have dainty, high voices, and while not especially loquacious, they manage to gently declare their requirements when necessary.

Of all the domestic cat breeds, the cougar-like Abyssinian is the most "wild" in appearance. The breed standard calls for the ideal specimen to be a regal-looking, medium-sized graceful cat with a distinctly ticked coat. Its conformation strikes a medium between the extremes of the cobby and svelte length types. It should have a slightly rounded wedge head, large and moderately pointed ears, and brilliant almond-shaped gold or green eyes. The coat is soft, silky, and finely textured with a lustrous sheen.

Abyssinian Colors: Ruddy, Red.

AMERICAN SHORTHAIR

- Easy to groom
- Friendly with children
- Affectionate and good-natured
- Healthy and robust
- Intelligent
- Good mouser
- Moderately quiet

Some naturalists consider the American Shorthair to be the original breed of domestic cat. It is believed that the ancestors of American Shorthair cats came to this country with the Pilgrims on the Mayflower in 1620. They were brought along to kill rats in addition to being family pets. The first shorthairs were registered in the Cat Fanciers' Association Stud Book in the early 1900s. Since that time the breed has come a long way, due to the many dedicated fanciers who have set high standards through selective breeding. Known for their stamina, vigor, intelligence, good temperament, and affection, it is not surprising that American Shorthairs are such popular cats in the United States.

The breed standard describes the American Shorthair as the only breed of true "working" cat. The conformation of the breed is well adapted for this and reflects its refusal to surrender its natural functions. This is a cat lithe enough to stalk its prey, but powerful enough to make the kill easily. Its reflexes are under perfect control. Its legs are long enough to cope with any terrain and heavy and muscular enough for high leaps. The face is long enough to permit easy grasping by the teeth with jaws so powerful they can close against resistance. Its coat is dense enough to protect from moisture, cold, and superficial skin injuries, but short enough and of sufficiently hard texture to resist matting or entanglement when slipping through heavy vegetation. No part of its anatomy is so exaggerated as to foster weakness. The general effect is that of the trained athlete, with all muscles rippling easily beneath the skin, the flesh lean and hard, and with great latent power held in reserve.

American Shorthair colors: White, Black, Blue, Red, Cream, Chinchilla, Shaded Silver, Shell Cameo (Red Chinchilla), Shaded Cameo (Red Shaded), Black Smoke, Blue Smoke, Cameo Smoke (Red Smoke), Tortoiseshell Smoke, Classic Tabby Pattern, Mackerel Tabby Pattern, Patched Tabby Pattern, Brown Patched Tabby, Blue Patched Tabby, Silver Patched Tabby, Silver Tabby, Red Tabby, Brown Tabby, Blue Tabby, Cream Tabby, Cameo Tabby, Tortoiseshell, Calico, Dilute Calico, Blue-Cream, Bi-Color, Van Bi-Color, Van Calico, Van Blue-Cream and White.

AMERICAN WIREHAIR

- Easy to groom
- Friendly with children
- Intelligent
- Loving and good-natured
- Playful
- Healthy and hardy
- Moderately quiet

The first American Wirehair, a red and white male named Council Rock Farm Adam of Hi-Fi, appeared in 1966 as a mutation in a litter of shorthair farm cats. After a few matings (Wirehair-to-American Shorthair and Wirehair-to-Wirehair) it was discovered that the coarse, resilient coat could be reproduced, and a new breed came into existence. In conformation Wirehairs most closely resemble American Shorthairs. The noticeable difference is the Wirehair's springy, crimped coat. Even the hair inside the ears and whiskers is curly. Like their shorthair cousins, American Wirehairs are hardy, good-natured, and affectionate cats that make ideal companions.

American Wirehair Colors: White, Black, Blue, Red, Cream, Chinchilla, Shaded Silver, Shell Cameo (Red Chinchilla), Shaded Cameo (Red Shaded), Black Smoke, Blue Smoke, Cameo Smoke (Red Smoke), Classic Tabby Pattern, Mackerel Tabby Pattern, Silver Tabby, Red Tabby, Brown Tabby, Blue Tabby, Cream Tabby, Cameo Tabby, Tortoiseshell, Calico, Dilute Calico, Blue-Cream, Bi-Color, Other Wirehair Colors (OWC)—any other color or pattern with the exception of those showing evidence of hybridization resulting in the colors chocolate, lavender, the Himalayan pattern, or these combinations with white.

BALINESE

- Needs daily grooming
- Good with children
- Sweet-natured and affectionate
- Playful
- Moderately vocal

The Balinese is identical in type and coat-pattern to the Siamese except that it has long and silky hair. The Balinese did not originate in Bali; it was developed by American breeders. Long-haired kittens had appeared infrequently in Siamese litters, and these "undesirables" were usually given away as pets. In the 1950s a few dedicated breeders discovered that the long-haired Siamese bred true and the breeders worked hard for recognition as a separate breed. Instead of the name "Long-Coated Siamese," the more exotic "Balinese" was chosen because of the cat's striking resemblance to a Balinese dancer. The vivacious, people-loving Balinese has a gentle and affectionate nature. It makes a charming pet and lives harmoniously with other animals. While it loves to talk, its voice is generally not as shrill as that of its relative, the Siamese.

The breed standard describes the ideal Balinese as a svelte, dainty cat with long, tapering lines, very lithe but strong and muscular. It has a long, tapering wedge head, long and straight nose, and fine wedge-shaped muzzle. The ears should be strikingly large and pointed, and the almond-shaped eyes are a deep vivid blue. The long, fine, and silky coat is without downy undercoat.

Balinese Colors: Seal Point, Chocolate Point, Blue Point, Lilac Point.

BIRMAN (Sacred Cat of Burma)

- Requires daily grooming
- Friendly with children
- Affectionate and sweet-natured
- People-oriented
- Active and playful
- Quiet

The Birman originated in the Far East and, in all likelihood, is an ancient breed. An exotic legend persists regarding its distinctive coloring. In the time of Buddha, so the story goes, the Khmer people of Southeast Asia erected many temples in honor of their gods. One hundred pure white cats lived in one of them, the Temple of Lao-Tsun. One day a venerable priest named Mun-Ha knelt in prayer before a statue of Tsun-Kyan-Kse, a golden goddess with sapphire eyes, who the Khmers believed controlled the transmigration of souls. Mun-Ha's favorite cat, Sinh, sat at his side. Invaders suddenly attacked the temple and struck down the old priest. Sinh jumped on his master's body, faced the goddess, and gazed solemnly into her sapphire eyes. At that precise moment Mun-Ha's soul entered the cat, and Sinh's white coat turned golden and his eyes became a deep blue. The cat's face, tail, and legs became dark, but the paws that touched the dead priest remained white as a symbol of purity. Sinh died seven days later and carried his master's soul to heaven. Next morning the white hair of all the temple cats turned golden and their eyes changed to sapphire blue. After that time the temple cats were considered sacred, and when one died, it was thought to carry the soul of a priest into paradise.

Legend aside, the breed's known history began shortly after World War I, when a male and female Birman were sent from Southeast Asia to Monsieur August Pavie and Major Gordon Russel, who then lived in France. The male died en route, but the female, pregnant at the time, reached her destination. Her kittens became the first Birmans born in Europe. The breed was first accepted for championship competition in the United States in 1967.

Birmans are large, long, and stocky cats with broad and rounded heads and almost round blue eyes. The hair is long and silky in texture, with a heavy ruff around the neck. The breed's most distinctive characteristics are white gloves on all four paws and white laces that extend partially up the back legs.

Birman Colors: Seal Point, Blue Point, Chocolate Point, Lilac Point.

BOMBAY

- Easy to groom
- Friendly with children and other pets
- Intelligent
- Trainable
- Good-natured and affectionate
- Likes attention
- Moderately quiet

The elegant jet-black Bombay was first created in 1958 by Nikki Horner by crossing Burmese with black American Shorthairs. Ms. Horner's goal was to create a cat that resembled a tiny panther. Her ambition was achieved after years of selective breeding, and the new breed was named for the black leopard of India. The Bombay was first recognized for championship competition by the Cat Fanciers' Association in 1976.

In conformation the Bombay closely resembles the Burmese. It is a medium-size cat with a pleasingly round head. Its close-lying, satiny coat has a high patent-leather sheen. Its huge eyes range from golden to deep copper in color. Bombays are active and intelligent cats that are extremely adaptable and trainable.

Bombay Color: Black.

BRITISH SHORTHAIR

- Easy to groom
- Friendly with children and other pets
- Healthy and robust
- Even-tempered
- Loving and devoted
- Intelligent
- Quiet
- Good hunter

The ancestors of British Shorthairs were common-place street cats, the hunters of vermin. When cat shows became popular toward the end of the nine-teenth century, many breeders concentrated their efforts toward selectively breeding these native short-hairs. Immediately after World War II, British Short-hairs were crossed with Persians to improve type. The end results were handsome cats that incorporated the best of two varieties: the compactness and sturdiness of the shorthairs, and the broad head and large round eyes of the longhairs. Today the Governing Council of the Cat Fancy, United Kingdom (GCCF) recognizes many varieties of British Shorthairs. They were approved by the Cat Fanciers' Association for championship competition in 1980.

British Shorthairs are large, strong, and exception-ally hardy cats. They have round and massive heads with round cheeks, a firm chin, widely spaced me-dium-sized ears with slightly rounded tips, large and well-opened eyes, and a medium nose with gentle dip. The short and resilient coat is very dense and well-bodied.

British Shorthair Colors: White, Black, Blue, Cream, Black Smoke, Blue Smoke, Classic Tabby Pattern, Mackerel Tabby Pattern, Silver Tabby, Red Tabby, Brown Tabby, Blue Tabby, Cream Tabby, Spotted Tabby Pattern, Tortoiseshell, Tortoiseshell and White, Blue-Cream, Bi-Color.

BURMESE

- Easy to groom
- Friendly to children and other pets
- Good apartment pet
- People-oriented
- Very intelligent
- Loving and devoted
- Trainable
- Charming companion
- Moderately vocal

Few breeds can trace their lineage back to a common ancestor; however, all Burmese in the

United States descend from one female named Wong Mau that arived in this country in 1930. Wong Mau's owner, Dr. Joseph G. Thompson of San Francisco, called her a Burmese because she came from Rangoon. American cat fanciers were unimpressed and considered Wong Mau to be a dark-colored Siamese. Thompson disagreed and established a selective breeding program. He bred Wong Mau to a Seal Point Siamese since there were no other cats of similar type available. Half the litter were dark brown like their mother; the other half resembled their father. Thompson discovered that the dark-colored cats bred true, and after several carefully planned breedings the Burmese was established.

The Burmese is a handsome, medium-sized "teddy bear" of a cat with a compact, muscular body, round head, sweet expression, and large golden eyes. The breed's most distinguishing feature is its short, glistening sable-brown coat that shades to a slightly lighter color on the underparts. (The Cat Fanciers' Association recognizes only the sable-brown color, although the British GCCF recognizes, in addition to sable, red, cream, blue, lilac, and chocolate, as well as various colored Tortie Burmese.) Burmese are terribly social cats that love human companionship. They live harmoniously with dogs and other cats, and are gentle with children. Burmese enjoy a good conversation, but they are not as long-winded or noisy as Siamese.

Burmese Color: Sable Brown.

COLORPOINT SHORTHAIR

- Easy to groom
- Friendly with children
- Superintelligent
- Very active
- Demanding
- Trainable
- Likes being with people
- Exotic appearance
- Extremely vocal

Colorpoint Shorthairs are exquisite-looking cats with long tapering lines, very lithe but muscular. They resemble Siamese in all respects except for their points, which come in a variety of colors and patterns. Colorpoints were created by breeding Siamese to other varieties, particularly American Shorthairs. From this hybridization breeders created cats of Siamese type with American Shorthair colors and patterns that were restricted to the points.

Colorpoints, with their long and tapering wedge heads, deep vivid-blue almond-shaped eyes, and gorgeous coloring, are fascinating animals. They are every bit as active and articulate as Siamese, and they make charming and lovable pets.

Colorpoint Shorthair Colors: Red Point, Cream Point, Seal-Lynx Point, Chocolate-Lynx Point, Blue-Lynx Point, Lilac-Lynx Point, Red-Lynx Point, Chocolate-Tortie Point, Blue-Cream Point, Lilac-Cream Point.

EGYPTIAN MAU

- Easy to groom
- Friendly with children
- Loving and devoted
- Very active
- Likes being with people
- Moderately vocal
- Exotic appearance

The Egyptian Mau, the only natural domesticated breed of spotted cat, is an ancient breed whose ancestors probably were favorites of the pharaohs. Tomb paintings from ancient Egypt bear a striking resemblance to modern Maus. One especially fine depiction from Thebes, of around 1400 B.C., shows a spotted cat hunting duck with its aristocratic master. Another painting from the tomb of Sennedjem, about 1300 B.C., shows the sun god Ra in the form of a spotted tabby, cutting off the head of the serpent Apophis.

The first Egyptian Maus were brought to the United States in 1953 from Cairo, via Rome, by Princess Troubetskoy. A medium-size and graceful cat, Maus look like they are on tip-toe when standing upright, because their hind legs are slightly longer than those in front. Maus come in three colors, and their silky coats are dense and resilient to the touch. The almond-shaped eyes (preferably gooseberry green in all colors) slant slightly upward toward the ears. Maus are much like Siamese but with softer and more lyrical voices. They are serene and loving cats, and terribly devoted to their owners.
Egyptian Mau Colors: Silver, Bronze, Smoke.

EXOTIC SHORTHAIR

- Requires regular grooming
- Friendly with children and other pets
- Good-natured and affectionate
- Intelligent
- Vivacious
- Quiet

Exotic Shorthairs were produced by serious breeders through crosses of Persians and American Shorthairs. The object was to produce a Persian-like cat with shorter fur. This stunning hybrid is similar in conformation to the Persian: round, massive head; short snub nose; large eyes, and a deep-chested cobby body. Its dense coat, however, is medium in length, ranging from about one-half inch to slightly over one inch long, a bit longer than other shorthairs. Exotics were accepted for championship competition by the Cat Fanciers' Association in 1967. The popular colors in the breed's infancy were chinchilla and shaded silver, but today Exotic Shorthairs come in many colors and patterns.

The breed standard describes the Exotic Shorthair as a medium- to large-size cat of cobby type—low on the legs, deep in the chest, equally massive across the shoulders and rump, with a short, well-rounded middle piece. The head should be round and massive, and set on a short, thick neck. The brilliant round and full eyes add a sweet expression to the face. The legs are short, thick, and strong. Exotics are extremely affectionate and peaceful creatures. They adapt to most situations and get along well with children and other animals. Exotics are not as vocal as most shorthairs.

Exotic Shorthair Colors: White, Black, Blue, Red, Cream, Chinchilla Shaded Silver, Chinchilla Golden, Shaded Golden, Shell Cameo (Red Chinchilla), Shaded Cameo (Red Shaded), Shell Tortoiseshell, Shaded Tortoiseshell, Black Smoke, Blue Smoke, Cameo Smoke (Red Smoke), Smoke Tortoiseshell, Classic Tabby Pattern, Mackerel Tabby Pattern, Patched Tabby Pattern, Brown Patched Tabby, Blue Patched Tabby, Silver Patched Tabby, Silver Tabby, Red Tabby, Brown Tabby, Blue Tabby, Cream Tabby, Cameo Tabby, Tortoiseshell, Calico, Dilute Calico, Blue-Cream, Bi-Color, Van Bi-Color, Van Calico, Van Blue-Cream and White.

HAVANA BROWN

- Easy to groom
- Friendly with children and other pets
- Good-natured and affectionate
- Active
- Good family companion
- Adaptable
- Trainable
- Moderately vocal

The Havana Brown, despite its name, originated in England, not Cuba. It was created in the early 1950s as the result of a carefully planned breeding program by crosses of Chocolate Point Siamese, Russian Blues, and black domestic shorthairs. The breeders' object was to produce a solid brown cat of foreign type that would breed true. The cat was named because its coat resembled the color of a Havana cigar. The first Havana Brown arrived in the United States in 1954, and the breed was officially recognized in 1959.

Havanas are medium-size cats with bodies similar in type to Russian Blues. They are dramatic-looking cats with their large, forward-tilted ears, clear green eyes, and tobacco-colored coat. Their glossy and lustrous coats are solid-colored to the roots—even their whiskers are brown! Havana Browns are sweet-natured and loving creatures that usually become very attached to their owners. They are not too vociferous, and they get along well with children and other pets.

Havana Brown Color: A rich, even shade of warm brown.

HIMALAYAN

- Requires daily grooming
- Friendly with children and other pets
- Loving and devoted companion
- Good apartment pet
- Fastidious habits
- Intelligent
- Trainable
- Moderately quiet

Himalayans are exquisite Persian-type cats with the Siamese color pattern. These outstanding-looking creatures possess the best qualities of both strains: the Persian's cobby body, large-boned short legs, round and massive head, short nose, large eyes, and long, glossy coat, and the Siamese's pale body color and darker mask, ears, legs, feet, and tail. Although several attempts were made in this country and Great Britain in the 1930s to produce colorpoint longhairs, the results were generally unsuccessful. Then in the 1940s, Brian Sterling Webb of England and Margarita Goforth of the United States, in separate breeding programs, seriously began to produce Persian-type cats with Siamese coloring. Mr. Sterling Webb's cats were called Colourpoint Longhairs and recognized by the GCCF in 1955. Mrs. Goforth's cats, named Himalayans after the rabbits with similar coat patterns, were first accepted for championship competition here in 1957. Today, Himalayans are one of the most popular breeds in the United States.

Himalayans are fastidious, good-natured cats that get along well with people and other pets. Their personalities range between the boldness of the Siamese and the serenity of the Persian. Their full and brilliant copper or deep vivid blue eyes give a sweet expression to their faces. Himalayans generally are quiet and easygoing, but they still enjoy "talking" with their owners. Their long and thick coats require a great deal of grooming.

Himalayan Colors: Seal Point, Chocolate Point, Blue Point, Lilac Point, Flame (Red) Point, Cream Point, Tortie Point, Blue-Cream Point, Seal Lynx-Point, Blue Lynx-Point, Chocolate Solid Color, Lilac Solid Color.

JAPANESE BOBTAIL

- Easy to groom
- Friendly with other cats
- Intelligent
- Loving and devoted
- Unique appearance
- Moderately vocal

The Japanese Bobtail is a native of Japan. Although cats probably arrived in that country centuries ago (historians disagree about the exact date) from China or Korea, the first written record of them in Japan appears in *A Tale of the Genji*, a novel written nearly one thousand years ago by the tutor-governess to the Japanese empress. Among the Japanese cats bobtailed breeds have existed for hundreds of years. The cat was always one of the favorite subjects of oriental artists, and bobtails appear in delicately shaded watercolors, paintings on silk, woodblock prints, and in their traditional tri-colored coat with front paw raised in a greeting, as a symbol of good luck, on the front of the Go-To-Ku-Ji temple in Tokyo. Bobtails appeared in this country in the 1960s, and were recognized by the Cat Fanciers' Association in 1969.

The gentle Japanese Bobtail is a medium-size lean yet muscular cat with a soft and silky coat. It has no perceivable undercoat and is practically nonshedding. The breed's outstanding characteristic is its short tail, about two inches long, with hair that grows outward to create a pompon or bunny-tail effect. There is a distinctive Japanese cast to the Bobtail's face, with its slanted eyes, high cheekbones, and long, parallel nose. Bobtails come in a variety of colors and patterns, the preferred being the traditional tri-colored *Mi-Ke* (mee-kay, meaning "three fur"), which is red, black, and white, or tortoiseshell with white. Japanese Bobtails have charming personalities. They are friendly, intelligent, and extremely loving. Their delicate voices are usually quiet, and they chat mostly when spoken to.

Japanese Bobtail Colors: White, Black, Red, Black and White, Red and White, *Mi-Ke* (Tri-color), Tortoise-shell, Other Japanese Bobtail Colors (OJBC)— include the following categories and any other color or pattern or combination thereof except coloring that is point-restricted (i.e., Siamese markings) or unpatterned agouti (i.e., Abyssinian coloring). "Pat-terned" categories denote and include any variety of tabby striping or spotting with or without areas of solid (unmarked) color, with preference given to bold, dramatic markings and rich, vivid coloring. Other Solid Colors: Blue or Cream. Patterned Self Colors: Red, Black, Blue, Cream, Silver, or Brown. Other Bi-Colors: Blue and White or Cream and White. Patterned Bi-Colors: Red, Black, Blue, Cream, Silver or Brown combined with White. Patterned Tortoiseshell: Blue-Cream. Patterned Blue-Cream. Dilute Tri-Colors: Blue, Cream, and White. Patterned Dilute Tri-Colors: Patterned *Mi-Ke* (Tri-color), Tor-toiseshell with White.

KORAT

- Easy to groom
- Friendly with other cats and good-natured dogs
- Intelligent
- Likes tranquil surroundings
- Loving and devoted
- Trainable
- Quiet

The Korat is an ancient natural breed named after the Korat plateau of Thailand (formerly Siam). It is a rare, highly prized cat, greatly loved by the Thai people, who regard it as a good luck symbol. In its native land the Korat is called the Si-Sawat, and males are prized as fighters. At one time, this stunning creature could not be bought, but had to be acquired as a gift. The first reference to Korats appears in *Cat Book Poems,* a manuscript book of paintings and verses about cats prepared in the old capital of Ayutthaya sometime between A.D.1360 and 1767. A few Korats were brought to the United States in the 1930s, but no serious breeding program was established until 1959. They were recognized first by the American Cat Association, the National Cat Fanciers Association, and the United Cat Federation in 1966, but by 1969 all other North American governing bodies had accepted them.

The Korat is a medium-size cat with a semicobby, muscular body, a distinctly heart-shaped head, and large ears. Its prominent eyes are usually luminous green, although an amber cast is acceptable. The Korat's fine and glossy silver-blue coat is tipped with silver, giving it an elegant, shimmery look. Korats are sweet-natured and affectionate cats that become very attached to one person. They are quiet, intelligent, and highly trainable.

Korat Color: Silver blue, tipped with silver.

MAINE COON

- Requires regular grooming
- Friendly with children
- Good-natured
- Healthy and robust
- Active and playful
- Efficient mouser
- Moderately quiet

The Maine Coon is an old American breed whose ancestry traces back to the cats brought to the northeastern United States by early settlers. Some far-fetched myths are attached to its origins: one is that it evolved from matings between domestic cats and raccoons (offspring from such breedings are genetically impossible); another is that it descends from Marie Antoinette's cats that were shipped to Maine in anticipation of her escape from prison during the French Revolution; and a third involves a strange "Captain Coon," whose reality has never been substantiated. Most authorities, however, believe that Maine Coons resulted from crosses between early Angoras or Persians and domestic shorthairs. The breed was more than likely named for its area of origin and distinctive color and markings. Brown Tabbies were (and still are) the most popular color, and the breed's bushy tail does resemble that of a raccoon. Maine Coons were popular show cats in the last century, one named Leo being designated "Best Cat" at the first organized show at Madison Square Garden in 1895. But as the more unusual breeds came into vogue the Maine Coon experienced a gradual decline in popularity until its resurgence in the 1960s.

Maine Coons are large-boned, solidly built cats. They tend to mature slowly. Their heavy, shaggy coats, well-tufted "snowshoe" paws, and bushy tails are ideal for harsh climates. Maine Coons require regular grooming, but their coats are less inclined to mat than most other long-coated breeds, except during heavy-shedding periods. The breed comes in practically every possible cat color or coat pattern. They are friendly and devoted (most love to hug), and males of the breed are reported to be more affectionate than the females.

Maine Coon Colors:

Solid Color Class

White, Black, Blue, Red, Cream.

Tabby Color Class

Classic Tabby Pattern, Mackerel Tabby Pattern, Silver Tabby, Red Tabby, Brown Tabby, Blue Tabby, Cream Tabby, Cameo Tabby, Patched Tabby Pattern.

Tabby with White Class

Tabby with White, Patched Tabby with White (Torbie with White).

Parti-Color Class

Tortoiseshell, Tortoiseshell with White, Calico, Dilute Calico, Blue-Cream, Blue-Cream with White, Bi-Color.

Other Maine Coon Colors Class

Chinchilla, Shaded Silver, Shell Cameo (Red Chinchilla), Shaded Cameo (Red Shaded), Black Smoke, Blue Smoke, Cameo Smoke (Red Smoke).

MALAYAN

- Easy to groom
- Friendly with children and other pets
- People-oriented
- Affectionate
- Playful and fun-loving
- Trainable
- Intelligent
- Moderately vocal

The Malayan is one of the newest breeds to be accepted by the Cat Fanciers' Association, being recognized in 1980. It is not a new breed, however, but a newly acknowledged series of colors. Malayans are really Burmese of other colors. Although the object of Burmese breeders was a rich, sable-brown cat, light-colored kittens appeared intermittently in Burmese litters, possibly due to a recessive gene acquired from crosses to Siamese in the breed's infancy. Such kittens were given away or sold as pets until the CFA ruled that Burmese of colors other than sable could be accepted if breeders would agree to register them as a separate breed.

Malayans are compact, medium-size cats, identical in conformation to Burmese. They have a short, close-lying coat that appears satiny in texture. Instead of the Burmese sable-brown color, Malayans come in delicate shades of champagne, blue, or platinum. They are enchanting and affectionate creatures that adapt beautifully to children, dogs, and other cats. Malayans are lively cats, always ready for fun and games. Like the Burmese, they express their viewpoints, but less noisily than Siamese.

Malayan Colors: Champagne, Blue, Platinum.

MANX

- Distinctive appearance
- Easy to groom
- Friendly with children
- Even-tempered and peaceful
- Intelligent
- Trainable
- Devoted to owner
- Efficient mouser
- Moderately vocal

The tailless Manx originated on the Isle of Man, a tiny island off the west coast of England in the Irish Sea. Its taillessness is the basis of several exotic legends. One says that the Manx was the last animal to board the Ark during the Great Flood and its tail was removed when Noah shut the door behind it. Another declares that Irish warriors used to ornament their shields and helmets with the tails of cats, and to prevent this, mother cats began biting off their kittens' tails at birth. A third proposes that the original Manx was a cross between a cat and a hare. Separate legends are attached to the Manx's geographical origin. Some say that Phoenician seamen brought tailless cats to Britain from their trading expeditions to Japan long ago. Another prescribes that two tailless cats abandoned a sinking ship of the Spanish Armada in 1588, swam to the Isle of Man, and created the breed.

The taillessness was most likely the result of a mutation in a litter of shorthairs that occurred years ago. One can find various tail-lengths in Manx, including: "Rumpy," or those that are completely tailless; "Stumpy," or those that have a short-tail stump; and "Taily," or those with a complete tail. Only the completely tailless Manx, however, can compete at purebred cat shows.

Manx are compact and well-muscled cats whose hind legs are longer than their forelegs. They mature slowly, with males becoming somewhat larger than females. Everything about the ideal Manx gives the impression of roundness: its head, muzzle, large eyes, broad chest, and curved rump. Manx come in almost every known cat color and coat pattern except colorpoint. Their short, plush double-coats are cottony underneath and glossy on top. They are superb ratters and can stand their ground with other cats and dogs. Although Manx are playful and affectionate, many tend to attach themselves to one person and act rather aloof to others.

Manx Colors: White, Black, Blue, Red, Cream, Chinchilla, Shaded Silver, Black Smoke, Blue Smoke, Classic Tabby Pattern, Mackerel Tabby Pattern, Patched Tabby Pattern, Brown Patched Tabby, Blue Patched Tabby, Silver Patched Tabby, Silver Tabby, Red Tabby, Brown Tabby, Blue Tabby, Cream Tabby, Tortoiseshell, Calico, Dilute Calico, Blue-Cream, Bi-Color, Other Manx Colors (OMC). Any other color or pattern with the exception of those showing hybridization resulting in the colors chocolate, lavender, the Himalayan pattern, or these combinations with white.

ORIENTAL SHORTHAIR

- Easy to groom
- Friendly with children and other pets
- Intelligent and very bright
- Trainable
- Elegant appearance
- Very active; acrobatic talents
- Loving and devoted
- Likes attention
- Vocal

The Oriental Shorthair is one of the newest and most spectacular-looking breeds. Actually it is a Siamese-type cat with a solid color, parti-colored, or patterned coat. It was created in the United States through selective crosses of Siamese and American Shorthairs, although the first British imports also had some Russian Blue in their ancestry. The CFA grant-

ed championship status to Oriental Shorthairs in 1977.

Oriental Shorthairs are practically identical to Siamese in conformation: long, svelte body and legs; elongated slender neck; elegant tapering wedge-shaped head; and long, thin tail. The major difference is one of color, and the Oriental's range of colors is dramatic. Most shades and patterns are recognized, including caramel, a café au lait color unknown in other breeds. The coat in all its colors is short and glossy, lying close to the body. Orientals also resemble Siamese in temperament and personality: they are athletic, saucy, chatty, and terribly demanding cats.

They also are extremely bright and nimble-pawed—some learn to open cupboard and closet doors or to lower window blinds at an early age. Orientals are affectionate and highly adaptable; they live peacefully with children and other pets.

Oriental Shorthair Colors:

Solid Color Class

White, Ebony, Blue, Chestnut, Lavender, Red, Cream, Caramel.

Shaded Color Class

Ebony Silver, Blue Silver, Chestnut Silver, Lavender Silver, Cameo.

Smoke Color Class

Ebony Smoke, Blue Smoke, Chestnut Smoke, Lavender Smoke, Cameo Smoke (Red Smoke), Parti-Color Smoke.

Tabby Color Class

Classic Tabby Pattern, Mackerel Tabby Pattern, Spotted Tabby Pattern, Ticked Tabby Pattern, Patched Tabby Pattern, Ebony Tabby, Blue Tabby, Chestnut Tabby, Lavender Tabby, Red Tabby, Cream Tabby, Silver Tabby, Cameo Tabby.

Parti-Color Class

Tortoiseshell, Blue-Cream, Chestnut-Tortie, Lavender-Cream.

PERSIAN

- Requires daily grooming
- Regal and charming
- Sweet-natured and easygoing
- Loving and devoted
- Good apartment pet
- Adores pampering
- Quiet

The dazzling and regal Persian is the aristocrat of the feline world. Although long-haired cats have been known in Europe for at least three hundred years, the Persian's history is unclear to a degree. Many authorities believe its ancestors were Angoras from Turkey and longhairs from Persia. Others speculate that certain Asiatic wildcats are part of its background. Whatever its genealogy, the Persian as we know it developed in Victorian England, where the breed became extremely fashionable in the last half of the nineteenth century. Queen Victoria owned two blue Persians. The early recognized colors included blacks, whites, tortoiseshells, chinchillas, and several-colored tabbies, but because of the royal preference blues were the most popular show cats by the late 1890s. Persians first appeared in the United States around the turn of the century.

The Persian is a medium to large sturdy-looking cat, low on the legs, with a cobby, deep-chested body that is massive across the shoulders and rump. Its round and massive head, large, widely spaced eyes, broad jaws, and full chin intensify the powerfully built appearance. But beneath this imposing exterior purrs a placid and gentle creature that luxuriates in the attention of its owner.

Persians come in more than thirty-six color and coat patterns, a formidable range that eclipses all other breeds. Peke-faced Persians occur in red and red tabby colors. Their large heads, short, depressed noses, and decidedly wrinkled muzzles make them look like the Pekingese dogs for which they are named. Like their canine namesakes, unfortunately, Peke-faced Persians are often predisposed to respiratory problems and excessive tearing of their large eyes.

Persians have soft and lyrical voices. They make charming pets and adapt gracefully to most environments. Daily grooming is essential to keep the Persian's long and thick coat tangle-free.

Persian Colors: White, Black, Blue, Red, Cream, Chinchilla, Shaded Silver, Chinchilla Golden, Shaded Golden, Shell Cameo (Red Chinchilla), Shaded

Cameo (Red Shaded), Shell Tortoiseshell, Shaded Tortoiseshell, Black Smoke, Blue Smoke, Cameo Smoke (Red Smoke), Smoke Tortoiseshell, Blue-Cream Smoke, Classic Tabby Pattern, Mackerel Tabby Pattern, Patched Tabby Pattern, Brown Patched Tabby, Blue Patched Tabby, Silver Patched Tabby, Silver Tabby, Red Tabby, Brown Tabby, Blue Tabby, Cream Tabby, Cameo Tabby, Tortoiseshell, Calico, Dilute Calico, Blue-Cream, Bi-Color, Persian Van Bi-Color, Peke-face Red and Peke-face Red Tabby, Persian Van Calico, Persian Van Blue-Cream and White.

DEVON REX

CORNISH REX

REX

- Easy to groom
- People-oriented
- Intelligent
- Trainable
- Loving and devoted
- Active and clownish
- Loves attention
- Ravenous appetite
- Moderately quiet

Curly-haired Rex cats are spontaneous mutations of the domestic cat. There are two distinct breeds—the Cornish Rex and the Devon Rex. Cats with wavy coats had appeared from time to time in Germany, Italy, and the United States, but the first serious attempts to preserve such fur began in 1950 when a curly-coated kitten named Kallibunker appeared in a normal straight-coated litter on a farm in Cornwall, England. When Kallibunker was mated to his ordinary short-haired mother, several curly kittens appeared in her litter that were later named "Rex" after a popular variety of curly rabbits.

Ten years later in nearby Devon a wavy-coated kitten named Kirlee was born to a tortoiseshell and white normal-coated female. Kirlee was thought to be a Cornish Rex, but when he was mated to one of Kallibunker's progeny, all of the resulting offspring were straight-coated. Geneticists soon determined that there were two different Rex genes, and these were named Cornish (Gene I) and Devon (Gene II). The two are not compatible, and each will yield curly coats only when both parents carry the same recessive gene. Separate selective breeding programs were established, and in 1967, Cornish and Devon Rexes were accepted for championship competition by the British cat fancy. They appeared in North America a few years later, and were recognized as separate varieties by the Cat Fanciers' Association in 1979.

Rexes are small- to medium-size slender and agile cats with comparatively small and narrow heads, oval eyes, and huge ears. The most conspicuous feature of both breeds is a dense and curly undercoat with no topcoat or guard hairs. Even the whiskers and eyebrows are crinkly! The Cornish has a tight, uniform marcel curl that looks like a 1930s permanent wave, while the Devon's hair is softer and wavier. Rexes need less grooming than most breeds; a good hand-stroking will make their coats shine. Rex cats are saucy, people-oriented little rascals that love to be where the action is. They are inquisitive and highly intelligent. Many learn to retrieve balls and toys without any formal training and to wag their tails when they are happy.

Devon Rex Colors: All colors and patterns acceptable.
Cornish Rex Colors: White, Black, Blue, Red, Cream, Chinchilla, Shaded Silver, Black Smoke, Blue Smoke, Classic Tabby Pattern, Mackerel Tabby Pattern, Patched Tabby Pattern, Brown Patched Tabby, Blue Patched Tabby, Silver Patched Tabby, Silver Tabby, Red Tabby, Brown Tabby, Blue Tabby, Cream Tabby, Tortoiseshell, Calico, Van Calico, Dilute Calico, Blue-Cream, Van Blue-Cream and White, Van Bi-Color, Bi-Color, Other Rex Colors (ORC)—any other color or pattern with the exception of those showing evidence of hybridization resulting in the colors chocolate, lavender, the Himalayan pattern, or these combinations with white.

RUSSIAN BLUE

- Easy to groom
- Little shedding
- Friendly with children and other pets
- Gentle and sweet-natured
- Good apartment pet
- Intelligent
- Trainable

- Likes warm and serene surroundings
- Adaptable
- Quiet

The origins of the Russian Blue are obscure, although most experts believe they are the descendants of blue cats of northwest Russia, with dense and plush beaver-like coats thick enough to withstand the bitter cold. Sailors from the Russian seaport of Archangel are said to have taken these cats to England in the mid-nineteenth century. They were first exhibited at British cat shows in 1880, and before the turn of the century were known by several different names, including the Archangel cat, Russian Blue, Spanish Blue, Maltese Blue, and Chartreuse Blue. The breed first appeared in the United States in the early 1900s.

The aristocratic-looking Russian Blue is a medium-size long-legged, slender cat that matures slowly. The breed's most outstanding feature is its bright blue double coat, similar to that of a beaver or seal, with silver-tipped guard hairs that add a distinctive shimmer to the fur. Round, wide-set eyes—amber in kittens, vivid green in adults—add a dramatic contrast.

Russian Blues are quiet and intelligent, and a perfect choice for people who don't want a demanding or noisy cat. Although most are impish during kittenhood, eventually they become dignified and serene adults that lavish their affection on one person. They are peaceful in nature, and live harmoniously with children, dogs, and other cats.

Russian Blue Color: Bright Blue.

SCOTTISH FOLD

- Easy to groom
- Distinctive appearance
- Friendly with children and other pets
- People-oriented
- Cuddly and affectionate
- Calm and easygoing
- Good apartment pet
- Quiet

All Scottish Folds can trace their ancestry back to one folded-eared cat named Susie, born in a litter of normal-eared farm cats in Perthshire, Scotland, in

1961. Ears that fold forward and downward rather than stand straight up are well known in many breeds of dogs, but prior to this spontaneous mutation they had never been seen in cats. Through a series of test matings of Susie and her offspring, it was learned that folded ears could be reproduced. Scottish Folds can only be shown in North America, as of this writing. They were accepted for championship competition by the Cat Fanciers' Association in 1978.

Folds are medium-size sturdy cats with flexible, tapering tails. Everything about them looks round: cobby body; well-rounded head blending into a short, thick neck; and expressive, brilliant eyes. To accentuate the roundness, the small folded ears resemble a snug-fitting cap on top of the head. Scottish Folds are gentle and affectionate creatures with an innocent and childlike expression. They like nothing better than to curl up warmly in the nearest lap. They are placid, undemanding cats that live harmoniously with children and other pets.

Scottish Fold Colors: White, Black, Blue, Red, Cream, Chinchilla, Shaded Silver, Shell Cameo (Red Chinchilla), Shaded Cameo (Red Shaded), Black Smoke, Blue Smoke, Cameo Smoke (Red Smoke), Classic Tabby Pattern, Mackerel Tabby Pattern, Patched Tabby Pattern, Silver Tabby, Red Tabby, Brown Tabby, Blue Tabby, Cream Tabby, Cameo Tabby, Tortoiseshell, Calico, Dilute Calico, Blue-Cream, Bi-Color, Other Scottish Fold Colors (OSFC)—any other color or pattern with the exception of those showing evidence of hybridization resulting in the colors chocolate, lavender, the Himalayan pattern, or these combinations with white.

SIAMESE

- Easy to groom
- Friendly with children
- Super-intelligent
- Highly trainable
- Affectionate
- People-oriented
- Dislikes solitude
- Brazen and demanding
- Active and acrobatic
- Loud and talkative

Although the Siamese is an ancient breed, its origins are obscure. No one knows if the "Royal Cat of Siam," the companion of kings and priests, and guardian of the royal palace, actually originated in

Thailand. Many legends and theories surround its origins: that it is a descendant of the ancient cat of Egypt; that its ancestry traces back to the sacred cat of Burma; and that it originated from the breeding of a rare albino cat presented to the king of Siam long ago. We do know that it was a highly prized breed in the Siamese capital of Ayutthaya hundreds of years ago, because a delicate illustration of a Seal Point appears in the manuscript *Cat Book Poems* prepared in that ancient city sometime between 1360 and 1767.

When the Siamese reached the West is another debatable point. The first to arrive in England, according to some breed historians, were Pho and Mia, a pair presented by the king of Siam to Mr. Owen Gould, British consul-general in 1894. Yet the breed must have been known in England at least thirteen years prior to that date because the catalog of the 1871 London cat show indicates that two Siamese were exhibited. The first recorded American Siamese belonged to Mrs. Rutherford B. Hayes (wife of the nineteenth President of the United States) in the late 1870s.

Siamese are handsome and elegant cats with long, narrow bodies; long, slim legs; tapering, wedge-shaped heads, and whiplike tails. Their fine and glossy hair lies close to the body. The lighter body color is accentuated by darker points or extremities: facial mask, ears, legs, feet, and tail. (Siamese kittens are born solid white or ivory; their color points begin to darken within several weeks.) Siamese are highly intelligent and clever creatures that can be a real handful. They are unduly curious, demanding cats that resent being left alone—they want their people nearby at all times! Siamese are easy to train; playing ball and retrieving are two of their favorite activities. Their athletic feats can take one's breath away, and most learn to open closet and cupboard doors with great expertise. Of all the cat breeds the Siamese is the most talkative. Their vocabulary is amazing, and they adore carrying on spirited "conversations" with their owners. If you're looking for an affectionate but lively companion, a Siamese may be a good choice. *Siamese Colors:* Seal Point, Chocolate Point, Blue Point, Lilac Point.

SOMALI

- Needs regular grooming
- Friendly with children

- Loving and devoted
- Sweet-natured
- Active and playful
- Charming companion
- Quiet

The Somali is a long-haired Abyssinian that looks like a tiny mountain lion. Like the Aby, the Somali's ruddy or red coat is ticked with black or brown, but its fur is longer, with a profuse neck ruff and breeches, and a bushy tail. Kittens with long hair had appeared in Abyssinian litters from time to time, but it was only in the 1960s that breeders concentrated on developing a long-coated Abyssinian. The new variety was named the Somali and was accepted for championship competition by the Cat Fanciers' Association in 1978.

Somalis are medium-to-large graceful cats whose conformation strikes a balance between the extremes of sturdy, cobby-bodied cats and long, svelte foreign types. Their large and expressive eyes may be green or gold. Although they are rather "wild"-looking, Somalis are quiet and sweet-natured, and they make charming and devoted companions.

Somali Colors: Ruddy, Red.

TONKINESE

- Easy to groom
- People-oriented
- Intelligent
- Trainable
- Adaptable
- Fastidious
- Chatty

The Tonkinese, once called the "Golden Siamese," was produced through crosses of Burmese and Siamese. The breed was developed in Canada in the early 1960s and first recognized by the Canadian Cat Association. It was granted provisional status by the Cat Fanciers' Association as of May 1, 1982.

The Tonkinese is a medium-size cat with a modified wedge-shaped head, wide-set oriental blue-green eyes, and a tapering tail. Males are proportionately larger than females. The short and glossy coat comes in five glorious colors. Tonks make very congenial pets—they are intelligent, playful and fun-loving, and they adore people. They are easy to groom and possess fastidious habits. Most Tonkinese train easily, and, like their Siamese cousins, adapt beautifully to harnesses and leads, and like to play ball or retrieve. Tonkinese are healthy and hardy cats. They have extensive vocabularies and delight in chatty conversations with their people.

Tonkinese Colors: Natural Mink, Champagne Mink, Blue Mink, Honey Mink, Platinum Mink.

TURKISH ANGORA

- Requires daily grooming
- Good-natured and sociable
- Loving and devoted
- Intelligent
- Trainable
- Quiet and dignified

The Angora is one of the oldest breeds of domestic cats. Its name is another form of Ankara, the Turkish capital. In spite of its early popularity, cross-breeding with other longhairs and the preference for the Persian type almost caused the Angora to disappear as a breed early in this century. The Turkish government and the Ankara zoo came to its rescue, though, and established a careful breeding program to save the cat regarded as a national symbol from oblivion. The breed was rechristened the Turkish Angora. In the 1960s, U.S. Army Colonel and Mrs. Walter Grant brought two unrelated pairs of white Turkish Angoras to the United States. These imports inspired American breeders to reestablish the breed in this country, and in 1970 the Cat Fanciers' Association officially recognized the Turkish Angora. Today's cats are almost identical to the original Angoras.

The Turkish Angora is a medium-size cat with a long, graceful body, long legs, wedge-shaped head, and long and tapering tail. It comes in a variety of colors and coat patterns, including the traditional pure white. The breed has a fine and silky coat with a longer ruff around the neck (and a profusely coated tail) that usually improves with age. The coat is not as thick or as long as that of a Persian, but it does need regular grooming. Turkish Angoras are extremely bright and entertaining creatures. They are good-natured and highly trainable. In their native land Turkish Angoras are sometimes called "swimming cats" because they are said to enjoy immersing themselves in the warm streams.

Turkish Angora Colors: White, Black, Blue, Cream, Red, Black Smoke, Blue Smoke, Classic Tabby Pattern, Mackerel Tabby Pattern, Silver Tabby, Red Tabby, Brown Tabby, Blue Tabby, Cream Tabby, Tortoiseshell, Calico, Dilute Calico, Blue-Cream, Bi-Color.

Meet a Few Additional Breeds

Other rare cats, and breeds that are recognized or accepted for championship competition by organizations other than the Cat Fanciers' Association, include the following.

Chartreux

The blue-haired Chartreux, one of the oldest natural breeds, is a native of France. Known in its present state for hundreds of years, it was acknowledged as a breed by two great eighteenth-century naturalists, Carl von Linné (better known as "Linnaeus") of Sweden, and his French counterpart, Georges Louis Leclerc de Buffon. The early history of the Chartreux is somewhat obscure, but supposedly they were bred originally in the Carthusian monastery near Grenoble, by the monks who are famous for producing the aromatic green or yellow Chartreuse liqueur. Many believe they are the same as the British Blue, because the two breeds are similar in conformation and coloring. Several cat fancy organizations have accepted the Chartreux for championship competition.

The gentle Chartreux is a large, robust, and

powerful solid-blue cat with a massive round head and large gold-to-orange eyes. Males range from ten to fourteen pounds; females are slightly smaller, weighing from six to nine pounds. Like the British Blue, the Chartreux is exceptionally healthy and hardy, and a good mouser. They are intelligent, affectionate, and good-natured cats that get along well with people and other animals. In fact, most Chartreux enjoy a good romp with children and dogs occasionally. Some have been known to stand on their hind legs. Chartreux are easy to groom.

Cymric

The tailless Cymric is a long-haired Manx. Kittens with long hair and no tails had appeared now and then in Manx litters, and in the late 1960s, American breeders elected to establish the variety as a separate breed. The Cymric (its name is a derivation of *Cymru,* the Welsh name for Wales) has been accepted as a separate breed by some cat fancy organizations. Except for its glistening medium-long coat, which comes in a variety of colors and patterns, the Cymric is similar in conformation to the Manx. Everything about it conveys the impression of curves and circles: round head with round muzzle and prominent cheeks; large round eyes; broad chest; and extremely broad and round rump with high hindquarters. Like the Manx, Cymrics are playful and affectionate, but they often become attached to one person and act rather aloof to others. Cymrics make delightful family pets; they are good-natured and they get along well with children. Daily grooming is essential.

Ocicat

The Ocicat was developed in the United States and traces its ancestry back to a spotted kitten named Tonga, which appeared in a litter sired by a Chocolate Point Siamese out of a cross-bred Abyssinian-Siamese queen. Tonga so resembled a tiny ocelot that the breed was christened the Ocicat. The American Shorthair, Siamese, and Abyssinian were used to develop the new breed. As of this writing the Ocicat has not yet been accepted for championship competition by any cat fancy organization.

Ocicats are large, exotic-looking, leggy cats with golden eyes and short glossy hair patterned very much like that of the Egyptian Mau. The first Ocicats were cream-colored with either dark chestnut or milk chocolate-colored spots; however, breeders have recently introduced bronze and silver in the breed as well.

Ragdoll

The controversial Ragdoll was developed about fifteen years ago by Ann Baker of Riverside, California, who placed severe restrictions on her clients regarding the Ragdoll's placement, showing, breeding, and perpetuation. The breed was named because of its ability to go limp like a rag doll when picked up. Ragdolls are recognized by several cat fancy associations.

Ragdolls are large, docile cats that are often misidentified with Birmans. They are much heavier than Birmans, though, with males weighing as much as twenty pounds. Their thick medium-to-long hair resembles rabbit fur. Some Ragdolls have seal, chocolate, lilac, or blue color points; some are bi-colored, and others have white mittens. Ragdolls are affectionate, intelligent, and quiet creatures that are extremely good-natured. They like being near people, and they enjoy attention. It is said that the Ragdoll feels no pain or fear, and that it will refuse to defend itself when challenged. It is, therefore, a defenseless breed, and anyone considering owning one must be prepared to be totally accountable for its well-being.

Safari

The Safari is a newcomer to the cat fancy. This controversial feral-domestic hybrid was developed in the mid-1970s by crossing the Geoffroy's Cat, a small, native South American spotted wildcat, with domestic shorthairs. Safaris are sinewy, long-bodied cats with massive heads. Their short, striking coats are patterned exactly like the tabbyish Geoffroy's Cat: a series of spots, stripes, leg bracelets, tail rings, cheek swirls, unbroken lines running back from the eyes, and frown marks on the forehead. Several domestic short-haired breeds have been crossed with the Geoffroy's Cat, but the most spectacularly marked Safaris have come from American Shorthairs and Siamese.

Safaris are loving, highly intelligent cats that frequently become attached to one person. They are not companions for the sedate—they play enthusiastically, and they love to climb!

Singapura

The delightful Singapura first arrived in the United States in 1975. It is a natural breed from Singapore, an island in the South China Sea, south of the Malay Peninsula. *Singapura* is the Malaysian word for Singapore. The Singapura is a smaller-than-average cat with a muscular body and legs, a short neck, round head, and noticeably large eyes and ears. Its short, tight coat is silky in texture and patterned much like that of an Abyssinian. The coloring is brown on a yellow-tinged old ivory base, with the chin, chest, and stomach the color of unbleached muslin. Singapuras are sweet-tempered and playful cats. They get along well with children and other cats and dogs, and although they are known to be reserved by nature, they do socialize with strangers.

Sphinx

The hairless Sphinx (also spelled Sphynx) first appeared in 1966 in a litter of normal-coated kittens born to a black and white housecat in Ontario, Canada. The breed, also called the Canadian Hairless, Moonstone, and Chat sans Poil ("Cat without Hair"), looks like the Mexican Hairless, a now-extinct cat known to the Aztecs. Although rare, Sphinx are accepted by a few cat fancy associations.

The Sphinx is a muscular, medium-boned, and

barrel-chested cat, higher in the rear, with a long and tapering tail. The head is a rounded wedge shape with large ears that are wide at the base and rounded at the tips. The eyes are round and slightly slanted. The Sphinx is completely hairless except for a fine, plush down on the face, the back of the body, the paws (up to the "wrist" or "ankle"), and tail tip. The fine down looks like velvet and feels like moss. The skin should be taut in adults, with a wrinkle pattern on the head. Until they mature, however, kittens look lost, as if they were wearing a sweater several sizes too large. There are no wrinkles on the body. Like hairless dogs, Sphinx cats possess a higher body temperature than other breeds, and they feel quite warm to the touch. Sphinx come in a variety of colors and patterns. They are sweet-natured and overly friendly, and are said to enjoy the company of people more than other cats.

III Welcoming Your New Cat

A home without a cat, and a well-fed, well-petted and properly revered cat, may be a perfect home, perhaps, but how can it prove its title.

—Mark Twain

You have decided that you want a cat as a pet. You and your family have carefully chosen your household's newest member; a cat, you hope, whose breed, sex, color, hair length, and temperament are right for your life-style. Owning a cat can be a great source of pleasure to an individual or a family. Along with the great gladness, however, comes responsibility. It is your duty to prepare and provide your cat with a clean and stimulating environment that is secure from harm.

Things to Have Ready

Preparing to welcome a new cat is like getting ready to bring a newborn baby home from the hospital. There are matters to attend to and supplies to purchase before the kitten arrives to assure that its first days in its new surroundings go smoothly. Have the following items (which can be purchased at pet stores and supermarkets) ready and waiting for the new arrival:

Bed or Basket

Cats spend a great deal of time sleeping, so you need a comfortable bed with a soft cushion, blanket, or fluffy bath mat. It may be an elaborate hooded "igloo-shaped" model, one made of plastic, a beanbag filled with plastic pellets, a wicker basket, or just a simple cardboard carton with an opening cut into the side.

Whatever style of bed you choose, place it in a warm, draft-free, and secluded area away from noise, bright lights, children, and other pets. Although your cat may eventually want to curl up on your favorite chair or lie close to you in bed at night, it should always have access to its own place of refuge, a cozy and warm bed, when it wants privacy.

Food and Water Dishes

A cat should have its own dishes for solid food and a bowl for water. Cat feeding containers are made of plastic, ceramics, glazed pottery, aluminum, and stainless steel. Most breeders prefer stainless steel dishes because they last indefinitely. Pick a style that is chewproof, easy to clean, and sturdy enough not to slide around the floor when the cat eats, and one that the cat cannot turn upside down. Cats prefer shallow food dishes; usually they do not like to eat out of deep bowls. Always place the food and water containers in the same location. Change the water frequently, and serve each meal in a clean dish. The same sanitary procedures you use in preparing and serving your meals should be observed for your cat. And always wash kitty's dishes in hot, soapy water, separately from the family's dishes.

Comb, Brush, and Grooming Aids

Every cat needs combing and brushing (even those with short and sleek coats), plus some other grooming. The different kinds of combs and brushes for longhairs and shorthairs are discussed in Chapter V, "The Well-Groomed Cat." Your pet supplies dealer can show you the necessary tools and help you select the right things.

Cat Carrier

You need a case to bring your cat home in, and for its first trip to the veterinary hospital. Carrying cases, like many other cat accoutrements, come in a variety of materials, sizes, colors, and prices. The least expensive is a folding cardboard "going home" car-

Popular types of cat carriers.

rier that can be purchased at most pet stores and humane societies. Although every cat owner should have one tucked away for emergencies, these are not recommended for frequent use because they are not leakproof or chewproof. If you will be traveling to cat shows, or for other occasions when your cat will go with you in the car, consider buying a sturdy wicker basket or lightweight plastic or fiberboard cat carrier with a luggage handle. The latter models come in a variety of shapes and subdued or brilliant colors—some are even fashioned like circus wagons or London buses—with mesh or clear plastic lids, or doors with metal bars. Should you plan to take your cat along on a plane trip, many of these carriers will fit underneath an airline seat. (*This information, however, is not applicable to the shipment of cats as air cargo.**)

Whatever its style, your carrier should be large enough to let your cat turn around or lie down in, well-ventilated, easy to clean, and have a secure latch. Line the bottom with newspapers and a soft towel, to give warmth as well as to absorb urine. Don't forget to label the case clearly with your name, address, and telephone number. Clean the carrier periodically, especially after your cat has been sick.

Litter Tray and Litter

Cat litter trays come in several different designs. The most common kind is a shallow rectangular-shaped plastic pan. Plastic, incidentally, is ideal for cleaning and disinfecting. Another style has a rimmed lid to help keep litter inside the pan, in the case of an overzealous scratcher, instead of all over your floor. Then there are trays with detachable hoods

---

*To learn more about shipping crates and matters pertaining to shipping cats as air cargo, consult Chapter XI.

(complete with small round entrance hole) for cats that like privacy or that spray when they urinate. Some of the hooded models come equipped with charcoal filters to suppress offensive odors. Jumbo pans for multicat households are also available. If you are bringing home a young kitten, it's easiest to start with the shallow rectangular-shaped pan and then change to some other style should the occasion arise.

Clear plastic pan-liners can be purchased from most pet stores and, while these are leakproof and make litter changing a breeze, they can be a real nuisance when one owns a cat that likes to poke holes in the plastic. Your pet-supplies dealer also sells special scoops (the most popular model being a slotted spoonlike device made of metal or plastic)

Cat litter pans made of plastic (from left to right): tray with rimmed lid; tray with detachable hood; shallow rectangular-shaped pan.

designed to remove fecal matter from the tray so you don't have to touch the soiled litter.

Although shredded newspapers, sand, sawdust, and wood shavings can be used in the litter pan, most owners prefer commercially manufactured cat litter. Several different kinds are available: litter made of white or gray clay, litter with scented granules to control odors, some made of alfalfa or chlorophyll pellets; each type has its good and weak points. Unless your kitten's breeder has recommended a specific type, you may want to experiment with different substances at first to determine which your pet prefers.

Scratching Post

You must positively provide a scratching post and place it in a prominent location, ideally near your kitten's sleeping quarters. Scratching is an instinctive reflex in a cat. Cats that go outdoors scratch on tree trunks, but those that are confined indoors will claw furniture, rugs, drapes, and other objects made of textured materials where there is nothing else to scratch. If you bought your kitten from a concerned breeder, it probably already knows how to scratch on a post. If it does not, however, you must teach the kitten how to use the post. Failure to do so will result in the establishment of a behavior pattern that is extremely difficult to break. There are several different kinds of scratching posts on the market, the most popular being a sturdy vertical piece of wood covered with carpeting or rough bark and mounted on a pedestal. Dr. Bonnie Beaver, associate professor at the College of Veterinary Medicine, Texas A&M University, advises in her book *Veterinary Aspects of Feline Behavior* that "in addition to being stable, the object should be tall enough (at least 12 inches) for the cat to rest on its hind limbs and reach out to claw. The texture of the scratching post is of little significance, but the preferred primary orientation of the fabric weave is longitudinal, which provides the cat with the most efficient conditioning of each claw." (See "Bibliography of the Cat" in Chapter XVI.) Scratching posts-cum-pedestal beds, or combination scratching posts with cat house and window-height pedestal, and even carpeted tree units that adjust to

A scratching post is necessary to deter the cat from clawing furniture. It can be a simple post (covered with a textured surface) on a sturdy base, tall enough for the cat to stretch out and claw, or it can be part of a floor-to-ceiling combination house and scratching post. Some have window-height pedestals so the cat can look outdoors.

fit eight-feet ceilings are available too. Because cats love to watch the world go by from high places, any one of these can be of practical use if you want to spend the extra money.

Toys

Kitten-play and play-fighting are laying the foundation, in a way, for the realities of life. Kittens develop their hunting and fighting skills and learn the art of offense and defense by playing with their mother and littermates, and when you take a kitten away from this environment, you must provoke play with stimulating toys. Always select toys of appropriate size that cannot be chewed or clawed apart, splintered, caught in your cat's throat, or swallowed whole. Cats adore soft objects they can pick up and carry around in their mouths, such as fur, felt, or rubber mice; sponge golf balls; or cloth toys shaped like booties, squirrels, caterpillars, spiders, and every other shape imaginable, not to mention fuzzy tiger and raccoon tails and pompons. Soft toys—especially mice—that can be gripped between the paws, held in the mouth, tossed in the air, and pounced upon will arouse your cat's natural hunting abilities. Many of these are filled with dried catnip leaves.* The catnip or catmint plant—or *Nepeta cataria,* as it is scientifically named—is intensely stimulating to most cats. They love to sniff it, lick and chew it, and roll in it until they become almost intoxicated with its scent. Research indicates that about 70 percent of all cats react to catnip in either high or low intensity, while the rest do not respond at all. The capacity to respond

---

*You can also purchase dried catnip leaves or aerosol catnip extract at most pet stores, or buy catnip seeds or plants from nurseries to grow at home.

seems to be inherited, and those that have inherited a high-intensity capacity pass into a state of ecstasy that extends from five to fifteen minutes. The effects, however, are not habit-forming and are perfectly innocuous. Beware, though, because not all "catnip" toys contain catnip leaves. Some are merely sprayed with catnip extract!

Hard-rubber or lattice balls with bells inside, Ping-Pong balls, and almost everything else that rolls can intrigue your cat for hours. Even such modest objects as a large sewing spool or crumpled sheet of paper can greatly amuse a cat. Some toys come with long elastic strings and can be suspended from doorknobs or refrigerator handles. Deluxe scratching posts are available with mice or balls attached to the tops on springs. Cats love to slap these around with their paws. They also adore playing hide and seek by concealing themselves in spacious brown paper grocery bags (remove handles, please) and cardboard cartons. Almost every cat enjoys playing games in which its owner takes part, even if the owner just dangles a piece of yarn or string, or swoops a peacock feather through the air.

Collar or Harness and Leash

Cat owners frequently disagree as to whether or not cats should wear collars. If one is used, though, it should contain an elastic insert or be made of Velcro and break away under pressure. A collar that expands or breaks away could prevent your cat from strangling should it get caught on something. When worn, the collar should be snug enough that the cat cannot hold it in its mouth or get its paws through, but loose enough that you can slip two fingers underneath.

Kittens should be collarbroken at an early age and allowed to become gradually used to wearing the device. Do expect much leaping, rolling over, and whirling about, the first few times your kitten wears its collar, in an attempt to remove the "millstone" from around its neck. If you plan to show your cat, incidentally, do not use a collar, because it could wear down the hair in the neck area.

A collar with identification is absolutely essential if your cat will go outdoors. One carrying an I.D. tag or a plastic pocket or tube containing a paper with your name, address, and phone number can help identify your cat if it strays from home. You will have to invest in a harness and leash if you plan to walk your cat outdoors. Then a harness in a figure eight, a figure H, or a standard shape plus a lightweight leather or nylon lead are required. (Instructions for training your cat to walk on lead will be found in Chapter VII).

Food

Ask the breeder what the kitten has been eating and have at least a week's supply of that food on hand. You may plan to change the diet eventually but wait until the kitten adjusts to its new surroundings. (The subject of nutrition is discussed in Chapter IV.)

Medical Supplies and Important Papers

Medical and first aid supplies are listed in Chapter VI, "Keeping Your Cat Healthy." You should also purchase a large manila envelope in which you can file such valuable documents as your cat's pedigree, registration, health and vaccination certificates, and eventually photographs and other important papers. Some of these can help trace your cat should it become lost (see Chapter XII).

Catproofing Your Home

You must make a few adjustments in your home to make it a safer place for the new arrival. Most cats are insatiably curious and will discover all kinds of household dangers, and every home or apartment contains countless potential hazards for an inquisitive feline. Your cat's actions, whether innocent or destructive, could cause it a great deal of harm, and cause you anguish, not to mention the dent it could put in your checkbook.

Cats are capable of doing an amazing amount of harm to themselves or to your possessions in a short period of time. Although your four-footed friend might get into trouble, you are most certainly to blame for not using common sense and taking adequate precautions. Follow these suggestions to make your home a safer place:

- To save wear and tear on upholstery and drapes, provide a scratching post and (if necessary) teach your cat how to use it.
- Securely screen all windows.
- Keep toilet bowl lids closed.
- Tape electrical cords on lamps, television sets, and so forth close to the wall so they don't tempt your cat. Cords on kitchen appliances such as coffeepots, toasters, broilers, and electric fry pans should *never* dangle, especially when the device is being used.
- Never leave items lying around that are small enough to be swallowed, for instance, pins, needles, thread, string, rubber bands, buttons, tinsel, bits of cellophane or aluminum foil. All of these are dangerous or possibly life-threatening when ingested.

- Check opaque trash bags before closing them.
- Keep drawers, closets, cupboards, and luggage closed. Keep dishwasher and automatic-dryer doors closed. All of these provide warm napping places in which your cat could be imprisoned. Be careful when closing refrigerator and freezer doors, too.
- Keep furniture polish, cleaning supplies, paint, paint thinners, gasoline, antifreeze, roach and insect killers, chlorine swimming pool preparations, and other dangerous items locked up and out of the reach of pets and children. (Other potentially toxic household items are listed in Chapter VI.)
- Securely close indoor and outdoor trash and garbage cans.
- Keep aquariums covered.
- Keep birds and other small pets like hamsters and gerbils caged. Should you wish to allow them a few minutes of freedom, confine your cat in another room so it won't attack them.
- Screen your fireplace.
- Remove valuable breakable objects from tabletops and other surfaces your cat can reach. Most cats love to knock things off tables and shelves just to see them fall.
- Place houseplants where your cat cannot reach them. This will not only discourage puss from nibbling on your gorgeous greenery but it may also save the kitten's life. Many houseplants are potentially harmful to animals, and some of these are listed in Chapter VI, "Keeping Your Cat Healthy." Should your cat have a fancy for plants, provide dried catnip leaves occasionally,

grow your own sprouts, or purchase a small kit of grass seeds that is commercially manufactured for cats. These come ready to grow in an aluminum tray; you simply add water, place the container in a sunny spot, and within a few days shoots begin to appear. Products such as VO-Toys' Kitty Kraze provide natural grass that satisfies the needs of most cats. Try adding a bit of chopped parsley to the food now and then to satiate your cat's craving for green plants.

It seems an appropriate time to mention that if kitty persists in chewing at your plants, walking across the dining room table, or knocking down objects, the best recourse is to have a child's water pistol or plant-mister ready for action. As soon as you see a misdeed, squirt your cat immediately. Pretty soon just reaching for the sprayer will produce results. It's worth the little extra thought and effort to make your household safe and your cat a happy family member. But don't become complacent. Just when you think, "Aha, he'll never be able to get that now," he probably will!

Welcoming the New Arrival

If you work during the week, try to bring home the new kitten on a Saturday morning so you can be with it the first few days to allay any fears. Take along the new carrying case, lined with newspaper and a soft towel, when you go to collect the kitten. The cat will feel more secure being confined instead of running loose while the car is moving. Loose and uncontrollable pets are dangerous in a moving car. Should you have to break to a sudden halt, the kitten could slide forward and be seriously injured. Worse yet, its roaming about or crawling under the gas pedal could cause an accident in which family members could suffer.

As soon as you arrive home, open the door of the carrying case and take the kitten out. The way a kitten is treated during the first days in a new home will greatly affect its personality and future actions. All the kitten's supplies should be prepared in their proper place. Let each family member greet the new arrival. Show the kitten the way to the litter tray and the bed, and then give it a chance to rest. Keep loud or boisterous children, other family pets, and well-meaning neighbors and friends away for the moment. Calm and relaxed surroundings are best for the first few days. The kitten is away from its mother and littermates for the first time and is not sure what is happening. It does not know where it is or who you are. You have to show the kitten that it is safe to give its love and trust to you.

Don't be alarmed if the kitten wriggles under a chair or the sofa and stays out of sight for a while. Many animal behaviorists think that hiding in a dark place is a cat's way of reverting to the security of its nest. Be patient; the kitten will come out before long and will want to investigate the new surroundings. Let the kitten explore to its heart's content, but follow it around (in case it gets into trouble) speaking in an affectionate tone. Feed the kitten at the usual times. It may be too overwhelmed at the moment for a real meal, but the offer of food, perhaps a sip of milk, and your affection will be very satisfying.

The first night in a new home can be an unhappy experience for a kitten that has always slept in the warm and cozy box where it was born. You have to decide *now* where the kitten will sleep for the rest of its life: in its bed in the kitchen or den, in its bed next to your bed, or on your bed or a child's bed. If you confine the kitten in a room other than your bedroom, it will probably cry out from loneliness, but going in to give a few pats and reassuring words now and then will help overcome this. If you succumb to its mournful wails, however, and let the kitten in your bed "just for the first night," it will expect to sleep there every other night. You may be exhausted at dawn, but creating good habits in the first twenty-four hours is a lot easier than correcting bad ones once they are established.

Lifting and Carrying

One of the first essentials is for every family member to learn the correct way to lift and carry the kitten or cat. Improper handling can not only frighten a feline, but it could also cause you or your children to be unintentionally scratched.

A cat should never be lifted by its forelegs, paws, tail, or especially by the scruff of its neck. Lifting a cat in such a manner can harm the nerves in the neck area as well as put a great deal of stress on the spinal cord. You may dispute this by saying that mothers always carry their kittens by the scruffs of their necks, but keep in mind that the kittens weigh only a few ounces and very little heaviness is suspended. Lifting an adult cat by the neck scruff is recommended only during certain emergencies or to produce passive immobility when the animal is almost unmanageable.

The correct procedure is to place one arm under the cat's chest with your fingers either holding its front elbows or between its front legs for support. As you lift the cat, place your other hand under its hindquarters to support the weight. Hold the cat securely as you lift. Don't grip too tightly, or the cat will struggle to escape. Once lifted, the cat may be happily cuddled with its weight resting in the crook of your arm. Hold the cat against your body for additional support, and keep it away from your neck and face.

Naming the Kitten

It is wise to select a name for your kitten and begin using it as soon as possible. Most cats learn to recognize their names, although many will not always respond when called. If you purchased a pedigreed kitten, its name may already have been chosen and registered by the breeder. Registered designations usually incorporate the breeder's cattery name. To clarify this: Suppose you buy a pedigreed kitten from a hypothetical couple named Philip and Margaret Smith. Your kitten could be registered as Phil-Mar Maid of the Mist, the cattery prefix being a contraction of Mr. and Mrs. Smith's first names. Once registered, the name cannot be changed, but you might pick "Misty" as the short call-name you will use most of the time. If your kitten has not yet been registered, you may be able to choose its name, and that can be anything you find appropriate, creative or whimsical.

People with two or more cats often name them with words that are frequently used together, such as Scotch and Soda, Lord and Taylor, Rags and Riches, or after famous couples like Romeo and Juliet, Antony and Cleopatra, or Tristan and Isolde. For three cats there are the three Bs, Bach, Beethoven, and Brahms, or the three musketeers, Athos, Porthos, and Aramis, for males and Faith, Hope, and Charity for females. If you are fond of opera, Shakespeare, Dickens, mythology, films, or the legitimate theater, here's where you can indulge your passion.

Should picking the right name be a difficult choice, you may want to consult the dictionary of celebrated cats and cats of celebrated people beginning on page 447. Hundreds of names appear along with sentimental or amusing anecdotes to help you make your selection.

The First Medical Examination

Your first trip with the kitten, preferably within forty-eight hours after it enters your home, should be a visit to the veterinarian for an examination. The kitten may need to be vaccinated against panleukopenia, rhinotracheitis, calicivirus, pneumonitis, and possibly rabies. Depending on its age, your kitten may already have received some or all of the necessary permanent inoculations. If you obtained a health and immunization record from the breeder or pet store (as suggested in the previous chapter), take it along so the veterinarian can determine if additional inoculations are required. He or she will also advise you about necessary booster shots.

Take along a fresh stool sample to be examined for worms. This is the time to seek the veterinarian's advice about diet, vitamin-mineral supplements, and health care. Should you discover that your cat has a serious medical problem or hereditary defect that may cause you heartbreak later, get a statement from the veterinarian, return the kitten immediately to the breeder or pet store, and choose another animal. It may seem cruel, but it is less traumatic in the long run to return the kitten now than to raise it and fall in love with it, and see it euthanized, perhaps, at an early age.

Choosing a Veterinarian

If you don't already have a veterinarian, ask the breeder of your kitten, the local cat club, or cat-owning friends for recommendations. The local veterinary association or the American Animal Hospital Association can supply you with the names of member veterinarians in your area (see "Useful Addresses" in Chapter XVI).

Select your veterinarian carefully, in fact, just as diligently as you did the family physician. Always choose him or her before bringing home your kitten. Don't wait until an emergency arises and everyone panics. Seeing and getting to know your cat while it is young will help the veterinarian a great deal. Some guidelines for choosing a veterinarian include:

- Office or hospital within a short distance of your home.
- Evening and weekend office hours if you work during the day.
- Clean, bright, pleasant-smelling and well-equipped facilities.
- Courteous and cheerful attitude from both veterinarian and staff.
- Kind but firm handling of your cat.
- Veterinarian and staff inspire confidence.
- Willingness to discuss problems, treatments, and fees.
- Ability to obtain medical care after office hours and on weekends and holidays during a *real* emergency. Accidents can and do happen at any time of the day. No critically injured cat should have to endure pain or lose its life because you can't reach the veterinarian.

- A reminder notice is sent when booster shots are necessary.

Do be a considerate client by arriving on time for appointments, paying strict attention to your veterinarian's instructions for home treatment, and by not pestering him with trivialities. Pay your bills promptly. Remember, as with everything else these days the cost of animal care has increased considerably.

Indoors or Outdoors?

Many people believe that cats should be allowed to roam free, and that preventing them from doing so is a violation of their natural rights. It is this author's belief that no cat should be allowed to go outdoors when it is unsupervised. The Tree House Animal Foundation of Chicago, one of the country's most progressive humane groups, suggests that "born free" may be a fine philosophy for Elsa the lion, but there are simply too many dangers outdoors to justify allowing a cat to roam. How right they are! Free-roaming cats can be lost, stolen, hit by cars, poisoned by toxic chemicals, infested with fleas and other external parasites, diseased, bitten or disabled in fights with other animals, or ensnared in leg-hold traps. So establish a pattern as soon as your cat sets foot in the house, and don't let it get a taste of roaming free.

Cats can live comfortably indoors and need a limited amount of exercise to remain in good condition. Most excercise when they bound around the house, sprint up and down the stairs or a cat tree, chase other family pets, or play with their owners. A collection of provocative toys, and large grocery bags or cardboard cartons with holes cut in the sides, will provide stimulating recreation. Although it has nothing to do with calisthenics, most cats love to sit in sunny windows, and you can buy or build a little window seat that fastens to the sill by brackets. Your cat can go outdoors with a little advance preparation. You can train it to walk on harness and leash, or you can buy or build an outdoor exercise pen. A sturdy wire-mesh enclosure at least three by four feet, with an escape-proof roof, is an ideal place for a cat to exercise in fresh air and sunlight.

Early Training

Litter pan and scratch post training should begin as soon as the cat enters your home. It may sound repetitious, but creating good habits in the first few days is much easier than trying to correct bad ones once they are adopted.

Litter Pan Training

Most cats are naturally fastidious creatures, and this charming quality is shared by all breeds, even the "all-American" domestic shorthair. By the time they are weaned, most kittens have been trained by their mothers to use a litter tray. If you have to housebreak your kitten, however, don't be downhearted, because it's usually very easy since most cats have a natural tendency to bury their body wastes.*

Fill the litter tray with three to four inches of commercial litter or any of the other previously mentioned materials. Be sure the tray is roomy and deep enough to contain your cat comfortably. Cats like privacy, especially when they perform the ritual

---

*Animal behaviorists say that this characteristic is predestined and that is is probably effected so the cat will not leave evidence to direct an enemy to its territory and home range.

of urination or defecation, so do place the tray in a secluded but accessible spot, such as the bathroom. Take your kitten to the tray the first thing every morning, after meals and play periods, and before it goes to sleep at night. It may be necessary to show the kitten what to do by taking hold of its front paws and making scratching motions.

Cats dislike using dirty or reeking litter trays. Scoop out the feces daily and flush them down the toilet. Add a little baking soda or cat litter deodorant occasionally, and stir the litter around to give the wet granules on the bottom a chance to dry. Change the litter regularly. How often you have to do this depends on the individual cat and its habits, but once a week is about average. Wash the pan with hot soapy water each time you change the litter, but do not use potentially toxic disinfectants.

Some cats are very particular about the material used inside the litter tray. Just remember that to avoid any training problems, it is best to stay with whatever substance your cat has been trained to use, and not to change.

If your cat has an accident away from the litter tray, don't spank it or push its nose in the mistake, especially if the misdeed has occurred in the past. Actions and consequences are interrelated to an animal, and it will not understand discipline for something that happened previously. So many young animals are intimidated by ill-advised owners in this manner, which may only make the kitten repeat its wrongdoing. Tell the kitten "No" firmly, then carry it immediately to the litter tray. If you catch your cat in the act of urinating or defecating away from its tray, squirt it with a water gun or plant-mister, or make a loud noise to get its attention and show your displeasure.

Clean up the accident and take care to eliminate all traces of pungence with a cat odor-control product or a mixture of equal parts white vinegar and water, sponged generously on the area and then blotted dry with paper towels. If you do not do this, your kitten may return to the same spot again and again. William Campbell, one of the country's leading animal behavior experts, recommends a "spot" feeding program to solve urinating and spraying problems. If your cat has a favorite spot for mistakes, advises Mr. Campbell, feed it there (after proper cleaning).

> If is has two spots, split each feeding into two dishes and place them at the spots. Leave the dishes down between feedings, washing them just before each feeding time. This should be done until four days have passed wherein the cat has not soiled in these areas. Then resume feeding at the regular place. If your pet regresses and soils or sprays again, re-start the "spot" feeding program until another four days' perfect performances have been achieved. . . . Keep this up until the problem is resolved.

Always check with your veterinarian when problems persist to be sure that no physical cause exists for the misdeeds before resorting to spraying with a plant-mister or other corrective procedures. One of the first signs of cystitis is when a cat squats to urinate frequently all over the house, or rushes constantly to its litter pan. The urine may be passed in small amounts and sometimes will be blood-tinged. Immediate veterinary attention is necessary.

Scratch Post Training

Scratching is an inherited trait of all cats for the purpose of removing frayed or worn claws and to expose the new, sharp claws underneath. To prevent your kitten from damaging valuable household furnishings, it is immediately necessary to provide a scratching post. Many owners don't think about scratching facilities, unfortunately, until they notice the mutilation of the furniture or other textured objects. And punishment for this misdeed has no permanent influence in putting an end to the scratching performance if the cat has no substitute on which to claw.

The post should be introduced to a new arrival as soon as possible. Dr. Benjamin L. Hart, in an article published in *Feline Practice* magazine, says that "cats tend to prefer, and develop a scratching habit towards, objects near their sleeping or resting areas, because they tend to scratch usually just after awakening. In addition to conditioning their claws, it appears as though scratching serves as a form of stretching for the front limbs. Therefore, the scratching post board should be located adjacent to where the animal sleeps." You may have to show your kitten what to do by moving its paws up and down the post. Praise and stroke the kitten when it uses the post. When you see it scratching household objects, squirt the kitten with the plant-mister or water pistol, and immediately take it to the post.

The Declawing Controversy

Serious problems occur when owners find it difficult to train their cats to scratch on a post and the animal starts to mutilate the furniture. They often resort to declawing to prevent the destruction of household furnishings.

Declawing is a highly controversial procedure that requires a general anesthesia. During the surgery the nails (including the cells from which they grow) and part or all of the terminal bone of the toes on the cat's forepaws are severed by means of a guillotine-type nail clipper. The toes are then sutured or bandaged tightly to prevent them from hemorrhaging. People who strongly oppose declawing say that it is cruel and unnatural, and likely to cause many problems. "For instance," says cat therapist Carole C. Wilbourn in her latest book, *Cats on the Couch,* "gangrene can set in and a foot may have to be amputated if the bandages are put on too tightly. Often hemorrhaging may start when the bandages are removed." (See "Bibliography of the Cat" in Chapter XVI.) Ms. Wilbourn adds that there are long-term problems. "Abscessed nail beds, or claws can begin to regrow and then are misshapen. Sometimes an entire nail bed is not removed, and some of the remaining claws begin to regrow. Also, it's possible for the bone to shatter, which can cause infection and continuous draining from the toe." Declawing causes certain psychological complications, too. A cat uses its claws to catch prey, to climb, and to defend itself, and without them may become more aggressive and more inclined to bite. On the other side of the coin, many veterinarians believe that declawing is neither cruel nor inhumane, and is *the* solution when you are faced with giving up your cat because of its destructive scratching.

Whatever your views about declawing, the procedure should be considered only after you have made a serious effort to train your cat to use a scratching post. Trim the cat's nails regularly. In addition to placing a post near the cat's bed, stand another one or two in other parts of the house or apartment, and spray them with catnip to induce the cat to use them. Correct mistakes immediately with the plant-mister. Praise the cat lavishly when it scratches on its post. Ms. Wilbourn also advises covering the furniture until the scratching post has become a strong habit.

Declawing should never be done automatically. It is an irreversible procedure that requires much predeliberation. But if you have exhausted all possibilities and opt for the procedure, most veterinarians recommend that it be done between six to eight months of age. They say that while cats of any age can be declawed, the younger cat adjusts better to life without claws. Cats that go outdoors unsupervised should never be declawed, incidentally.

IV Nutrition and the Cat

Early man used to throw left-over food and bones at animals lurking outside his cave. His intention was to discourage them, but it merely convinced certain animals that man could simplify the eternal quest for food by handing it to them, almost on a plate. The cat was among those animals, and since then it has moved right into the home. However, its approach remains unchanged. When meat is being prepared, children are eating cereal, or a cow is being milked . . . the cat is there.

—Dr. Frank Manolson and David Hardy,
Living With Your Cat

The expression "you are what you eat" holds true for cats, too, and good nutrition is the most important thing you can provide for your cat. It is the foundation for a healthier, more active, and longer life. A lot of owners, however, know little about feline nutrition and rely on misinformation or old wives' tales. Cats are classified as carnivores, or meat-eaters. Although the cat is a true carnivore, however, it cannot flourish on an all-meat diet, which could cause nutritional deficiencies. Few people consider that the cat's prehistoric ancestors instinctively ate a complete and balanced diet, consuming the stomach, intestines, internal organs, and flesh of their prey to meet protein, carbohydrate, and vitamin and mineral requirements, and the muscles, fat, and bones to satisfy their energy, growth, and maintenance needs. Even today wildcats satisfy their nutritional requirements by consuming the entire carcass of their kill.

Modern domestic cats, of course, are largely dependent on people for food. Feline nutritionists know that cats have special dietary requirements totally unlike those of dogs or people, and that they need to eat a well-balanced diet to be healthy, active, and happy during their various life-stages.

To understand the basics of feline nutrition, a concerned owner must become acquainted with the essential nutrients and their importance, the different kinds of cat foods, how to evaluate a food, and how to feed a cat.

The Essential Nutrients

Cats require a balanced diet containing all the essential nutrients to maintain optimum health and well-being through various stages of their lives: kittenhood, adulthood, pregnancy and lactation, and old age. The essential nutrients—protein, carbohydrates, fat, vitamins, minerals, and water—are found in food and work in several ways, including providing heat and energy, regulating body processes, and supplying material for growth and repair of body tissues. No single nutrient will maintain good health. Each has its specific purpose and affinity to the cat's body and must be present in proper quantities in the diet. A deficiency or excess or imbalance of certain nutrients can cause a cat to become sick. A cat's diet ideally should achieve the following:

1. The food should be nutritionally adequate.
2. The diet should supply sufficient calories to meet the cat's energy requirements.
3. The food should contain the required nutrients in a form that can be utilized by the cat.
4. The food should be acceptable to the cat so that it is eaten in adequate amounts.

The table that follows the brief descriptions of the essential nutrients lists the nutrient requirements presently accepted for cats.

Protein

Cats need proportionately more protein in their diets than dogs do. Proteins, often called the "building blocks" of the tissues, are composed of twenty-three units known as amino acids. They serve as building material for body organs, muscles, skin, coat, nails, and blood. The cat's body can manufacture twelve of the twenty-three amino acids; the other eleven are called "essential amino acids" because they must be derived from outside protein sources in the diet. Although cats can utilize both animal and vegetable proteins, animal proteins are of greater nutritional value. Meat, fish, poultry, eggs, cheese, and milk all are excellent sources of animal proteins. Whole egg protein, according to *Nutrient Requirements of Cats,* a publication of the National Academy of Sciences, supplies nearly optimum concentrations of the amino acids needed by cats. But when eggs are fed as a source of protein, they must be cooked and not given raw. Raw eggs contain a carbohydrate-protein complex, avidin, that combines with biotin (one of the B-complex vitamins) in the intestines to impair its absorption. Fresh meat and fish should also be cooked. Certain raw fish and shellfish, for example, contain an enzyme called thiaminase that causes thiamin (vitamin B_1) deficiency in the cat. Sources of vegetable proteins include soybeans, legumes, and grain products.

Carbohydrates

Carbohydrates supply energy and fiber to the diet, and they consist chiefly of sugars, starches, and cellulose. Cellulose provides little energy value, but it does add bulk to the diet and regulates the distribution of water in the intestines, influencing the formation and elimination of the feces. Cats do not actually require carbohydrates in their diets, but they can utilize cooked starches and sugars. Some sugars, incidentally, cannot be tolerated by adult cats. The sugar lactose, which is found in milk, often cannot be properly digested and passes into the large intestine to cause diarrhea. Cats are also unable to taste the sweetness of sugar.

Fat

The fat requirement, like the protein requirement, is higher for cats than for dogs. Fats are the most concentrated source of energy, and they make the cat's food more palatable and attractive. Fats supply essential fatty acids needed to maintain overall good health, and they are necessary for a healthy skin and shiny coat. They also carry the fat-soluble vitamins through the body.

Vitamins

Vitamins are essential for normal physiological function and as constituents of enzymes used in numerous metabolic processes. They have no caloric value and do not supply energy. Vitamins are divided into two classifications based on whether they will dissolve in oil or water. The fat-soluble vitamins—A, D, E, and K—are measured in international units and require fat in the diet in order to be transported through the body. The water-soluble vitamins—B complex and C—are measured in milligrams and micrograms, and dissolve in water. The vitamin requirements of cats are slighly higher than those of most other animals.

Minerals

Minerals are necessary for the development of bones and teeth, muscle and nerve function, and the maintenance of other body processes. Their actions within the body are interrelated—that is, one mineral's function depends on another's, and therefore they should be considered as a group and not as separate entities. "As a species," reports Dr. J. F. Alberson in a monograph, *The Nutrition of the Cat,* "cats have a lower per pound per day mineral requirement than do most other carnivores and excrete the excesses provided in the diet as soluble salts in the urine under normal conditions. However, under abnormal circumstances, not scientifically precisely identified at present, certain mineral excesses have been demonstrated to be contributory to the formation of bladder stones (uroliths), 'sand,' or 'gravel' in cats." (This subject is discussed more fully under "Feline Urologic Syndrome" in Chapter VI.)

NUTRITIONAL REQUIREMENTS OF CATS[a]

Nutrient	Unit	NCR Recommended Allowances per Kilogram[b] of Food on a Dry Basis[c]	Important for	Sources
Protein[d]	%	28	Growth and cell repair.	Meat, fish, poultry, eggs, cheese, milk.
Fat[e]	%	9	Energy and coat condition.	Butter, lard, animal and vegetable oils; meat fat.
Linoleic Acid	%	1	Healthy skin and hair.	Vegetable and animal fats.
Minerals: Calcium	%	1	Building bones and teeth; nerve function; muscle contractions.	Milk, milk products, meat and bone meal; sardines.
Phosphorus	%	0.8	Growth; building bones and teeth.	Eggs, milk and milk products, cereal grains, meat, poultry, fish.
Potassium	%	0.3	Growth; muscle coordination; fluid balance.	Potassium salts, animal tissues. Present in most cat foods.
Sodium Chloride[f]	%	0.5	Regulating body fluids; muscle strength.	Table salt; fish and fish meal. Present in most cat foods.

Nutrient	Unit	NCR Recommended Allowances per Kilogram[b] of Food on a Dry Basis[c]	Important for	Sources
Magnesium	%	0.05	Muscle function; heart activity; tooth and bone formation.	Whole grains, soybeans, green leafy vegetables (eaten raw).
Iron	mg	100	Blood building; enzyme activity.	Liver, muscle meat, kidneys, egg yolk, whole-grain cereals, yeast.
Copper	mg	5	Blood regeneration.	Liver, kidneys, dried beans, corn-oil margarine. Supplied in most diets as trace mineral salts.
Manganese	mg	10	Kidney function; bone formation; reproduction.	Fish, whole-grain cereals, egg yolk. Supplied in most diets as trace mineral salts.
Zinc[g]	mg	30	Protein synthesis; growth; healthy skin and hair.	Muscle and organ meats, eggs. Supplied in most diets as trace mineral salts.
Iodine	mg	1	Normal thyroid function.	Iodized salt, sea salt, seaweed, fish, fish meal, shellfish.
Selenium	mg	0.1	Interacts with Vitamin E.	Fish, egg yolk, milk, meat, whole-grain cereals.

Nutrient	Unit	NCR Recommended Allowances per Kilogram[b] of food on a Dry Basis[c]	Important for	Sources
Vitamins:				
Vitamin A	IU	10,000	Vision, healthy hair and skin, bone and tooth development.	Liver, egg yolk, cheese, butter, milk, fish oils, yellow and dark-green vegetables.
Vitamin D	IU	1,000	Formation and maintenance of bones and teeth.	Fish-liver oils, egg yolk, liver, irradiated yeast, sunlight.
Vitamin E[h]	IU	80	Fetal development. Protects essential fatty acids from oxidation.	Vegetable oils, wheat germ, whole-grain cereals, egg, liver.
Thiamin (B₁)	mg	5	Proper utilization of carbohydrates.	Wheat germ, brewer's yeast, whole-grain cereals, liver, eggs, milk.
Riboflavin (B₂)	mg	5	Helps release energy from proteins, carbohydrates, and fats.	Meat, liver, kidney, milk, eggs, whole-grain cereals, dried beans and peas.
Pantothenic Acid	mg	10	Growth. Healthy skin and hair.	Liver, kidneys, whole grains, eggs, dark-green vegetables.
Niacin (B₃)	mg	45	Joins with thiamin and riboflavin to promote energy production in cells.	Liver, poultry, meat, whole grains, eggs, wheat germ, brewer's yeast.

Nutrient	Unit	NCR Recommended Allowances per Kilogram[b] of Food on a Dry Basis[c]	Important for	Sources
Pyridoxine (B₆)	mg	4	Growth; formation of red blood cells; helps nervous system to function.	Liver, egg yolks, meats, whole grains, brewer's yeast, wheat germ.
Folic Acid	mg	1.0	Blood regeneration.	Liver, kidneys, wheat germ, yeast, dark-green leafy vegetables.
Biotin	mg	0.05	Growth; healthy skin and hair.	Liver, kidneys, egg yolk, dark-green vegetables, yeast.
Vitamin B₁₂	mg	0.02	Red blood cell formation. Helps nervous system to function.	Liver, kidneys, meat, fish, whole grains, eggs, yeast.
Choline	mg	2000	Growth. Liver function.	Liver, egg yolk, plant foods.
Inositol	mg	20	Liver function.	Meats, whole grains, yeast.
Vitamin C	Metabolic synthesis		Counteracting retarded growth; healthy teeth, gums, and skin.	Unlike humans, cats synthesize or manufacture adequate amounts of vitamin C in their bodies.
Vitamin K	Intestinal synthesis		Needed for normal blood clotting.	Synthesized or manufactured by intestinal bacteria.

a. Recommended allowances (and subsequent footnotes) from *Nutrient Requirements of Cats*, no. 13, rev. 1978. National Research Council of the National Academy of Sciences.

b. One kilogram equals 2.2 pounds.

c. "Dry Basis" refers to the value of all foods when measured without moisture.

   Nutrient levels selected have satisfactorily maintained adult cats and have supported growth of kittens. It is probable that they would be adequate for gestation and lactation, but few such studies have been conducted. Since diet processing (such as extruding or retorting) may destroy or impair the availability of some nutrients, sufficient amounts of such nutrients should be included to ensure the presence of recommended allowances at the time the diet is eaten.

d. Quality equivalent to that derived from unprocessed mammalian, avian, or fish muscle. Processing may lower protein quality and necessitate higher concentrations.

e. No requirement for fat, apart from the need for essential fatty acids and as a carrier of fat-soluble vitamins, has been demonstrated. The figure of 9 percent is listed only because approximately this amount is necessary to develop a diet with the necessary caloric density of dry matter. Fat does favorably influence diet palatability.

f. Since reliable individual estimates of the need for sodium and chlorine are not available, the need for both elements has been expressed as a recommended allowance for sodium chloride.

g. When cats are fed vegetable-protein-based diets, zinc requirements may be in excess of 40 ppm (Aiken *et al.*, 1977).

h. Higher levels may be necessary when large concentrations of unsaturated fats, such as tuna oil, are included in the diet.

Water

Water is an essential nutrient, and its importance is often overlooked in the cat's dietary requirements. Compared to most other animals, cats appear to survive with a minimum of drinking water. Many owners say they never see their cats drinking water, and this may be so when they are eating canned foods, because most of the water is being supplied by the food. Cats are rather eccentric creatures—they may turn up their noses at water in their drinking bowl, and then go right to the bathroom or kitchen and lick dripping tap water with great enthusiasm. It is important, however, to keep fresh water available at all times.

Types of Cat Food

Pet food manufacturers have invested a great deal of time and money in developing and improving their products. Cats and dogs, in many cases, eat a better-balanced diet than a lot of people do. This is because most of the products manufactured for cats contain all the required nutritional elements in accordance with the recommendations established by the National Research Council of the National Academy of Sciences. Commercial cat food is available in several different types, and each has its advantages and disadvantages.

Dry Food

Dry food, the most economical of commercial cat rations, comes in bite-size crunchy nuggets that are easy for cats to pick up in their mouths. All brands are dry-form blends of cereals or grains, meat meals, poultry meal, fish meal, and sometimes dairy products, and vitamins and minerals. They contain around 90 percent solid matter and 10 percent moisture, and they supply between 300 and 350 calories per cup. Dry foods are convenient to store and easy to feed to cats. But because the drying process strips the raw ingredients of some of their nutritional value and fat and water content, they are the least palatable type of ration to cats. The big advantage to serving dry foods, conversely, is that they contain a wide variety of protein sources and reduce the chance of cats becoming addicted to their food. They also promote good dental health by providing exercise for the cat's teeth and gums.

The feeding of dry foods is a disputed matter of opinion among cat breeders and veterinarians. Some think that their high mineral content is a contributory element in inducing urinary tract problems, particularly feline urologic syndrome (FUS). (See Chapter VI.) It is believed that several factors, including low water intake and feeding a diet composed mostly of dried foods (especially those with a high magnesium and phosphorus content), appear to make cats more inclined to FUS. At the present time nobody knows what actually causes FUS, but it is generally supposed that cats inclined to that disease should not eat a lot of dry food.

Most brands of dried foods provide total nutrition for cats. They can be fed dry (with water on the side), moistened with water or milk (not so much as to make the food mushy), or with a little added meat to enhance the taste.

Soft-Moist Food

Soft-moist food is a combination of meat, poultry, or fish and/or their by-products, soybean meal, fat, vitamins, and minerals. Most brands are packaged in airtight foil or cellophane pouches, each packet containing a complete meal. Soft-moist foods have a moderately long shelf life, and they do not require refrigeration because they contain humectants that keep them from becoming dry or decomposed. This kind of food is more palatable to cats than the dry form because of its high protein, fat, and water content. Soft-moist foods contain 75 percent food solids and 25 percent moisture, and supply about 125 calories per 1.5 ounce package. They are formulated to be nutritionally complete.

The major disadvantage to some brands is their high phosphorus content. Manufacturers of soft-moist foods for dogs add sugar not only for flavor and energy but also as a preservative to control the growth of bacteria. "Unlike the sugar preservation process used in soft-moist dog foods," reports Dr. Mark Morris, Jr., one of the world's leading animal nutritionists, in *Feline Dietetics*, "pH control using phosphoric acid is utilized in some soft-moist cat foods to control bacterial growth. The result is that the utilizable phosphorus content of these products is high, which may have implications in cats susceptible to Feline Urologic Syndrome (FUS)."

Canned Foods

Canned food comes in two different types. *Complete and balanced canned food* is a combination of fish, meat, poultry and/or their by-products, various cereals or grains, fat, vitamins, and minerals to provide total nutrition. Most brands are sold in 12- or 16-ounce cans and are less expensive than the smaller "gourmet" cans of food. Depending on the ingredients, most brands contain about 25 percent solid food and 75 percent water, and supply about 500 to 600 calories per can. *Canned "gourmet" foods* form the largest segment of the feline food market, and are the most expensive as well. They consist of highly palatable foods such as chicken, turkey, liver, kidney, beef, tuna, salmon, mackerel, shrimp, and endless combinations of these and other animal or marine foods. They are usually sold in 6-ounce cans and supply about 250 calories per container. Some but not all of the "gourmet" brands contain varying amounts and combinations of vitamins and minerals. While they are undoubtedly the most palatable of cat foods (because they contain more protein and fat than either dry or soft-moist rations), in many cases "gourmet" brands are nutritionally incomplete and should be fed only as part of the diet.

Special Diets

The dry, soft-moist, and canned Science Diet feline products of Hill's are precisely formulated to meet the nutritional requirements of cats. They are total rations, designed to be fed straight from the container, and require no supplementation. Their high nutritional density provides for most efficient utilization of food and reduces the stool volume considerably.

Therapeutic diets, such as Prescription Diets, available only through veterinarians, are formulated to aid in the management of several disease conditions. Those available for cats are: c/d, a diet with less mineral matter to prevent urinary stoppages; k/d, a diet with specially selected protein and careful balance for impaired liver and kidney function; p/d, a high protein and high calorie diet; h/d, a low-sodium formulation for heart disease; and r/d, a low-calorie diet for weight reduction.

Evaluating a Cat Food

Every package or can of cat food lists the product and brand name; the manufacturer's name and address; the guaranteed analysis, or the minimum percentages of crude protein and crude fat and the maximum percentages of crude fiber and water (additional guarantees may appear, but these are not mandatory by law); a list of ingredients in order of their predominance; the net weight of the container; and feeding instructions. The label will also contain a statement regarding nutritional completeness— whether the food is formulated as part of a cat's diet, or if the ration is complete and balanced and meets the requirements established by the National Research Council of the National Academy of Sciences. If the food is nutritionally complete, the label (by law) will include such words as *complete, scientific, balanced, perfect,* or *100 percent complete and balanced*. If it does not, you must assume that the food is not nutritionally adequate and you should not feed it as a steady diet. Another way to evaluate a cat food is to examine it. Canned, dry, and soft-moist foods should always look and smell fresh.

Feeding Your Cat

Although the cat is a true carnivore, it cannot thrive on a meat-only diet, and, indeed, its tastes range far beyond meat. With domestication, the cat has learned to eat almost every kind of food, including vegetables and fruits. Cats need meat as a source of protein, but a complete and balanced diet is vital to their health. Wild and feral (semiwild) cats relish rodents, birds, flies, grasshoppers, butterflies, and crickets, and they eat them entirely for a well-balanced diet.

Cats are very fastidious creatures with a keen sense of taste, and they are able to distinguish flavor differences at thresholds far below those of dogs or man. Their highly developed senses are also stimulated by the odor, texture, temperature, appearance, and even the shape of the food. "Cats eat slowly and seemingly with difficulty," says Dr. Mark Morris, Jr.

> Their teeth are so short and ill-placed that they can tear, but not grind their food. Hence they are selective in their eating habits and certain characteristics should be understood. A cat will eat solid food or liquid food, but it is not characteristic of cats to eat combinations of liquids and solids. They are generally reluctant to eat solid chunks from a fluid mixture. Many cats love to "crunch" their food and one of the easiest ways of feeding is to select a top quality dry food product, put it in a bowl in a quiet convenient place and let the cat eat whenever the mood indicates.

Cats are considered to be one of the most difficult animals to feed. And experts on feline nutrition don't always agree as to how they should be fed. Some believe cats should eat a variety of commercial foods and that if this practice is started during kittenhood, you will have no problems getting the animal to eat different kinds and flavors of foods, or changing the diet if it becomes necessary*. Others feel that cats do not need variety, and that they can do nicely on one well-balanced diet. These experts say that feeding

---

*When it is necessary to introduce a new food, add it gradually to the present diet over a four-to-seven-day period (increasing amounts each day) until the cat accepts the new food completely.

cats different kinds of food only makes them finicky eaters. Such cats may learn that if they turn their backs on offered food and go through the motions of covering it up as they do waste matter discharged from their bodies, or expressing their displeasure with contemptuous meows, different food will be presented. A possible drawback, though, of feeding one diet is that cats can become almost addicted to that food to the point of starvation and refuse to eat anything else.

However you choose to feed your cat, always give it fresh and appetizing food. Cats prefer routine: they like to eat at the same times, in the same location, and from the same clean dishes every day. Place a plastic place mat (pet stores sell models specially designed for cats) under the dishes to make cleanups easier. Keep distractions at a minimum during mealtimes. Most cats are eager eaters, but they like to consume their food in privacy in a quiet place.

There are two ways to feed your cat: scheduled or portion feeding and ad libitum or self-feeding. Portion feeding involves giving the cat a measured quantity of food at specific times each day. With this method you can adjust the amount of food necessary to maintain, gain, or lose weight. Feeding a cat at the same times each day encourages a steady appetite and regular routine. Give it at least one-half hour to eat, then remove the uneaten portion and wash the dish. Ad libitum or self-feeding involves keeping a dish of food available at all times. Dry and semimoist foods are ideal for self-feeding; canned rations are not practicable because they spoil easily. Your cat has access to food twenty-four hours a day and can eat as much or as little as it wants. Self-feeding offers many advantages to professional breeders and cattery owners, as well as to individuals who work. You don't have to be at home for a scheduled feeding, and your cat is less likely to become bored from spending a lot of time alone. Cats are exceptionally intelligent and usually eat just the right amount of food, but if yours is a glutton or prone to gaining weight, self-feeding is not recommended.

Regardless of which feeding program you follow, don't forget to provide fresh drinking water at all times. You may offer a little milk after the solid foods have been eaten, but only if your cat can agreeably digest it. Some adults cannot, and develop diarrhea. Keep in mind that milk is a food, and *not* a drink to replace water.

Most cats enjoy table scraps and treats, but you must remember to feed the right tidbits and not let them compose more than 10 percent of the total diet. Table scraps or people snacks usually contain lots of carbohydrates, which can upset a cat's dietary balance as well as add extra calories. An occasional snack will not hurt when given in moderation. But choose things intended for cats, or something from your garden, raw or lightly steamed, and do not offer spicy leftovers or calorie-rich treats. Be sure to remove small or brittle bones when you feed meat, chicken, or fish, as they may stick in the cat's throat or stomach, or may splinter and pierce the intestinal wall.

If your cat is receiving adequate nourishment through a well-balanced diet of commercial cat foods, vitamin and mineral supplements are not imperative, but they will help round out the cat's diet and prevent deficiencies if the foods are not balanced or nutritionally adequate. Supplements are available in powder, liquid, and tablet form, formulated in correct amounts and proportions for kittens, adults, pregnant and lactating queens, and geriatric cats. The supplements should be recommended by your veterinarian and offered in the correct amounts. As many problems exist today from excess vitamin-mineral consumption as from deficiencies.

How Much and How Often to Feed Your Cat

No two cats have exactly the same requirements. The quantity of food consumed will be influenced by such factors as breed, sex, weight, temperament, environment, climate, activity level, and life stage. The amount of food offered each day will vary, for instance, because big cats usually eat more than small ones, active breeds (like Siamese) usually need more food than sedate ones (like Persians), altered cats need less than sexually active queens and toms, kittens require more food than older cats, and cats that roam free eat more than those confined indoors, and so forth. The best principle is to feed enough food to satisfy the cat's appetite and to support growth or maintain normal body weight and condition during a particular life stage.

From weaning time to around fifteen months, growing kittens are experiencing marked physical changes and need a balanced diet consisting of twice as many calories per pound of body weight as adults. Cats take fifteen to eighteen months before they reach maturity, and the caloric requirements should be gradually decreased when the primary growth period is completed. Now a cat needs a balanced diet to supply energy and maintain its adult body weight at a constant level. Although an adult cat can get by on one good meal a day, most experts usually recommend two feedings.

Queens need more food during pregnancy and lactation. They should be healthy and svelte, not overweight, before they are mated. During the first three weeks of pregnancy the queen's desire for food increases slightly. Quality, not quantity, should be the criterion. From the fourth week until the time of delivery, the queen's food intake should be gradually increased. She will need about 25 percent to 40 percent more than her normal maintenance since the fetuses are growing rapidly. The increase should be in foods with high protein levels—such as cooked eggs, cottage cheese, poultry, fish, beef, lamb, organ foods such as kidney, tripe, and giblets—rather than adding extra carbohydrates. After delivery the queen's need for food increases dramatically. The second through the fifth week of lactation is a crucial time for nutrition. A nursing queen should eat four to six times a day. The amount of food needed depends on the number of kittens in the litter, but it can be two to three times more than the queen's daily maintenance requirements. Once the kittens begin weaning, a gradual decrease in the queen's food intake will help to reduce the production of milk. (More about feeding during pregnancy and lactation, and the nutrition of young kittens will be found in Chapter VIII.)

As a cat grows older it needs less food, a result of lower metabolism. Generally speaking, cats start to show signs of age around eight years, although true old age usually commences at nine years. The geriatric cat may not suffer from a specific illness, but it is beginning to experience bodily changes that accom-

pany old age. It should eat a balanced and exception-
ally digestible diet with less (but higher-quality) protein to reduce the demands on the kidneys and fewer
fats to prevent obesity. Obesity is just as dangerous for
elderly cats as it is for older people. It's often
preferable to feed smaller and more frequent meals.

Most commercial cat foods list the caloric content
and recommended feeding amounts on the package.
These are estimates. Start with these guidelines and
then adjust the calorie intake to fit your cat's needs.
You may wish to follow this recommended feeding
schedule:

Home Cooking

There is nothing wrong with feeding your cat a
homemade diet (although most veterinarians generally do not recommend this) if you have the time and
the inclination to do it. It can be satisfying to a
creative cook to make cat food from scratch, free of
preservatives, additives and artificial flavors and coloring. The diet, however, *must* be balanced and
provide the required amounts of essential nutrients
and food energy. Unfortunately, many homemade
diets are formulated incorrectly and do not contain
all the nutrients a cat needs. The animal frequently is
offered or chooses to eat one food that it likes best to
the total exclusion of others. Another problem is that
people tend to anthropomorphize, or ascribe human
tastes to their cats. But if you are looking for
nutritious recipes that you can prepare at home, you
may wish to consult a few books on the subject. Some
of those dealing with home cooking (as well as all
phases of cat nutrition) are: Anitra Frazier and
Norma Eckroate's *The Natural Cat*; Joan Harper's *The*

Recommended Feeding Schedule

Age	Number of Feedings	Meal
Weaning to 3 months	4	Breakfast, lunch, midafternoon, and dinner.
3 to 6 months	3	Breakfast, lunch, and dinner.
6 to 15 months	2	Breakfast and dinner.
15 months to 8 years	1, or preferably 2	Breakfast and dinner.
Pregnancy, especially after the fourth week	3	Breakfast, lunch, and dinner.
Lactation, especially from the second through the fifth week	4 to 6	Breakfast, (midmorning), lunch, (midafternoon), dinner, and bedtime.
Beyond 8 years	3 to 4	Breakfast, lunch, and dinner. Three meals a day are recommended unless your cat is very old and needs smaller but more frequent portions.

Healthy Cat and Dog Cook Book; Terri McGinnis's *Dog and Cat Good Food Book*; and Jean Powell's *Good Food for Your Cat*. And for fat cats, Mordecai Siegal's charming and informative *The Good Cat Book* contains some receipes for low-calorie Chinese dishes, such as Meow Shu Pork and Shanghai Steamer, that both you and your cat can savor.

My own cats love an occasional homecooked meal, and here are the receipes (formulated in my own kitchen) for four of their favorite dishes:

Oeufs à la Sardine

    1 egg lightly beaten
    5 sardines, chopped
    1 tablespoon wheat germ
    chopped greens

Grease frying pan lightly with butter or oil until hot. Pour in egg mixture and scramble, adding sardines and wheat germ. Cool to room temperature, garnish with chopped greens and serve. This recipe serves two cats.

Câté Maison

    1 lb. beef liver (or chicken hearts, livers, and
        stomachs)
    1 lb. fish (flounder, haddock, sole, cod, etc.),
        carefully boned
    Pinch salt and pepper
    1 cup toasted wheat germ
    ⅓ cup miller's bran
    About ½ cup beef broth
    1 tablespoon melted butter

Simmer beef liver (or chicken) and fish separately in covered saucepans until cooked. Drain. Combine liver/fish in a blender, season with a pinch of salt and pepper, then mash. Place mixture in a bowl. Add wheat germ, miller's bran, the butter, and enough beef broth to make the mixture reach the consistency of a pâté. Mix well. Feed a small amount at one time as a treat. Store remainder in a covered jar in the refrigerator or freeze in serving-size portions.

Kitty Cat-soulet

    1 lb. lean lamb or beef
    Mixed vegetables (broccoli, carrots, peas, potatoes, green beans, spinach, zucchini—any combination your cat prefers), lightly cooked and chopped into bite-size pieces
    A little cooked chopped onion
    Small pinch of garlic
    Pinch of sea salt or ½ teaspoon kelp
    Toasted wheat germ
    Fresh parsley or alfalfa sprouts

Simmer meat in covered saucepan until tender. Drain and cut into cat bite-size pieces. Add chopped vegetables, the onion, and seasonings. Cool. Sprinkle with a little toasted wheat germ and garnish with fresh parsley or alfalfa sprouts. Serve. Freeze remainder in serving-size portions.

Chicken Cat-ciatore

    1 boned chicken breast, diced into cat bite-size pieces
    1 carrot, steamed and diced

　　1 cup whole wheat macaroni or spaghetti, or 1 cup
　　　　cooked brown rice, millet, or kasha (buckwheat
　　　　groats)
　　Pinch of sea salt or ½ teaspoon kelp
　　Pinch of garlic
　　1 small can tomato sauce or stewed tomatoes
　　Pinch of dried parsley or other herbs

Add pasta or rice to boiling water and cook until
done. Drain pasta in strainer. Add a little oil to a
skillet and stir-fry the diced chicken. Add tomatoes,
carrot, herbs, pinch of garlic, and salt or kelp.
Simmer for several minutes, then add the pasta or
rice. Cool. Sprinkle with a little cheese. Serve. Freeze
remainder in serving-size portions.

Common Feeding Errors

　　Veterinarians say that a great many multipet owners ask if it is all right to give dog food to cats. A look
at some of the differences between the nutritional
needs of cats and dogs is enough to answer this
question.

- Cats require almost four times as much protein
  and three times as much fat as do dogs.
- Cats usually require more than twice the amount
  of B-complex vitamins than do dogs.
- Cats cannot convert some of the amino acids of
  protein into needed vitamins, as do dogs. A
  recent discovery involves the amino acid taurine
  in the development of the cat's eye. A deficiency
  of taurine in the cat can cause a progressive
  retinal degeneration of the eye that can result in
  blindness. Many dog foods contain insufficient

levels of taurine because dogs evidently do not require it.

- Cats have no taste response to sugar and will not respond to the sweetening of food.
- Dog food contains an excess of mineral ash because dogs have a much higher requirement. Most cat foods contain optimum ash levels. Although there are differences of opinion among veterinarians over the significance of ash content of cat food, it is believed that a high ash diet, among several other factors, may contribute to kidney stone formation and cystitis.

Another mistake is for owners to feed their cats excessively oily fish—especially red-meat tuna—that is manufactured for human consumption. These are rich in polyunsaturated oils that oxidize and destroy vitamin E. Such a diet can cause a vitamin E deficiency in cats and lead to a disease known as pansteatitis (steatitis), or yellow fat disease, which can be fatal. Fortunately most manufacturers of cat foods now add vitamin E to their all-fish foods to prevent this disease, and red tunafish or other oily fish produced for humans should not be fed.

Cats and Greens

Most cats adore nibbling on grass and plants. They seem to ingest greenery as a food, especially when their diet is low in fiber, perhaps seeking natural roughage to help hairballs in the stomach pass through to the bowels, or to encourage vomiting to rid the stomach of unfit contents. "The cat's liking for grass (the coarser the better) appears to be strictly for utilitarian purposes," says Dr. Mark Morris, Jr. "A small amount acts as an emetic, clearing out the stomach. A large amount seems to act as a purge. It is not digested." But cats still crave grass and greenery even when the diet is well-balanced and adequate. "This behavior is not confined to the domestic cat," reports Dr. Frank Manolson in *Living With Your Cat* (see "Bibliography of the Cat" in Chapter XVI). "Lions in game preserves can be seen in the morning grazing like cattle. Although no one knows for sure why they do it, one can only assume that fresh grass contains nutrients lacking in the regular diet."

A cat's eager longing for greenery is the main reason why it tries to chew houseplants. Many hundreds of plants have been identified as producing toxic substances in sufficient amounts to cause harmful effects in animals. (Many of these plants and their toxic parts are listed in Chapter VI.) It is most important, therefore, to keep potentially dangerous plants out of the reach of cats and to provide them with some nonharmful greens on which to chew. Cultivating pots or containers of green grass, oats, wheat, rye, alfalfa sprouts, parsley, and catnip and placing them strategically around your house will not only satisfy your cat's need to graze but will help keep kitty away from more dangerous houseplants.

Obesity

It is estimated that from 30 percent to 40 percent of the pets in the United States are overweight. That's not surprising. Americans probably have greater access to information about nutrition and exercise than any other people in the world, yet obesity is a common problem of both children and adults. And obese pets are frequently owned by overweight people.

What Is Obesity?

Obesity is one of the major health hazards of today's pets. It can be defined as an increase of body weight that exceeds skeletal and metabolic requirements and physical exertion or, more simply, an excessive accumulation of fat in the body. Obesity is an aesthetic judgment; what is "fat" to one person may be "just right" to another. The major signs of obesity in a cat are: (1) excessive flesh over the rib cage; (2) protruding or droopy stomach; (3) puffy jowls; and (4) little or no neckline between the head and body. A good way to test whether your cat's

A good way to find out whether or not your cat's weight is proper is to place your hands around its rib cage. If you cannot feel each rib without probing, the cat is probably too fat. If the ribs stick out prominently, the cat may not be getting enough to eat, or may be affected with an illness which needs professional attention.

weight is correct is to put your hands around its rib cage. If you cannot comfortably feel each rib without probing, your cat is probably overweight.

The Problems of Obesity

A fat cat is nothing to laugh about. Overweight cats, like overweight people, have a shorter life expectancy than their leaner counterparts. Obesity, veterinarians say, can precipitate any or all of the following conditions:

1. Congestive heart failure.
2. Respiratory difficulties.
3. Kidney problems.
4. Problems from excessive wear on the joints, such as osteoarthritis.
5. Gastrointestinal problems, such as indigestion, constipation, and flatulence.

A candidate for feline Weight-Watchers?

6. Diabetes mellitus.

7. Skin problems (especially irritation and infection in the rolls of fat).

8. Heat intolerance caused by layers of fat under the skin.

9. General lethargy.

10. Reduced chances of conception. After pregnancy, increased chances of difficult delivery.

11. Increased susceptibility to viral and bacterial infections.

12. Increased surgical and anesthetic risks, plus protracted healing of wounds.

The Causes of Obesity

Obesity can be caused by hereditary influences, and glandular or hormonal defects, but in cats as in humans the primary cause is dietary, or simply that the cat is eating more food than it needs. When a cat eats too much and does not expend enough energy to maintain normal body weight, and when more energy or calories are consumed than the body can utilize, fat forms.

Controlling Obesity and Feeding Guidelines

An obese cat should receive a complete physical examination from a veterinarian to determine the nature of the corpulence. If the condition is caused by overeating and not by a medical problem, the only way your cat will lose its excess fat is by eating fewer calories every day. The first step is for your veterinarian to determine the optimum weight for the cat and then establish a reduced-calorie regimen to accomplish that goal. This will generally involve:

1. A complete and balanced diet including all the essential nutrients, reducing the daily food in-

take for gradual weight loss. (Crash or starvation diets are never recommended for animals.)
2. Feeding smaller portions at each meal.
3. Avoiding foods with high fat contents.
4. Eliminating table scraps and high-calorie treats. Raw or lightly steamed vegetables are a good substitute.
5. Providing fresh water at all times.
6. Establishing some sort of exercise routine, such as walks on harness and leash, or planned owner-cat play periods.

Weigh your cat once a week. There will probably be little weight loss for the first fourteen days; but if your cat isn't loosing weight by the third week, consult your veterinarian. He may suggest the use of a commercially prepared low-calorie diet, such as Prescription Diet r/d, which is available in canned, soft-moist, or dry form. You'll be pleasantly surprised at the changes as the weight comes off, and your cat will have more energy to play and exercise. As soon as the cat attains its ideal weight, it should eat a good-quality maintenance ration at a level that maintains the optimum weight. Weigh your cat every week, and any upward variation in weight of more than 10 percent from normal should be accompanied by a reduction in food intake or a return to the weight reduction program until the ideal weight is reattained. Obesity is often difficult to control because so many owners lack the self-control necessary to keep themselves as well as their pets on a strict diet. Don't be swayed by those persuasive eyes or mournful meows when you are preparing food!

Lack of Appetite

Lack of appetite, or the inability to eat (anorexia), are more difficult to deal with. These conditions can be caused by nutritional deficiencies, infection, physical or metabolic disorders, fear, anxiety, depression, jealousy, other abnormal psychological attitudes, or simply because you are offering unappetizing meals. Cats are considered to be one of the most difficult of domestic animals to feed. Their appetites are greatly affected by how food is prepared and presented. They are fastidious eaters with keen senses of smell and taste, and an interest in the appearance and the texture of food as well. They like to dine from clean and shallow dishes and will often refuse food that is stale or served in dirty containers. Cats often do not eat when they cannot smell their food. And it is equally important to provide the correct texture and moisture content to the food, along with the right flavor. Temperature is important, too. Most cats prefer their rations at room temperature and will not eat food served directly from the refrigerator or food that has been heated up. Some cats need to be fed in separate rooms, away from other animals or family members.

Changes in routine eating pattern and feeding environment can make a cat go off its food. Queens and stud males sometimes lose their appetites during breeding season, especially when there is a member of the opposite sex nearby. Boarding in a cattery or moving to new surroundings can also affect the appetite. All these causes, however, should only be temporary, and revert to normal with attention and observant care.

The young kitten that refuses to eat is a critical

problem. Good nutrition is vital to growth, and because its tummy holds so little, a missed meal is lost nourishment. Perhaps the kitten misses the companionship of its mother and littermates during mealtimes. You could try to perk up its appetite by sprinking a few granules of brewer's yeast or wheat germ, or drizzling a little butter, bacon fat, or broth over the food.

If you notice a marked decline in your cat's appetite that persists for a day or two, consult your veterinarian to determine if the condition is being caused by a more serious problem.

V   The Well-groomed Cat

The exquisite cleanliness of the cat has probably led to its having been compared, by all peoples, in all ages, to a woman. The love of dress is very marked in this attractive animal; it is proud of the lustre of its coat, and cannot endure that a hair of it should lie the wrong way.
> —Champfleury,
> *The Cat: Past and Present,*
> translated by Mrs. Cashel Hoey (1885)

A clean and well-groomed cat is a healthier, happier, and better-looking pet. The coat will sparkle and the cat will be less susceptible to flea and tick infestation, hairball formation, and common skin disorders. Most cats keep themselves immaculately clean, but self-grooming is not enough. Daily attention from you is essential to keep the cat looking its very best, and this applies to shorthairs as well as longhairs.

Grooming should begin as early as possible—during kittenhood ideally—and the routine that is established should be as gentle and pleasant as possible so that your cat will not only learn to tolerate grooming but look forward to it each day. Apart from its health aspect, grooming is of psychological importance, too. Even though cats are not social creatures (in the sense that social animals such as dogs form dominance hierarchies), they do derive great pleasure from interactions with their owners.* Through the act of grooming you demonstrate concern and affection for your cat. Your cat, in turn, not only learns that grooming makes it feel better, but it also gains attention and praise from looking good. If you do not groom your cat regularly, the coat will immediately shows signs of inattention and the cat will sense your neglect as well.

Regular grooming sessions are the best way to spot potential health problems, too. During combing or brushing, be on the lookout for danger signs. Examine the skin for the presence of external parasites, disease, or inflammation. Check each of your cat's body openings. Turn the cat over and examine its abdomen for signs of tenderness or lumps under the skin. The early discovery and professional treatment of problems not only could spare your cat a great deal of pain and suffering but will cost you less money in the long run.

The Basic Grooming Aids

To keep your cat looking good, you will need a few tools and supplies that will cost very little. The following items (pictured in the photographs) can be purchased at any pet store:

---

*See Chapter VII, "The Nature of the Beast," for more about behavior.

Combs. The kind of comb you select depends on your cat's hair length. For shorthairs select a metal comb with rounded ends to the teeth. The teeth should not be excessively tapered, especially for single-coated breeds, such as the Siamese, or the coat may become darkened or damaged. Longhairs require several combs: a metal one with long back and long tapered teeth, spaced half fine and half medium. The ends of the teeth should be rounded to prevent skin scratching or coat loss. You'll also need an extra-fine comb for the facial hair and the long tufts between the toes.

Brushes. A natural-bristle brush is recommended for cats, especially longhairs. The best models have tufts of bristles that are graduated in length for deep penetration through the hair. Synthetic

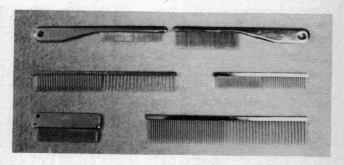

Combs: (Top) Fine-tooth comb for short-haired and long-haired cats. It is ideal for combing and fluffing the hair around the head of long-haired cats upward and outward. Fine-tooth comb with handle, very useful for short-haired cats because the ends of the teeth are rather blunt. (Center) Half-fine/ half-medium combs for long-haired cats. (Bottom) Extra-fine-tooth comb (also used as a flea comb). Half-fine/half-medium Belgium comb. This is preferred by exhibitors for long-haired cats because it has long, tapered teeth.

bristles cause hair breakage and excessive static electricity. Some shorthair owners like a rubber brush with short, round-tipped bristles for polishing the coat or removing dead hair. A fine wire slicker helps to remove dead hair and light tangles.

Nail trimmer. Select a nail trimmer designed for cats. The all-purpose tools suggested for use on both cats and dogs won't perform as efficiently. You'll also need a small container of Kwick-Stop powder.

Detangler and mat removing tool. Special products and tools are available from your pet supplies dealer to speed up the removal of mats and tangles. If you comb your cat regularly, you'll never need them!

Powder brush. A soft bristle or "complexion"-

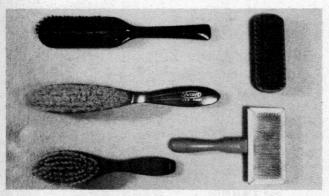

Brushes: (Top) Tufted natural-bristle brush for long-haired and short-haired cats. Rubber brush with short, round bristles for removing dead hair and to polish the coat of a short-haired cat. Soft bristle brushes for powder cleaning the coats of white or light-colored cats. Fine-wire slicker to remove dead hair or tangles on long-haired cats.

type brush to use when powder-packing white and light-colored long-haired cats.

Cotton balls and swabs.

Soft toothbrush.   To clean the hair under the eyes of Persians, Himalayans, and other longhairs when it is stained.

Cornstarch or grooming powder.

Coat conditioner.   These are antistatic formulations with protein, mink oil, and other conditioners to facilitate brushing, to help remove tangles, eliminate dryness and flaking, add a gloss to the hair, and enhance the natural coat color.

Coat dressing.   A nongreasy antistatic brushing aid that puts a high gloss on the hair without adding oil to the hair shaft.

Shampoo.   There are dozens of different shampoos for cats: tearless, flea and tick, protein, texturizing, and medicated, and products with optical brighteners for different hair colors. Cats (and dogs) have a slightly more alkaline skin and hair than humans, so be sure to select a shampoo that is pH-balanced for pets and not people.

Hair conditioner.   These are used on dry and brittle coats. Superconditioners such as Ring 5 Hair Care are formulated to restore moisture to the skin and coat, to bring back lost elasticity, and to restructure the hair shaft.

Chamois, silk scarf or black velvet square.   To apply finishing touches on certain breeds.

It is not necessary to buy all of these tools and supplies. Check the grooming instructions for short-haired and longhaired cats which follow to determine the items you need.

Grooming Short-haired Cats

Short-haired cats are very easy to groom. There are two types of shorthairs, those with a single coat, and those with a double coat. The short-haired single coat is glossy and fine in texture, and lies close to the body. Some of the breeds with this coat type are the Siamese, Burmese, Korat, Havana Brown, Bombay, Colorpoint Shorthair, and Oriental Shorthair. The short-haired double coat is composed of two sets of hair: longer guard hair to give the coat its coloring, and a dense undercoat to provide warmth. Some of the breeds with this coat type are the American Shorthair, Abyssinian, Manx, and Russian Blue.

Regular brushing or a gentle hand massage will loosen the dead hair. If there is a great deal of shedding, moisten your hands slightly and stroke the coat backward (from tail to head) to help loosen it. Don't forget the underbody and legs. Finish by

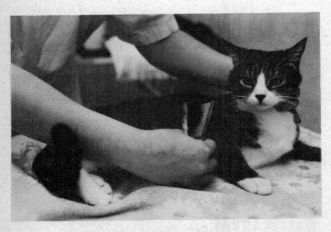

Combing a short-haired cat.

stroking, combing, or brushing the coat from head to tail in the natural direction of its growth. Spray the hair lightly with coat conditioner or coat dressing. Stroke the fur with a chamois, silk scarf, or piece of black velvet to polish the coat. The goal is to make the short-haired single coats appear glossy and slick, and the short-haired double coats look plush.

Grooming Long-haired Cats

Daily combing and brushing is essential for long-haired cats. If you cannot find the time to comb your cat every day, three times a week is the absolute minimum. Longhairs should be combed first and then brushed. Use the medium-spaced side of the comb for the body and tail hair, and the fine-spaced side for the hair on the cat's head and legs. Before you begin, spray the hair lightly with coat conditioner or coat dressing to reduce static electricity, or sprinkle a little grooming powder onto light-colored cats. The correct technique is to place the teeth close to the skin

After combing or brushing, spray the hair lightly with a coat of conditioner or coat dressing.

and comb upward to lift out all the dead hair, remove
mats and tangles, and straighten the undercoat. Only
a few dead hairs may come out at certain times of the
year, but during the heavy shedding seasons in late
spring and (to a certain degree) early fall, the dead
hair practically comes out by the combfuls. A thorough combing is vital at shedding time, otherwise
during self-grooming your cat will ingest large
amounts of dead hair that can form into hairballs
(these are explained later in this chapter). Be sure to
comb the hard-to-get-at areas on the flanks, the
underbody, and between the legs. A long-haired cat
should be trained during kittenhood to lie on its back
while its stomach is being groomed. It is easy to lift
and stretch each leg while your cat is in this position
to comb between and around it. Comb the tail
carefully and try not to pull out excessive coat or
make a possible stud tail condition more serious.
Comb the facial hair, paying particular attention
around the base of the ears. After you have finished
combing, use the natural-bristle brush to remove any
remaining dead hair.

Once the coat is powder cleaned or bathed (these,
too, are discussed later in this chapter), a few additional steps will make your longhair look glamorous.
On breeds whose standards call for round-tipped ears
(such as Persians), the small tufts of hair that grow
above the natural line around the ear tips may be
pinched off with your thumb and index finger. Then
shake out the tail. Any straggly hairs near the tip that
spoil the profuse look may be pinched off with
your fingers in the same manner. Don't overgroom,
though.

Complete the picture by combing your cat to make

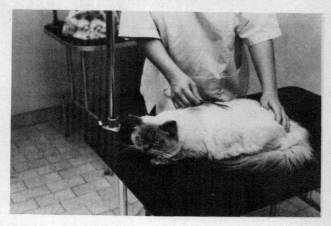

Using the medium-shaped side of the Belgian comb on a long-haired cat's body coat.

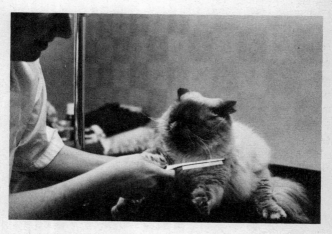

Occasionally during the grooming process, a cat may voice its displeasure.

the hair stand out from the body. Use the extra-fine-tooth comb to bring the hair on the forehead upward, and then comb it toward the nose. Bring the cheek hair outward and forward and the chin hair upward. Comb the hairs at the base of the ears up and out. Use your extra-fine-tooth comb to pull out the long tufts of hair from between the toes, then comb them forward. Comb the front and hind legs upward. Switch to the medium comb and start at the shoulders and work toward the tail (some people do the reverse and start at the tail), lifting the coat and fluffing it upward and outward. Comb the frill on the front of the chest up and out, then fan out the hair around the neck to frame the face. The exception to these actions are long-haired tabbies, which are combed to emphasize their markings. Instead of bringing the hair up and out, comb it in the direction of its growth.

Tangles and Mats

Tangles and mats are best removed with a liquid detangler like Ring 5 Untangle, and a dematting tool or soft wire slicker-brush. If the use of a tool sounds frightening, your thumb and fingers will be a fine substitute. Here's an easy way to demat a cat: Saturate all the matted hair to the skin and allow the detangling product to stay on the fur until the hair almost dries. Try to separate the mats by breaking large clumps into smaller sections. As each section is separated (with fingers or tool), carefully brush it.

If the coat has become one solid mass to the skin, all the hair may have to be clipped off with an electric clipper. Although it may sound cruel, clipping is certainly more humane than painfully tugging out large clumps of mats. Don't attempt to clip the cat yourself, however, if you have no previous experience. Have it done by a professional groomer or, if the cat needs to be tranquilized, by a veterinarian. You may be pleasantly surprised after the clipping, especially if the groomer can save the neck ruff and some of the tail hair. Your puss may well resemble a mini-lion! And clipping often results in a profuse regrowth of coat.

Hairballs

Daily combing and brushing helps to retard the ingestion during self-grooming sessions of dead hair that can form into hairballs. To explain how hairballs form, one must understand self-grooming, an important activity for all cats. It has been estimated that most cats spend about 30 percent of their waking time grooming themselves. Cats self-groom in several ways: by licking their fur, by cleaning their heads with saliva-moistened paws, by scratching their fur with claws, or by pulling at their claws with their teeth.

During self-grooming the loose dead hair, according to Dr. Benjamin L. Hart in a column from *Feline Practice*, sticks to barblike, backward-projecting filiform papillae on the cat's tongue.* And because of the backward angle of the barbs, the hair is easily swallowed by the cat. Generally it passes through the system and is eliminated with the bowel movements. But in cats that self-groom excessively (especially longhairs), or during heavy shedding periods in hot weather, the dead hair can collect inside the stomach

---

*Dr. Hart also comments that "rubbing up against the side of furniture, doorways or other objects with the side of the face appears to be a type of grooming but instead is a form of scent marking with specialized glands located in the corners of the mouth and in the supraorbital region."

and form into a ball several inches wide. Some cats will normally cough up hairballs, but once a large mass passes from the stomach to the intestines, it cannot be regurgitated. If the mass cannot pass through the intestinal tract, constipation and other serious problems may occur. It has been estimated that hairballs are the most common cause of constipation in cats. When an intestinal impaction occurs, a cat must be treated to make the hairball pass. Treatment generally consists of an enema or mild laxative to help lubricate the mass, along with a fast of about twenty-four hours. If the hairball does not pass normally from the body, it may have to be surgically removed.

The best hairball deterrent is regular combing and brushing. The more dead coat you remove, the less hair your cat will swallow. But keeping in mind that your cat will still do a great deal of self-grooming, it is also important to provide a commercial hairball preparation to relieve the hairballs as well as prevent their formation. Hairball medicines such as Petromalt are a combination of emulsified petroleum jelly and vitamins flavored with malt or other tastes palatable to a cat. About one-quarter to one-half teaspoon is placed on the cat's nose or front paw, where it will be promptly licked off and swallowed to lubricate the mass and move it through the intestinal tract. There is no benefit, by the way, in feeding salad oil, butter, or margarine to a cat as a treatment for hairballs.

Stud Tail

While you are combing or brushing your cat, be especially watchful for stud tail, a condition where waxy secretions build up at the base of the tail. It occurs when the sebaceous glands near the base and top of the tail secrete a dark, oily substance from the pores that causes the hair to become greasy and discolored and to smell rancid. Stud tail occurs in cats of both sexes as well as in neutered males and spayed females, but as the name suggests, it is most often seen in breeding males. If the condition is ignored, the exudation will irritate the skin, damage the hair follicles, and eventually cause a thinning or permanent loss of hair.

Cats affected with stud tail should be bathed frequently. It is not necessary to shampoo the entire cat, however, just the discolored tail area. Work the shampoo into the skin, using your fingers or a soft toothbrush to clean the area. Massage gently, trying not to cause friction, because the more you rub, the more you will stimulate the glands to secrete. Regular shampoo may not remove the grease in stubborn cases, and you may have to clean the tail with either (a) a waterless hand cleaner (available in most supermarkets) or (b) liquid dish detergent.* Rinse thoroughly to be sure that no traces of shampoo, waterless cleaner, or dish detergent remain in the coat. Pat the hair dry with a towel, then dust on a little fuller's earth (available at most pharmacies), cornstarch, or medicated powder, making sure the granules get deep into the damp hair. Allow the coat to dry naturally, then brush out the powder. Between spot shampoos or regular baths the continued use of the powder will help to control this offensive condition.

---

*Neither product is meant to be licked off or ingested by the cat. Rinse thoroughly.

Blackheads or Feline Acne

Occasionally during the regular grooming session you may notice dark specks that resemble blackheads on your cat's chin. The condition is called feline acne or chin pyoderma and is restricted to the chin and lip area. It occurs in certain cats (especially those that do not clean their chins meticulously) when dirt or food particles clog the pores. Blackheads appear in the early stages; if the condition is neglected, pustules and small cysts often form and the entire chin area may become swollen and infected. Feline acne is more common in short-haired cats, but it does occur in longhairs. The presence of longer hair around the chin seems to shield the dirt and food specks from becoming embedded in the pores.

Should you notice this condition before it has become a severe infection, wash the chin area with an antibacterial soap and water. Scrub the area gently with a soft toothbrush. Rinse thoroughly with clear water, then dry carefully. You can pat a little corn-starch or rubbing alcohol onto the chin to ensure dryness. Clean your cat's chin every day with anti-bacterial shampoo and water to remove bacteria and sebum from the clogged pores. Rubbing alcohol or human acne cleaners (such as Stri-dex pads) may help to remove the blackheads. Do consult a veterinarian. Severe cases respond favorably to antibiotic therapy.

Bathing Your Cat

Cats that are combed and brushed regularly seldom need bathing. The concerned cat owner will want to heed this advice, because although cats usually love to play in water, the majority of them passionately dislike baths. How often a bath is necessary depends on many circumstances, including among others the length of the hair (longhairs usually need bathing more often than shorthairs), the type of fur (some cats have oily hair, which needs more frequent bathing), and how much time your cat spends outdoors getting dirty. There are times when a bath is imperative, such as when your cat becomes very soiled, or when you want to help loosen and remove an excessive amount of dead hair. Bathing, like other good grooming habits, should begin during kittenhood. The earlier your cat becomes used to a bath, the better the chances of having it accept the experience without being panic-stricken.

The kitchen or bathroom sinks are the ideal places to bathe a cat. Animals usually become frightened when they have to stand on slippery surfaces, so a folded terry towel on the sink bottom will give better footing. Should you own a real escape artist (that is not declawed), try slanting a window screen inside the sink. As soon as the cat is placed on the screen, it will stay in place by hooking its nails into the mesh instead of you. It is often necessary to have two people to bathe a cat, one to steady the animal and the other to do the shampooing.

Assemble all necessary supplies in advance: a flexible shower head that attaches to the faucet, or a plastic cup for wetting and rinsing; a washcloth for cleaning the face; the soft toothbrush to scrub stained hair; shampoo; hair conditioner (if necessary); and several large bath towels. If you plan to fluff your cat's hair with a hair dryer after the bath, prepare a drying table in advance by laying down a large terry towel on top, assembling your comb and brush, and plugging in the hair dryer so that it is immediately ready to switch on. Do as much advance preparation as possible, because once you get the cat into the tub, you will want to concentrate totally on controlling it and completing the shampoo within a reasonably short time. Your cat should be thoroughly combed or brushed and the nails trimmed before the bath. Place a little bit of cotton into each ear (if this upsets your cat, forget it, and hold your thumb over each earhole as you wash that area), and if you don't use a tearless shampoo, drop a little mineral oil into the corner of each eye to prevent burning and irritation.

Fill the sink with a few inches of warm water, add some shampoo and swirl it around with your fingers. Cat hair tends to resist wetting, and mixing the shampoo in the water helps to moisten the hair faster. Stand your cat in the sink or on the screen with its back toward and face away from you, so that if an escape is attempted, the cat will leap up and claw at the air, not you. Wet the cat all over except for the head. Most animals are more relaxed when you shampoo from back to front and wash the head last.*

Pour shampoo over the coat and work up a lather by squeezing the fur as if you were washing a delicate sweater. Wash the neck, the body, the underbody, the tail, and the legs and feet. Talk quietly and reassuringly, and move carefully so that you don't startle your cat. Wet the head last. If the cat seems frightened by the water, pull the plug and let it drain before you do this. Clean the face and ears with a washcloth and tearless shampoo. Stubborn stains on the hair under the eyes should be gently cleaned with the soft toothbruth. If your cat is very dirty, you may have to

---

*Wash the head first, however, if the cat is infested with fleas.

rinse lightly and shampoo a second time using the same procedure.

Empty the sink before the final rinse. Using warm water and the spray attachment (or plastic cup), start at the forehead and rinse down the neck and back toward the tail, then over the sides of the body and down the legs. Rinse every trace of shampoo out of the hair and keep rinsing until clear water rolls off your cat. A thorough rinse will wash away any remaining dirt or dead hair as well as the soapsuds. If your cat's hair needs conditioning, apply the product now, following package directions. Greasy coats are often enhanced by a final rinse of water mixed with a little white vinegar.

Squeeze the excess water from the coat, wrap your wriggly friend in a towel, then carry the cat to the drying table. Blot the hair with towels to absorb all the excess moisture. If you want the hair to dry naturally, confine the cat inside its carrier near heat, or in a draft-free room (the bathroom is good) until the hair is completely dry. Should you wish to expedite the drying process on shorthairs, or want to make your longhair look fluffier, use a hair dryer.* Set the dryer on "Warm" rather than "Hot," because too much heat at too close a range strips natural oils and moisture from the hair. Point the dryer nozzle at the area to be combed or brushed, and use short, quick strokes on shorthairs, and long sweeping strokes to lift rather than flatten the coat on longhairs.

When the bathing and drying process is complete, it's the ideal time to tell your cherished companion

---

*When cats are introduced to the sound of a hair dryer early in life, most will tolerate blow drying.

how elegant he or she looks and to offer a very favorite treat.

Coat Rusting

Coat rusting is a term describing the brownish-red spots on the ends of a cat's hair caused by dampness, food stains, too much sunlight, or excessive licking. Darker-colored cats usually are more susceptible, although creams and other light colors can be affected. The discoloration of the hair ends can be reduced by bathing your cat with a shampoo formulated to remove oxidation from the hair shafts. These are available in specific formulations for various hair colors, and are sold in pet stores everywhere.

Dry Shampoos

When the weather is cold, when your cat is sick, pregnant, or old, and to remove greasy spots, clean the coat with a dry shampoo. Such products are sold by pet stores in powder, liquid, or foam form. They are applied to the hair according to package directions, allowed to dry, and then brushed out.

Bathing Alternatives: Powder-Packing and Coat Dressings

In addition to commercially prepared dry shampoos a cat's coat may be cleaned with cornstarch, grooming powder, or coat dressing.

Powder-packing is a method of cleaning white and light-colored cats that may be used in place of shampoo-and-water bath, provided the cat is not very dirty. The animal, of course, must be thoroughly combed beforehand and all tangles and mats removed from the hair.

Spread a large towel on top of a sturdy table, then place your cat on top. You want to literally "pack" the cat's coat with cornstarch or grooming powder safe for use on cats. (Some groomers and exhibitors use talcum powder, but this author frowns on such use because talcum can irritate the lung tissues when inhaled.) Both substances will be easier to apply if they are put into a powdered-sugar shaker.

Begin by shaking the cornstarch or grooming powder onto the body hair, and work it well into the coat. Use your fingers to separate a longhair's coat into layers so the powder reaches the skin. Sprinkle extra powder on any greasy problem areas. Powder the body, the tail, the underbody, and the front and back legs. Do not sprinkle powder onto the head.

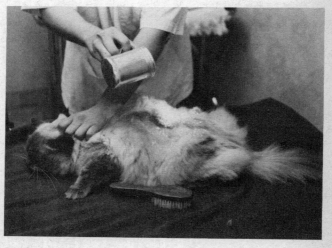

Powder-cleaning a white or light-colored long-haired cat. Cornstarch or grooming powder is easy to apply from a powdered-sugar shaker.

Instead, dip a small soft-bristle brush or a toothbrush into loose powder and brush it carefully into the facial area, taking care not to get it near the cat's eyes, to irritate the tear ducts, or its nose, to inflame the nasal passages. Confine the cat for twenty minutes to one-half hour, or long enough for the powder to absorb the grease and oil. Bring the cat back to the table and brush the powder out of the coat. If your hair dryer has a "Cool" or "Warm" setting, it can help to remove the powder quickly. Just remember to position the dryer nozzle so that the powder blows out and away from the coat and not onto another part of the cat. Hair that still appears dirty should be dusted with powder a second time, then brushed out.

Powder-packing is also an accepted practice to prepare white and light-colored Persians and other longhairs for show. The rationale is that the powder tends to add body and make the coat stand out fuller. The cat usually is bathed five to six days before the show to allow the body to return to the coat. Immediately after the bath, while the hair is still damp, the coat is packed with powder in the manner previously described, then allowed to dry naturally. Because of the amount of powder applied to the coat, you have to confine your cat to a cage or other restricted area before the show. The day before the show, the powder is brushed out of the hair. Remember one important fact about powder-packing: be sure all traces of powder are out of the coat by judging time, or your cat could be disqualified from competition.

Black and dark-colored cats are never powder-packed. Instead of a soap-and-water bath, however, their coats can be cleaned by shaking cornmeal (not cornstarch!) into the hair in the manner previously mentioned, and then brushing it out, or by applying a nonoily antistatic liquid coat dressing such as Ring 5 Coat Gloss. Spray the dressing well into the coat (on longhairs you'll have to part the hair as you spray to be sure the skin gets wet). Towel away the excess moisture, then dry the hair naturally or with a blow-dryer. Dirty coats may need two applications of coat dressing.

Nail Trimming

Cats usually have five toes and nails (including a dewclaw) on each forefoot and four toes and nails on each hind foot.* Extra toes (a condition known as polydactly) are sometimes present, however, and cats may have six or more toes on each front foot and five or more on each hind foot. The nails are enclosed in sheathes and are retractile, meaning that a cat can push them out or draw them back into their coverings at will. The claws on the forefeet are shaped like a half-crescent, while those on the hind feet are generally shorter than the front claws and have less of a hook to the nails.

It is important to accustom your cat to having its paws handled and nails trimmed at an early age. When regular nail cutting begins during kittenhood and the process is conducted with a soothing voice and gentle handling, a cat should peacefully accept having its claws trimmed. But if you cut the nails sparingly, you'll find your cat may resist the process and a battle will take place each time nail trimming is necessary.

---

*The dewclaw is the toe on the inside of each front leg just above the paw.

The frequency of trimming depends on how often your cat goes outdoors, how active it is, and how fast the nails wear down normally. An outdoor cat that comes into contact with trees will seldom need to have its nails trimmed, while an indoor cat with no scratching facilities may need to have its claws shortened every few weeks. Let common sense be your guide, though, and if the nails start scratching you or the upholstery or drapes, clip them. You can trim the nails yourself or have them done by a veterinarian or professional groomer.

How to Cut the Nails

Place your cat in a comfortable position on a sturdy table or in your lap. Take hold of a front paw with your hand. Always begin by cutting the nails on the forepaws. The sharp edges of freshly cut nails can lacerate your skin easily. Should you trim the nails on the hind feet first, and should your cat kick, you could be dangerously scratched. Press on the top and bottom of one toe with your thumb and index finger to force the nail out of its sheathe. It's not necessary to pinch hard, just the slightest pressure will pop the nail outward. Inside the transparent, downward-curving nail you will notice a pinkish area, called the "quick," which contains the nerves and blood supply. Clip the nail tip back with the trimmer, but do not cut into the quick. Take your time and look at the nail closely to determine exactly where to cut. Accidentally nicking the quick will cause the nail to bleed. If this happens, dip a Q-Tip into a quick-stop powder (available from pet stores) and press firmly against the nail tip for a few seconds to stop the bleeding.

If your cat is very fussy, have another family member steady it with one hand while the other hand

The cat's nails are enclosed in sheathes. Before each nail is trimmed, you must press on the top and bottom of the toe with your thumb and index finger to force the nail outward.

Look at the nail carefully to determine exactly where to cut. Then clip the nail tip off with the trimmer.

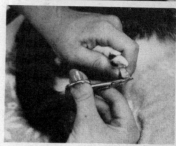

grips the skin at the back of the neck in restraint. As soon as the nail-trimming session is over, your cat will probably rush to its scratching post and "file" the nails in protest.

Ear Cleaning

Ear cleaning usually is an easy job because cats keep themselves so clean. Check your cat's ears every week, although, unless there is a specific problem, they will require cleaning about once a month. All that is necessary is to moisten a cotton ball or Q-Tip with warm water or mild ear-cleaning lotion and to swab gently over the part of the ear that is visible to you. Never probe deeply into the ear. Not only can you push dirt deeper into the canal, but you could cause damage.

If you suspect that your cat has an ear problem, consult your veterinarian. Frequent shaking of the head, scratching of the ears, tilting of the head to one side, a foul odor or excessive brown wax, indicate infection or the presence of ear mites, which require immediate professional attention. (See Chapter VI.)

Eye Care

Check your cat's eyes every day and always keep them clean. It is normal to find a little matter on the inside corner. This can be wiped away with a cotton ball moistened with warm water. Never rub over the eyes with cotton, however, because you could scratch the eyeball with the fibers. Some white and light-colored breeds with short noses, especially Persians, have a persistent discharge from one or both tear ducts, which causes the hair under the eyes to become discolored. The area should be cleaned frequently with warm water and cotton to keep the hair stains from becoming permanent. Use fresh cotton at the corners and under each eye to keep potential infection from spreading.

During the daily eye-cleaning sessions, check to see that the eyes are clear and bright. Any thick discharge, or the prominent appearance of the third eyelid or nictating membrane (the fold of skin at the inside corner of the eye, which is normally barely visible) is an indication of potential trouble. Never ignore minor eye problems. Abnormalities and irritations must be checked by a veterinarian as soon as possible.

Dental Care

Domestic and wild cats have fewer teeth than any other carnivore. Kittens have twenty-six deciduous or temporary teeth. These are softer and thinner than the permanent teeth and start pushing through the gums at around two to three weeks of age. The permanent teeth begin to replace the baby teeth between fourteen to sixteen weeks of age. Unlike puppies, which usually suffer from swollen and sensitive gums during this period, kittens have few teething problems, although they have been known to chew at the time. While your kitten is teething, check its mouth frequently to see that the permanent teeth are pushing through the gums properly. Consult your veterinarian as soon as any problems develop, especially a retained deciduous and permanent tooth in the same location. The permanent teeth, sixteen in the upper jaw and fourteen in the lower jaw, should be in place by six months of age.

Cats may experience the same dental problems as humans: loose or extra teeth, retained baby teeth, plaque buildup, gum inflammation, bad breath, and root abscesses. Cats seldom develop tooth cavities, probably because they eat foods lower in carbohydrates than foods people eat. The most common problem is the buildup of plaque between the teeth and around the gumline that occurs most often in young cats that eat soft food, and in older cats. Another potentially serious problem, although uncommon, that occurs in longhairs is loose hair twisting around the lower canines. Unless the hair has been ignored and pushed into the gumline, it can be easily removed with eyebrow tweezers.

To protect your cat's teeth and, more importantly,

its health, see a veterinarian regularly and adopt a home dental hygiene program in conjunction with regular checkups. Feed some dry food daily and offer small crunchy cat treats to help clean the teeth and prevent plaque from building up. To retard the accumulation of tartar, clean the teeth with a salt solution of a paste of bicarbonate of soda and water either by brushing or by wiping over the teeth with a piece of gauze wrapped around your index finger.

VI Keeping Your Cat Healthy

The cat in the environment of civilization must be fed, looked after, and guarded in its moments of freedom.
—Rush Shippen Huidekoper, MD, *The Cat* (1895)

The most important part of being a responsible pet owner is keeping your cat healthy. From the moment a new kitten or adult cat enters your home, its physical health depends on two people—you and your veterinarian. Have your veterinarian give your cat a thorough physical examination every eight to ten months. Cats and dogs mature almost five times as fast as human beings do, and more and more small-animal practitioners are recommending frequent health checks on the theory that early detection and treatment of problems can quicken the recovery process and prolong life.

It is your responsibility, though, to recognize warning signals and report them quickly to your veterinarian. Early diagnosis and treatment of disease can prevent a great deal of pain and suffering. Help your veterinarian by learning to use your senses of touch, sight, and smell to know the signs of feline good health. Every cat is a distinct being with peculiar characteristics that distinguish it from others. Once you learn what is normal for your cat, any subtle changes in general appearance, behavior, temperature, and other factors that accompany illness will be clearly apparent.

Signs of a Healthy Cat

General appearance. The cat should be in good flesh with a sinewy and smoothly muscled body. It should be active, alert, and lively.

Gait. The movement should be graceful, smooth and agile, with no limping, stumbling, stiffness, or dragging of limbs.

Coat. Although the hair may vary in density, the coat should be glossy (dark colors usually are more glossy than light) and unbroken, with no bare patches. Longhairs should not be matted and tangled.

Skin. The skin should be smooth and supple. Its coloring may range from pale pink or silver to brown or black. It may be unpigmented or pigmented (normal in some cats with spotted, striped, or blotched coat patterns). There should be no evidence of fleas, mites, dandruff, crusts, lesions, pustules, or any other infection.

Eyes. The eyes should be clear and shining, with no excessive tearing, mucus discharge, or sensitivity to light. The third eyelid (also called the "haw," or nictating membrane) at the corner of each eye near the nose, should be almost invisible. Unlike dogs, cats usually do not have eyelashes. The skin folds of the eyelids should be smooth. Roll down the bottom lid with your thumb to examine the lining of the eye. It should be pink, and not ashy or bright red.

Ears. The skin on the external earflaps (or *pinnae*) and inside the ear should be pale pink. Brilliant pink, red, or brownish skin indicates trouble. Smell the ears: healthy ones smell clean, while unhealthy ears smell foul. A little wax is normal, but excessive amounts are not. There should be no pawing at the ears or excessive shaking of the head.

Nose. A healthy nose should be cool and slightly moist with no sticky or yellowish secretions.

Mouth. Examine your cat's bite: the insides of the upper incisors should touch the outsides of the lower incisors when the mouth is closed. An overshot bite (the upper front teeth extend beyond the lower front teeth) or an undershot bite (the lower front teeth extend beyond the upper front teeth) are abnormal. The teeth should be firmly implanted and not loose. They should be white in a kitten, but may yellow slightly with age. There should be no tartar buildup on the teeth or around the gumline. The gums and tissue inside the mouth should be pink, never bluish or ashy. The breath should smell pleasant.

Body. There should be no masses, lumps, or bumps, especially around the nipples.

External genitalia. Body openings should function properly with no abnormal discharges. Membranes should be smooth and pink.

Urination. Become familiar with your cat's urinary

patterns, because fluctuations may indicate changes in body chemistry. Urine should be clear yellow with a characteristic aroma, never orangey.

Defecation. Diet influences the volume, color, and odor of a cat's feces, but the stool should be well-formed, typically brown in color, and it should be eliminated regularly. Stools should not be loose, strangely colored, blood-streaked, or putrid-smelling.

Temperature. A cat's normal rectal temperature registers between 100.5° F to 102.5° F (38° C to 39° C). Do remember, however, that excitement, exercise, or heat can temporarily cause the temperature to rise.

Heartbeat and pulse. The average heartbeat of a cat at rest varies from 110 to 140 times per minute, or about twice the normal human rate. The beat should be firm and steady. You can feel the heartbeat while your cat stands by pressing your fingers against the rib cage in back of its left elbow. The pulse rate will equal the heartbeat; it is taken over the femoral artery on the inside of the thigh, while your cat stands or lies on its side, by pressing two fingers on the inside of the back leg, just about where it joins the body. To determine the rate per minute, count the pulse beats for fifteen seconds, then multiply by four. A cat's pulse and heartbeat, though, may be so accelerated that they are difficult to measure, and in evaluating illness, owners should be more influenced by the character of the pulse, that is, whether it is strong and steady as opposed to rapid and shallow.

Respiration. A healthy cat at rest normally

breathes from twenty to forty breaths per minute. A cat breathes in and out through its nose as its chest contracts and expands smoothly. Like dogs, cats release body heat less efficiently than man, and in very hot weather or extreme excitement disperse heat by panting and rapid breathing. Observe how your cat breathes at rest and you'll soon be able to tell when abnormalities occur.

Signs of a Sick Cat

It's not difficult to know when your cat is sick. Any deviation from normal good health will ordinarily be coupled with one or more changes in body functions and behavior. An observant owner who is immediately able to recognize these changes and report them to the veterinarian can be an invaluable help in the discovery and diagnosis of early illness. These are the most common signs:

Any change in appetite or fluid intake.
Excessive weight gain or loss.
Fever.
Behavioral changes: apathy, depression, listlessness, viciousness.
Shivering or trembling.
Difficult or shallow and rapid breathing.
Limping, lameness, or difficult movement, especially when getting up or lying down.
Bloody, frequent, or uncontrollable defecation.
Constipation.
Blood-tinged, orangey, or cloudy urine.
Constant straining to urinate or inability to urinate.
Bladder enlargement.

Abdominal swelling or tenderness.

Swellings or tumors of the breasts.

Swellings or lumps on or beneath the skin.

Abnormal discharges from any body opening.

Prolonged vomiting.

Prolonged sneezing or coughing.

Nasal discharge: sticky, yellowish, or greenish.

Partial covering of each eye by the third eyelid.

Any eye problem.

Ear problems: foul odor, excessive wax, abnormal head shaking.

Pale gums.

Foul breath.

Excessive salivation.

Intense biting and scratching at the skin and coat.

Hair loss, baldness, open sores, pustules, lesions, excessive external parasite infestation, or any other skin problem.

Dehydration or excessive loss of body fluids. An easy way to determine if your cat is dehydrated is to pinch a fold of skin along the middle of its back and then release it. The skin should go back into place *immediately*. If it returns to place slowly, the animal is somewhat dehydrated. If it stays pinched together in an A-shape, the cat is extremely dehydrated and requires immediate fluid therapy from a veterinarian.

Vaccinations

The most helpful preventive is vaccination against five feline communicable diseases. The principle of immunization is to trigger an animal's immunity system to produce defensive antibodies. When a vaccine is injected into the cat's body, it causes in effect a mild version of the disease and the tissues react to produce immune bodies against the agent. There are five cat diseases for which vaccines have been produced.

Feline Panleukopenia (FPL)

Feline panleukopenia (FPL), also known as feline infectious enteritis (FIE) and inaccurately called feline distemper, is a member of the parvovirus group. It is a dreaded, highly contagious, and potentially fatal viral disease that is known throughout the world. The extremely hardy virus is spread by direct contact with an infected cat or through contact with its excretions. Parvoviruses are, in all likelihood, the most resistant viruses known, and FPL can live on many surfaces at room temperature up to one year and are resistant to most disinfectants. Unvaccinated cats of all ages are susceptible to FPL, although the disease is most common in young kittens. The death rate is extremely high. In fact, FPL can develop so rapidly and so severely in youngsters that death occurs before the owner is aware that the kitten is sick. Symptoms appear within two to ten days after exposure and include loss of appetite, depression, lethargy, fever, vomiting frothy yellow fluid, and diarrhea. The feces are soft and yellowy and may be blood-tinged.

Feline Upper Respiratory Diseases

Feline upper respiratory diseases are also highly contagious. They are known throughout the world and often reach epidemic proportions where cats are gathered together in groups—boarding catteries and breeding colonies, for example. Upper respiratory diseases are caused by a number of organisms and spread through the air or by direct or indirect contact. Cats shed the viruses in eye, nose, and mouth discharges, and the calicivirus may be present in the feces from one to three weeks. Upper respiratory diseases primariy affect the linings of the nasal passages, the eyes, and frequently the mouth. The severe congestion of the nasal passages causes a cat to lose its appetite because it cannot smell its food. In certain diseases ulcers may develop on the tongue and inside the mouth and make eating very painful. A cat can lose weight quickly, and as it becomes more debilitated it may be susceptible to bacterial infections such as pneumonia. The symptoms of upper respiratory tract infections are very similar and it is often hard to distinguish between them. They may occur individually or in combinations, and they can infect every cat in your household within a few days. Vaccines are available for three of these diseases.

Feline rhinotracheitis (FVR) is caused by a herpes virus similar to that which produces cold sores in humans. It is the most universal and serious of the feline upper respiratory diseases. Symptoms appear within two to twelve days after exposure and include paroxysms of sneezing, an abundant purulent eye and nose discharge, swelling of the eyelids, a retching cough, anorexia, listlessness, drooling, depression, and fever of over 104° F (40° C) in many cases. Ulcers may develop inside the mouth and make eating painful. Unvaccinated cats of all ages are susceptible, although kittens and old or debilitated cats are especially liable to the ravages of the disease. FVR is known to cause genital lesions and abortion in pregnant queens.

There are many strains of *feline calicivirus (FVC)*,

another upper respiratory infection. Symptoms appear from one to nine days after exposure and are somewhat like those of FVR, including ulcers on the tongue and inside the mouth that make eating difficult and painful. The heavy eye and nose discharges characteristic of FVR, however, are usually not present. Although the disease lasts a few days and most cats recover, some strains can cause pneumonia.

Feline pneumonitis (FPN) is a highly infectious upper respiratory infection spread by a rickettsial organism, *Chlamydia psittaci*. Symptoms appear from six to fifteen days after exposure and resemble those of a bad cold in human beings: mild redness in one or both eyes, a little sneezing, sniffling, runny eyes and nose, slight rise in temperature, and sore throat. Kittens usually are more susceptible than adult cats. Fortunately, pneumonitis is rarely fatal and can be successfully treated with the tetracycline antibiotics.

Rabies

Rabies is a fatal viral disease that infects cats, dogs, coyotes, wolves, skunks, raccoons, foxes, and bats. All warm-blooded creatures are susceptible to rabies and the disease can infect humans. The virus is present in the saliva of an infected animal and is spread through biting or by licking over cuts in the skin. The incubation period varies from ten days to several months, depending on the location of the bite and how long the virus takes to reach the brain. Two forms of the disease exist: (1) the furious form, in which the animal becomes vicious and eager to attack anything that moves, including people and other animals; and (2) the paralytic, or "dumb," form, in which the muscles of the mouth and throat become paralyzed and force the lower jaw to fall open. There is an excess of saliva due to difficulty in swallowing. The paralysis spreads quickly and causes death within a few days. If you or your cat (even when it is vaccinated) are ever bitten by a rabid animal, call a veterinarian or physician immediately for instructions. There is no cure, and rabies is always fatal once it appears in an animal. It can be prevented by vaccination, however, and periodic reimmunization.

Vaccination Schedule

Vaccinations should begin in early kittenhood. When you buy a cat and the seller indicates that it has been immunized, find out which vaccinations were given and when, and inform your veterinarian. Sev-

IDEAL VACCINATION SCHEDULE FOR CATS*

Disease	Type of Vaccine**	Initial Vacci-nation (age in wks)	First Booster (age in wks)	Additional Boosters
Panleukopenia	Killed or modified live†	8	12	yearly
Pneumonitis	Modified live†	8	12	yearly
Rhinotracheitis	Modified live†	8	12	yearly
Calicivirus	Modified live†	8	12	yearly
Rabies‡	Killed or modified live†	12	—	yearly

*This vaccination schedule assumes a healthy kitten weaned by an immune mother. Consult your veterinarian for further interpretation or modification to fit your specific situation.

**Combination vaccines are available for cats, which allow several vaccinations to be given in one injection.

†Pregnant cats should not be vaccinated with modified-live vaccines due to possible effects on the fetus.

‡Not all veterinarians recommend rabies vaccine for cats kept inside all the time. Check with your veterinarian for the pros and cons. The rabies vaccine is usually given at the first booster visit.

eral kinds of vaccines can be used to immunize cats, and most veterinarians make their selection based on local conditions and experience. The suggested vaccination schedule above was prepared by Valerie Matthews, DVM, for *Cat Fancy* magazine and reproduced with their permission.

Feline Urologic Syndrome (FUS)

Feline urologic syndrome (FUS) is one of the major disease complexes affecting cats. It occurs in cats of all ages and all breeds. Lon D. Lewis, DVM, Ph.D., comments in a monograph about the disease (see "Bibliography of the Cat" in Chapter XVI) that it affects nearly 1 percent of all cats and accounts for 5 percent to 10 percent of all veterinary hospital admissions. Without proper nutritional management it recurs at a rate of 50 percent to 70 percent. "Cats are particularly susceptible to urologic problems," adds Dr. Lewis, "because they normally have prolonged intervals between urinations. Many cats urinate only once a day and some only once every two to three days. The cat also has a more concentrated urine than many other species, which increases mineral concentrations and promotes crystallization and calculi formation."

The major conditions that constitute the feline urologic syndrome are as follows: *Cystitis* is any acute or chronic bladder infection. It damages the bladder wall and causes mucus, blood, and other organic fragments to collect in the bladder. When the bladder becomes inflamed, or when the cat eats certain foods, or when the urine is retained too long, the normal acid pH of the urine changes to aklaline. Salts that usually dissolve in the acidic urine form into struvite crystals that combine with the debris from the inflamed bladder to create gritty substances known as "stones" or "plugs." This condition is called *urolithiasis. Urethral blockage* occurs when the stones or plugs obstruct the urethal (or discharge) passage and stop the flow of urine. Urethal obstruction is more common in males because of their long and narrow urethras. The female's urethra is wider and not as easily obstructed; small stones are often passed without too much pain. Once the urethra becomes blocked, the cat cannot urinate, the kidneys stop functioning, and waste products back up in the body, resulting in *uremia,* or a kind of self-poisoning that causes coma and death within forty-eight hours.

The actual cause of FUS is not completely understood, and many factors such as excessive mineral intake, diets that consist primarily of dry food, vitamin deficiencies, urine pH, low fluid consumption leading to greater urine concentration, viral and bacterial urinary tract infections, anatomic defects, obesity, and stress may be involved. According to T. D. Phillips, DVM, a veterinarian specializing in nutrition, FUS is characterized by the formation of struvite crystals in the bladder or urethra. "Struvite is a name for the chemical compound magnesium ammonium phosphate," said Phillips. "For many years, we have had evidence that the amount of ash or mineral matter in a cat's diet has a bearing on whether or not the pet would suffer with FUS. But recently, we have narrowed the focus to the element magnesium, a trace mineral found in bone." Phillips referred to experiments that show that the more magnesium in the diet, the more likely it was that FUS would occur. Analysis of various commercial cat foods showed that some labeled "low ash" were, in fact, higher in magnesium than is recommended for cats prone to FUS. "The safe limit for magnesium is not more than .1% on a dry weight basis," Dr. Phillips added. He suggests talking over the question of choosing low magnesium foods with a veterinarian, who can give expert advice on the subject. It is most important, too, always to provide fresh water, especially if dry food is being fed. Veterinarians advise that a high water intake tends to dilute the urine and make the formation of struvite crystals less likely.

Early clinical signs of FUS, in order of their progression, are:

- Changes in urinary habits: urinating in unusual places away from the litter pan.
- *Frequent* unsuccessful attempts to pass urine or the passing of small quantities of urine. In these efforts a cat will squat very close to the ground or its litter pan and strain. Owners sometimes equate these actions with constipation and give the cat a laxative. A laxative can be fatal when the urethral passage is blocked, and can cause the distended bladder to burst.
- Crying from painful urination.
- Blood-stained urine, often accompanied by a strong, ammonia-like odor.
- Listlessness; poor appetite; excessive thirst.
- Frequent licking of the penis.

Signs that the condition is severe or that the urethra is blocked with stones are vomiting, depression, dehydration, urinelike odor to the breath, and a painful and distended bladder. The bladder when palpated may feel as large as an egg or an orange. It will often rupture and cause death before uremic poisoning occurs. Contact your veterinarian immediately when any of these signs appear. Time is critical, especially if blockage has occurred. FUS can be treated successfully if it is detected early. But when the condition has been allowed to progressively worsen, or when it recurs, surgery may be necessary.

Feline Infectious Peritonitis (FIP)

Feline infectious peritonitis (FIP) is a mysterious disease that strikes domestic and wild cats of all ages, but most often those from one to four years old. There is no effective treatment.

Edward A. Hoover, DVM, Ph.D., who has investigated feline viruses at the Department of Veterinary Pathobiology at Ohio State University and conducted several investigations under the sponsorship of the Morris Animal Foundation, reports:

> FIP is caused by a virus and is contagious by contact or through the air. Many cats can be infected with the virus, but only a few will actually develop the FIP disease. Cats exposed to the virus who do not develop the disease develop mild infections and immunity to FIP. Many cats continue to carry the virus, increasing the chances that other cats will be exposed. The factors that determine which cats infected with the virus will develop the disease are not yet understood. . . . Mysteriously, about 40 percent of all cats with FIP infection are also infected with feline leukemia virus, which may harm their ability to avoid and fight off FIP.*

*Morris Animal Foundation Newsletter, July 1981.

The primary sign of the disease is inflammation or swelling of the stomach due to fluid buildup. The onset of FIP is gradual and marked by a loss of appetite, loss of weight, fever, weakness, and dehydration. The signs may be apparent only after several weeks, and erroneously thought to have appeared suddenly. Diagnosis of FIP is difficult because other symptoms resemble many feline diseases.

Feline Infectious Anemia (FIA)

Feline infectious anemia (FIA), also known as *Haemobartonella felis,* is a disease that strikes cats of all ages, but most often those from one to three years old. Kittens can be born with the parasite, infected in the womb from their mother. FIA is caused by a microscopic protozoan parasite that attacks and destroys an infected cat's red blood cells. The parasites can be carried by fleas, mosquitos, and other blood-sucking insects, and injected into the bloodstream of healthy cats through their bites. It is also believed that the organism can be transmitted from cat to cat through bite wounds.

The onset of FIA is gradual and marked by a loss of appetite, excessive thirst, listlessness, and a general malaise. The blood-cell loss is manifested by progressive acute anemia, and the cat develops a high fever, becomes weak, emaciated, depressed, and, in severe cases, jaundiced. The disease is often said to resemble malaria in human beings. Diagnosis is made by blood test, and this may need to be repeated several times because the parasite is not always discernible during certain life-cycle stages. If the anemia is in an early stage, treatment involves antibiotics and vitamins. Blood transfusions and fluid therapy are necessary in extreme cases. Cats that are severely anemic and jaundiced, however, rarely survive.

Feline Leukemia Virus (FeLV)

Feline leukemia virus, also called FeLV, is the most serious infectious disease of cats. It is the leading cause of death from disease among pet cats in the United States. The virus is part of a group that causes cancer in a number of species. Dr. William D. Hardy, Jr., Head of the Veterinary Oncology Laboratory of Memorial/Sloan-Kettering cancer center in New York reported at a Carnation Symposium on Feline Diseases that the FeLV virus belongs to the family *Retroviridae*. "Like other viruses of the same genus," said Dr. Hardy, "it consists of a circular protein shell (envelope) enclosing a core containing the genetic material, which for these viruses is a single-stranded ribonucleic acid (RNA). Since these viruses are oncogenic and contain RNA, they are commonly referred to as oncornaviruses. Oncornaviruses are found in many vertebrate species and it is known that an oncornavirus from one species can infect other species. For example, FeLV is now known to have been an ancestral rat virus which first infected cats about five million years ago."

The FeLV virus is spread from cat to cat primarily by the saliva and the urine. Once the virus infects a healthy cat, it gravitates toward the bone marrow, where it lives and grows in the cells. In many cases it depresses the cat's immune response so that the animal cannot cope with infections or the cancer cells that are growing in the body, and its presence makes the cat susceptible to other bacterial and viral infections. The major problem of this virus is that it does not cause just one disease but a number of fatal proliferative and degenerative diseases, which members of the veterinary community are more likely to refer to as the Feline Leukemia Virus Associated Disease complex. The diseases known to be caused by FeLV are: lymphosarcoma (a cancerous disease of the lymphoid tissues and the most common type of cancer in cats), FeLV nonregenerative anemia, FeLV panleukopenia-like syndrome, myelogenous leukemia, thymic atrophy (fading kitten syndrome), and a number of immunosuppressive diseases, such as haemobartonellosis, FIP, septicemia, glomerulonephritis, skin disorders, chronic oral ulcers, upper respiratory diseases, and general unthriftiness. Fetal resorbtions and abortions are also thought to be connected with FeLV infection.

The first signs of FeLV are not very specific: loss of appetite, weakness, listlessness, lethargy, persistent gum infection, pale mucous membranes, difficult breathing, and loss of weight. A cat can become infected with FeLV, can carry the virus for life and never show any signs of the disease. Asymptomatic carriers, as these are called, are a constant problem for catteries and multiple-cat households because these animals are just as capable of spreading the virus as a cat with clinical disease. It is most important, therefore, that breeders and multiple-cat owners routinely test their cats for FeLV to determine that they are negative. A veterinarian can make a rapid and accurate diagnosis by testing a sample of the cat's blood. The test indicates whether the cat is or is not carrying the FeLV virus; it does not diagnose cancer. Your veterinarian can give you more information and advice about treatment. Some of these diseases respond well to medical care and long-term remissions can be obtained, while others, like lymphosarcoma, are usually fatal.

Veterinary researchers at Ohio State University have worked for more than ten years to develop a FeLV vaccine. *DVM,* the Magazine of Veterinary Medicine, reports that a new vaccine could be approved by the U.S. Department of Agriculture and available for veterinary use within a few years. Hopefully, it will be administered to cats as routinely as panleukopenia vaccine is today. Although FeLV is not considered a threat to human health, most physicians and veterinarians advise that a person undergoing chemotherapy or immunosuppressive therapy not keep FeLV positive cats in their households.

A Guide to Parasite Infection

A parasite is an animal that lives in or on an organism of another species, from whose body it obtains nourishment. It is important for every cat owner to learn as much as possible about internal or external parasites (including how to recognize them in many instances), for these destructive creatures suck your cat's blood, debilitate it, and make it more vulnerable to disease. Worse yet, they often transmit other viral and bacterial diseases.

An animal's age, physical condition, and amount of infestation will influence the severity of the problem. A few parasites may not make a cat ill, but large numbers can cause severe infirmity and, when ignored, even death. Kittens and undernourished, weak, sick, and old cats are more susceptible to internal or external parasite infection. Healthy animals are better able to fight off parasites, but even they can become weak and debilitated under intense exposure.

Internal Parasites and Their Treatment

Internal parasites are common ailments of cats, and even the most responsible and meticulous owner cannot always shield his or her cat from infection. They seem to be most common in kittens and young cats, although cats of any age can be infested. Some of the most common kinds of internal parasites are listed on the following chart, along with notes on their appearance, where they live in the cat's body, the manner of infection, and common symptoms.

Other internal parasites that can infect cats include stomach worms, threadworms, lungworms, flukes, eye worms, (these appear most often on the West Coast), and the intestinal protozoans or single-celled animals *Coccidia* and *Toxoplasma gondii*. All internal parasites must be specifically identified by laboratory analysis (in most cases by microscopic examination of a fresh stool sample) and treated by a veterinarian. Quite often you will be able to tell when your cat has tapeworm, because segments break off and pass out with the feces. These are about one-quarter inch long, creamy colored, and move in the feces when they are fresh. Sometimes they dry on the hair or skin around the anus and look like kernels of rice attached to the cat.

Once the type of internal parasite is identified, your veterinarian will dispense the correct medication for worming, the dosage of which depends partly on your cat's age and physical condition. If you don't know the type of worm present, *never* buy an over-the-counter worming preparation. Worming medi-

Feline Internal Parasites

Parasite	Appearance	Location	Manner of Infection	Symptoms
Roundworms	White; 2 to 4 inches long; $\frac{1}{8}$ inch wide. Resemble small earthworms.	Roundworms live free in a cat's intestines.	1. Very young kittens can be infected by drinking mother's milk contaminated with worm larvae. 2. By ingesting soil or feces infested with worm larvae from another cat.	Poor appearance. Dull, brittle coat. Listlessness. Bloated abdomen or potbelly. Intermittent diarrhea. Worms in feces. Coughing or vomiting up worms.
Hookworms	Grayish and threadlike; $\frac{1}{4}$ to $\frac{3}{4}$ of an inch long.	Hookworms live in the cat's intestines, where they "hook" onto the intestinal wall and suck blood.	1. Kittens can be born with worms, infected in the womb from their mother. 2. Very young kittens can be infected by drinking mother's milk contaminated with worm larvae. 3. By ingesting soil or feces infested with worm larvae from another cat. 4. Larvae from infected soil can penetrate through skin (this is rare).	Poor appetite. Anemia (leading to emaciation). Pale gums due to anemia. Dull, brittle coat. Intermittent, bloody diarrhea.

Feline Internal Parasites

Parasite	Appearance	Location	Manner of Infection	Symptoms
Tapeworms	White, flat, and with many egg-filled segments from 5mm. to 10mm. long. Often grow several feet long.	Tapeworms live in a cat's intestines and attach their heads to the intestinal wall.	Several species infect cats: The most common type is carried by fleas and usually ingested when a cat, biting itself in relief, swallows the flea. Other types are acquired through eating raw meat or body organs of infected rabbits, toads, rodents, squirrels, or raw fish, crayfish, and snails.	Signs vary with worm species, severity of infection, age, and physical condition of cat, but include: Dull, brittle coat. Excessive or irregular appetite. Thinness. Listlessness Poor condition. Mild and foul-smelling diarrhea.
Whipworms	Creamy colored and slender, 2 inches long. Shaped like a whip.	Whipworms live in the cat's large intestines in the cecum and attach their heads to intestinal wall.	Acquired by eating the egg-infested feces of an infected cat, or by ingesting the infective larvae from contaminated soil or feces.	Mild infections produce few signs except poor appearance. As infection increases, the cat becomes emaciated and suffers from foul-smelling (often bloody) diarrhea.

Feline Internal Parasites

Parasite	Appearance	Location	Manner of Infection	Symptoms
Heartworms (once thought only to occur in dogs)	Creamy colored; 1/8 inch wide. Adult males reach a length of 6 inches; adult females grow up to 12 inches long.	Adult heartworms live in the right side of the heart and pulmonary artery. After reproduction, females release young worms (microfilariae) into the cat's bloodstream, where they circulate and can live up to five years. Microfilariae need the mosquito to complete their life cycle. When mosquitoes bite infected dogs or cats, they ingest microfilariae while sucking blood. Within fourteen days larvae develop and migrate to mosquitoes' mouths, ready to be deposited into other cats and dogs.	Through the bite of a contaminated mosquito. Infective larvae pass through the mosquito's mouth into a healthy cat's skin. There they develop for three to four months, enter the bloodstream, and move to the heart, where they mature and reproduce young worms.	Coughing. Lethargy. Labored breathing. General weakness. See a veterinarian immediately if you suspect heartworm. In advanced cases the heart, liver, and lungs may be severely damaged and a cat can die of circulatory failure.

cines are potentially dangerous, and medications formulated to kill internal parasites can cause great harm when administered in excessive amounts, too frequently, or for the wrong species of worm. A lot of cats die every year because of their owners' casual attitudes about worming. Follow your veterinarian's instructions to the letter.

In the case of heartworm, a blood test and X rays are necessary to diagnose the presence of microfilariae. If the test is positive, a veterinarian may be able to treat the cat and return it to a negative state. Heartworm was once thought to infect only dogs, and to be found in the eastern and southern coastal areas of the country. The problem has spread throughout the United States, and now we know that cats are vulnerable too. Because it is passed by mosquitoes, there is a direct relationship between the number of dogs or cats with heartworm and the number of mosquitoes in any area. Prevention is the only solution to the problem. If you live in an area heavily infested with mosquitoes and your cat goes outside, check with your veterinarian to learn about possible preventive measures.

Toxoplasmosis

One protozoan parasite already mentioned, *Toxoplasma gondii,* is of special concern to pregnant women. In the past few years an alarming number of articles about the disease toxoplasmosis have appeared in women's magazines that were especially disparaging to cats. People can and do catch diseases from pets, although this is a rare occurrence. Illnesses that are transmitted from animals to people are called zoonoses. Toxoplasmosis is such a disease, and it is caused by the *Toxoplasma gondii* parasite. It can be spread by handling or eating raw meat or through contact with cat fecal material. *Toxoplasma gondii* can infect any animal, but only cats spread the parasites via infective oocysts or egg spores shed in their feces. Then when flies or cockroaches eat the infected fecal material, they become intermediate hosts of the disease and spread it to other animals like birds and rodents. Healthy cats become infected when they eat birds or rodents containing infective organisms.

In most mammals, including human beings, *Toxoplasma gondii* can cross the placenta during pregnancy and infect the developing fetus or fetuses. The infection is most dangerous to women in their first three months of pregnancy; if the disease is not diagnosed and treated promptly, it can cause miscarriage or birth defects in the fetus. These occurrences are rare, however, and before you panic and make plans to give the cat away, it is important to put the facts in perspective. The major source of *Toxoplasma* infection in humans is eating raw or undercooked meat—steak tartare, for instance.* The only way someone can get toxoplasmosis from an infected cat is to touch its feces, or something contaminated with its feces, and then put his or her hands into the mouth.

Women in the first trimester of pregnancy should observe the following simple precautions:

● Wear rubber or plastic gloves before you change the litter or clean the litter tray, or temporarily assign these duties to another family member.

---

*In *The Well Cat Book* (see "Bibliography of the Cat" in Chapter XVI), Dr. Terri McGinnis says that infection rates of greater than 80 percent have been found in people consuming large quantities of raw meat.

- Change the litter every day. Research indicates that it takes from two to four days for the oocysts to become infective.
- Clean the litter pan with scalding water and a disinfectant safe for cats.*
- Wear gloves while gardening or cleaning sandboxes, to avoid coming into contact with contaminated soil.
- Wash your hands after handling your cat.

Proper feeding is the best way to protect your cat from becoming infected with *Toxoplasma* parasites. Feed it dry or canned commercial rations, or cooked homemade food, but never anything raw. Don't let the cat kill and eat birds or rodents, because they could be diseased. But it is *most* important for pregnant women to wash their hands after handling raw meat, and to cook the meat thoroughly before it is eaten. Cats affected with *Toxoplasma* organisms display a variety of symptoms including fever, diarrhea, enlarged lymph nodes, and poor appetite. A veterinarian can perform a fecal examinaton or take a sample of your cat's blood to determine the presence of *Toxoplasma gondii*. And for your own peace of mind, you can ask your physician to take a sample of your blood and have it tested for *Toxoplasma* titer.

External Parasites

External parasites are organisms that live on the skin and sometimes feed off the cat's blood. They are extremely debilitating and irritating. Many cause anemia as a result of their bloodsucking. If your cat suddenly starts scratching and biting its coat, or if you

---

*Dr. McGinnis recommends a 10 percent ammonia solution.

see irritated or bare patches on its skin, it may be infested with external parasites, and steps to eradicate them should begin immediately. To save your cat a great deal of discomfort, you should check regularly for their presence. Once a week, during combing and brushing, part the hair to the skin and examine the cat from head to tail under a good light, especially on the abdomen, around the front and back legs, and on the head and ears. Fleas, ticks, lice, and mites are some of the external parasites that can infest cats. By knowing how to identify them and understanding their habits, you can learn to protect your cat against these dangerous pests.

Fleas

Fleas are the most common external parasites of cats. In some parts of the country they are a menace in the summer; in other areas they are a problem fifty-two weeks a year. Fleas are tiny, dark brown, wingless insects with piercing/sucking mouth parts. They bite the host animal and suck its blood. They also have long legs that make it easy for them to hop from cat to cat, cat to dog, and even from animal to human, searching for a host to feed on. Although there are many different flea species, manufacturers of insecticidal products say the cat flea, or *Cteno-cephalides felis,* is by far the most prevalent species found on cats and dogs.

Adult fleas live and breed on the cat. They are difficult to see, especially on longhairs, because they move quickly through the hair. The first signs may be a glimpse of a small dark bug scurrying through the fur, or the presence of small black specks on the skin, in the cat's hair, or on the comb after grooming. These are flea excrement, made up mostly of blood sucked from the cat, passed through the flea's digestive system, and eliminated as dried blood. Adult females lay eggs, which drop off and hatch into wormlike larvae and complete their life cycle to become adult fleas.

Fleas should be eradicated immediately because they transmit several viral, bacterial, and blood-borne diseases, and they are the intermediate host for a species of cat tapeworm. The parasite *Haemobartonella felis*, which causes the previously mentioned feline infectious anemia, can be transmitted by fleas. The flea's bloodsucking also causes anemia in young or sick cats. When a flea bites, its mouth pierces the cat's skin and sucks its blood. The flea deposits saliva under the skin during this action, which causes the cat to itch considerably. Cats often develop hypersensitivity to the flea saliva, resulting in a condition known as feline flea allergy dermatitis, in which the cat's persistent scratching and biting destroys the coat and causes the skin (generally on the back near the tail, the abdomen, and between the legs) to become red and thick and infected. Flea allergy dermatitis must be treated by a veterinarian.

Flea Control

If your cat is infested with fleas, control involves treating not only the cat but also its environment. Begin by thoroughly vacuuming all the carpets, floors, baseboards, cracks, and crevices in your house. Wash the cat's bedding. Fumigation is often necessary in the house: do it yourself with a household fogger, or hire a professional exterminator if you have a heavy infestation.* A second fumigation within five to seven

---

*Using a fogger entails removing all people and live animals from the house for several hours while the fogger is working.

days may be required to kill eggs that were not previously affected. If your cat goes outdoors, treat the lawn, patio, or other areas where it spends time, with a yard and kennel dust or spray. In addition to these steps both inside and outside your home, if you have more than one animal, each one has to be bathed with an insecticidal shampoo.

Once the fleas on the cat are destroyed, the use of feline-safe flea collars or tags, dips, powders, sprays, or shampoos will help prevent reinfestation. Such insecticidal products are usually safe for kittens and adult cats when they are used according to package directions.* A flea collar should be removed from its sealed pouch and aired for at least twenty-four hours before it is placed on the cat. Fasten the collar comfortably around the neck and cut off any excess. The ideal fit is loose enough for you to slip your finger comfortably between the collar and the cat's skin, but not so loose that the cat can slide the collar into its mouth. Check the neck every day for the first week or so to make sure there is no hypersensitivity to the insecticide. Do not use flea collars and other insecticides simultaneously. Remove the collar before using other products, if it gets wet (unless the label indicates this is safe), or when you notice skin inflammation or loss of hair. A flea tag hangs, like an identification disc, from your cat's regular collar.

Insecticides can be potentially dangerous to felines, and you must exercise caution when using them and follow directions explicitly. The labels should clearly state that the products are formulated for use on cats. Consult your veterinarian before you use a combina-

---

*Kittens should be at least sixteen weeks old before wearing a collar.

tion of insecticides at one time, since such concentrations could produce toxicity.

Ticks

Ticks are members of the wingless arachnid family and they are the hardiest and most dangerous blood-sucking parasite. Although they do not plague felines as severely as they do canines, several species that do infest cats can cause certain diseases that vary geographically, including Rocky Mountain spotted fever, tularemia, thulerioses, and some forms of encephalitis in humans.

The most common adult ticks are grayish-brown in color, with four legs jutting out from each side of their oval bodies. When they bite, they force their fishhook-shaped mouths into the skin and suck the cat's blood. This not only lowers the animal's resistance to disease and eventually causes anemia, but it leads to intense itching and frenzied scratching that result in secondary skin infections.

Ticks are found in moist and warm areas: woods, beaches, high grass, and low bushes. They mate on the host animal, then the female drops off and looks for an out-of-the-way place to lay her eggs. Inside your house this could be in the baseboards, the carpets, under the furniture, or behind the drapes and picture frames. The eggs hatch and complete their life cycle to become adults.

Remove ticks as soon as you discover them. To do this, soak the ticks in alcohol or petroleum jelly to help paralyze them and loosen their grip. Then grasp each tick as close to the skin as possible with tweezers and carefully pull it straight out, making sure that no part of the head is left in the skin. Protect your fingers with a piece of paper if you don't have tweezers. Once the tick is pulled out, swab the area with an antiseptic, then wash your hands thoroughly with soap and water. To eradicate ticks, follow the suggestions under "Flea Control."

Lice

Louse infestation, fortunately, is not a common problem of healthy and well-groomed cats. Lice are small, pale pests that spend their entire life cycle on the host animal, and they spread primarily through body contact. Two kinds of lice infest cats: the biting variety, which feeds off hair and skin debris and moves slowly through the fur; and the sucking variety, which attaches itself to the cat's skin and feeds on blood and tissue fluid. As with fleas and ticks, the constant bloodsucking of lice can cause anemia in young or debilitated cats. Symptoms of infestation are similar to those for fleas and ticks: intense itching, biting, and scratching of the skin. A good way to confirm the presence of lice is to look for eggs or "nits" that will be laid by the female. They will be pale in color and stick to the cat's hair. Feline-safe flea and tick shampoos and dips will also kill lice.

Mange Mites

Although body mange is not common in cats, felines can be infested by several varieties of mites that burrow into the skin and hair follicles. There are two common kinds of mange: the first, sarcoptic mange or scabies (caused by *Notoedres cati,* or the feline sarcoptic mange mite), is an extremely contagious condition. It frequently starts on the ear tips, spreads to the face, eyelids, and neck, and can extend to the feet. It is characterized by intense itching, scale formation, and skin irritation. The second type is demodectic or red mange (caused by *Demodex cati,* or the feline demodectic mange mite), which is manifested by extensive hair loss and thick, reddened skin. Infections in cats usually affect the eyelids and areas around the eyes. Early diagnosis and treatment by a veterinarian is most important in both manges. Treatment usually involves clipping the hair around the lesions, medicated baths, and possibly oral medication or injections.

Ear Mites

Ear mites are tiny pests that live in a cat's ears and are very irritating. They complete their entire life cycle in the ears, and they spread by direct contact. The ear mite, or *Otodectes cynotis,* bites into the soft folds of a cat's ear and sucks lymph and serum. Like fleas, ear mites inject saliva into the wound, which causes intense itching and scratching. The frenzied scratching sometimes produces a hematoma under the skin of each *pinna,* or sores on the ear. When ear mites are ignored, a secondary bacterial infection may develop that could spread to the inner ear and cause hearing difficulties, loss of equilibrium, convulsions, and even death. Although ear mites are not usually visible to the naked eye, you can suspect their presence by certain signs: head shaking, violent scratching, smelly and dark brown wax in the ears, scratch marks, loss of ear hair, or sores around the edges of or behind the ears. It's best to have a veterinarian perform the first treatment, since he or she will have to remove deeply embedded wax and debris and prescribe a feline-safe insecticide to kill the mites. Once this is done, you can continue treatment at home. The cat should be isolated from any further source of infection. If the cat sleeps with the tip of its tail curled up near its ears, the tail tip may need treatment too.

Skin Problems

Although cats have fewer dermatological problems than dogs or people do, they can experience a variety of skin disorders that may be caused by bacteria, fungi, viruses, hormone imbalances, and nutritional deficiencies. Early identification of any skin problem is vital. Most disorders can be treated successfully in their early stages, but when they are ignored, they can become chronic and difficult to cure.

Ringworm is one of the most serious diseases of cats. It is caused not by a worm, as its name might imply, but by an external fungus, the spores of which grow down the hair follicles and destroy the hair. Ringworm gets its name from the infected areas taking the form of a round or oval shape. It starts in small patches, usually on the cat's head. At the onset of the disease the hair becomes coarse and brittle and eventually breaks off or falls out in stubby patches. The skin becomes scaly and mildly itchy. If the disease goes untreated, it spreads rapidly over the body, and the cat's licking and scratching can cause secondary bacterial infection. Ringworm can be readily transmitted to other pets and to humans. If you suspect this disease, wear gloves when you handle your cat and consult a veterinarian immediately. Diagnosis involves an examination of skin scrapings, the use of a Wood's lamp (an ultraviolet light), and possibly a culture of the fungus.

Treatment consists of clipping the dead hair from infected spots, the application of a topical antifungal medication to dry the scabs and keep them from spreading to other parts of the body, and oral doses of the drug griseofulvin.* Ringworm takes from several weeks to several months to cure, depending on how advanced the disease was at the time of the discovery. As the cat is being treated at home, pick up any scaly matter or hair that drops off and burn it. Wash your hands with antibacterial soap before touching any part of your body.

Feline acne is an eruption on the cat's chin and the edges of the lips that is characterized by pustules and inflammation of the hair follicles. It is very common in cats that fail to clean their chins properly. This problem is discussed under "Blackheads or Feline Acne" in Chapter V.

Seborrhea, better known as dandruff, can occur in cats, and when it does, the condition is similar to that experienced by human beings, in other words the skin becomes dry and flaky. As the condition progresses the cat's licking and scratching can further irritate the skin. Dandruff in cats can result from a number of causes, the most common being a nutritional deficiency of fatty acids. Diets deficient in essential fatty acids can be improved by adding small amounts of vegetable oil to the food daily.

Eczema is an inflammatory condition of the skin derived from many different causes. Eczema appears in several forms, in which the skin can be dry and scaly in appearance, or moist, bright red, and pustular, or both. The cat's constant licking and scratching of the affected areas aggravates the skin and causes more irritation and damage. Treatment should be prescribed by a veterinarian. A number of topical

---

*Griseofulvin should *not* be given to pregnant queens, because it is known to cause fetal death or birth defects.

products provide temporary relief, but most stubborn cases of eczema must be treated internally.

Abscesses, or localized collections of pus in confined spaces, are also a common and serious problem of cats. Unlike abscesses in dogs and humans, they extend deep beneath the skin in cats and cause a great deal of pain and discomfort. Abscesses form when bacteria enter the body through a break in the skin. Cats possess a great amount of bacteria in their mouths, and these can be deposited in the body through deep puncture wounds from cat bites, or by licking open sores. Symptoms of abscess include fever, anorexia, and lethargy, and swelling, heat, and pain at the location of the infection. Abscesses require immediate professional attention and antibiotic therapy.

Plants That Are Poisonous to Cats

According to a report by the director of Research and Data Services of the Humane Society of the United States, more than seven hundred plants have been identified as producing physiologically active or toxic substances in sufficient amounts to cause harmful effects in animals. Poisonous plants cause at least five different types of reactions, and their toxic qualities are classified as muscular, neuromuscular, neurotic and blood poisonous, and irritating. While ingestion of the different toxins produces various symptoms, some of the most visible signs of poisoning include trembling, excessive thirst, increased salivation, dilated pupils, frequent swallowing, foul mouthodor, vomiting, cramps, panting, diarrhea, rapid or weak heartbeat, paralysis, convulsions, and coma.

If your cat ingests any toxic part of a plant, call

your veterinarian or nearest Poison Control Center to learn the correct emergency treatment. First aid depends on the type of poison ingested. Vomiting is not induced in all cases, especially if your cat eats a plant containing calcium oxalate crystals, which cause intense burning and swelling of the mouth, tongue, and throat. Here is a list of the most common house, garden, and vegetable plants, ornamental plants, trees, shrubs, and wildflowers, along with their toxic parts:

Poisonous Plant	Toxic Part
Aconite	Roots, foliage, seeds
Alocasia	All parts
Amaryllis	Bulb
Anemone	All parts
Apple	Seeds (when eaten in large quantities)
Apricot	Bark, stem, leaves, pits (when eaten in large quantities)
Arrow grasses	Leaves
Atropa belladonna	All parts
Avocado	Leaves, stems
Azalea	All parts
Baneberry	All parts
Bayonet	Root
Beargrass	All parts
Belladonna (deadly nightshade)	All parts
Bird-of-paradise	All parts
Bittersweet	Leaves, unripe fruit, stem

Black cherry	Leaves, twigs, bark, pits
Black locust	Bark, shoots, foliage, seeds
Black-eyed Susan	All parts
Bleeding Hearts (Dutchman's-breeches)	Leaves, roots
Bloodroot	All parts
Bluebonnet	All parts
Boxwood	Leaves, twigs
Buckeye (horse chestnut)	All parts
Bunchberry	All parts
Burning bush	Leaves, fruit
Buttercup	All parts
Cactus	All parts
Caladium	All parts
Castor bean	Seeds, beans
Cherries, most wild	Berries
Cherry tree	Leaves, tree bark
Chinaberry	Fruit, berry, bark
Chokecherry, wild	Leaves, pits, twigs, bark, seeds
Christmas rose	Rootstalk, leaves, sap
Clematis	All parts
Cone flower	All parts
Corn cockle	Seeds
Corydalus	All parts
Cow cockle	Seeds
Cowbane	All parts
Cowslip	All parts
Creeping Charlie	All parts
Crocus, autumn	All parts

Crown of thorns	All parts
Cyclamen	Tuber
Daffodil	Bulb, entire plant
Daphne	Bulb, entire plant
Death camas	Bulb
Delphinium	Seeds, young plants
Dieffenbachia (dumb cane)	All parts
Eggplant	Foliage, sprouts
Elderberry	Leaves, tree bark, buds, young shoots
Elephant's ear	All parts
Emerald Duke	All parts
Euonymus	All parts
False flax	Seeds
False hellebore	Roots, seeds, leaves
Fanweed	Seeds
Four-o'clock	Roots, seeds
Foxglove	Leaves, seeds
Golden chain	Beanlike capsules containing seeds, flowers
Golden glow	All parts
Heartleaf	All parts
Hellebore	All parts
Hemlock, poison	All parts
Hemlock, water	All parts
Hens-and-chicks	All parts
Holly	Berries
Horsebeans	All parts
Horse nettle	All parts
Hyacinth	Bulb, flowers
Hydrangea	All parts
Indian splurge tree	Bark, buds, leaves

Iris (blue flag)	Roots, leaves, bulb
Iris, wild	All parts
Ivy, English	All parts
Ivy, glacier	All parts
Ivy, parlor	All parts
Jack-in-the-pulpit	All parts
Jasmine	All parts
Java beans	All parts
Jequirity bean	Seeds
Jerusalem cherry	All parts
Jessamine, yellow	All parts, rootstalk, flower nectar
Jessamine, Carolina	All parts, rootstalk, flower nectar
Jimsonweed (thorn apple)	All parts
Jonquil	Bulb, entire plant
Lantana (red sage)	All parts
Larkspur	All parts; seeds
Laurel, cherry	All parts
Laurel, mountain (calico bush)	All parts
Lily, calla	All parts
Lily, climbing or glory	All parts
Lily, spider	Bulb
Lily of the valley	Leaves, flowers, roots
Locoweed	All parts
Lupine	All parts
Majesty	All parts
Mandrake	Roots, foliage, unripe fruit
Marble Queen	All parts
Marsh marigold	All parts

Matrimony vine	Leaves, shoots
Mayapple	Unripe fruit, roots, foliage
Mistletoe	Berries
Mock orange	Fruit
Monkshood	All parts
Moonseed	Roots, berries (these resemble grapes)
Morning glory	Seeds, roots
Mother-in-law	Leaves
Mountain mahogany	Leaves
Mushroom (fly agaric and amanita)	All parts
Mustards	Seeds
Narcissus	Bulb, entire plant
Nephthytis	All parts
Nightshade	All parts
Oak	Foliage, acorns
Oleander	All parts
Oleander, yellow	All parts
Peach tree	Leaves, pits, tree bark
Peony	Roots
Periwinkle	Seeds, roots
Philodendron	All parts
Philodendron, split-leaf	All parts
Pimpernel	All parts
Poinciana	All parts
Poinsettia	Leaves, sap, stem
Poison ivy, oak, and sumac	All parts
Pokeweed	All parts
Poppy	All parts
Porthos	All parts

Potatoes	Foliage, sprouts, green parts (not the tuber)
Privet, common	All parts
Red Princess	All parts
Rhododendron	All parts
Rhubarb	Leaves, blades
Rosary pea	Seeds
Saddleleaf	All parts
Scotch broom	Seeds
Skunk cabbage	All parts
Smartweeds	Sap
Snow-on-the-mountain	Sap
Snowdrop	All parts
Solandra (trumpet flower)	All parts
Staggerweeds	All parts
Star-of-Bethlehem	Bulb
Sweet pea	Stem, seeds, pods
Tansy mustard	Flower
Tobacco	Leaves
Tomato	Leaves
Tulip	Bulb
Tung tree	Nuts
Umbrella plant	All parts
Violet (pansy)	Seeds
Virginia creeper	All parts
White snakeroot	All parts
Wisteria	Seeds, pods
Yew	All parts, especially berries

Household Dangers

In addition to plants that can cause illness (and even death), there is also a real danger if your cat swallows many household objects. Harmless-looking items like thread, string, yarn, rubber bands, pieces of cork, aluminum foil, cellophane or plastic wrap, and pins and needles can be deadly when swallowed. As string, yarn, or rubber bands pass through a cat's digestive tract, they can wrap around the intestines and draw them into accordion-like pleats or cut through the intestinal wall. Foil, cork, and cellophane and plastic wrap cause intestinal blockage. A needle or a pin may become lodged in the pharynx or the base of the tongue, or could fatally penetrate the stomach or intestinal wall.

Every home contains countless potential hazards to the curious cat. The most common danger is poisoning. Pets most often become poisoned when they taste, chew, or swallow toxic substances out of curiosity or boredom. And since cats lick their fur during self-grooming, the accidental ingestion of potentially dangerous substances is an absolute threat to your cat's life. The garage, the basement, or other storage areas, as well as every room in your house contain chemicals that could poison your cat, and other substances that may seem harmless to you but could prove fatal, should your cat swallow them in large amounts. Some of these include ammonia, ant and roach killers, antifreeze (pets are attracted to its sweet taste and it's *deadly*), antiperspirants, barbiturates, battery acids, birth control pills, bleach, brake fluids, carburetor cleaners, cleaning fluids, chlorine swimming pool preparations, charcoal starters, depilatories, detergents, dishwashing compounds, drain cleaners, fabric dyes, furniture polish, fertilizers, hair dye, home permanent solutions, indelible pencils, insecticides, marking crayons, metal cleaners, oven cleaners, oil paint, paint and varnish removers, paint thinners, phenol and its various derivatives, photographic developer and fixer, rust and corrosion inhibitors, silver polish, shoe polish, weed killers, and many, many more.* Cats are sometimes poisoned accidentally when their owners try to treat them with medicines designed for human beings. *They are highly susceptible to poisoning by aspirin and aspirin substitutes, and these drugs should be avoided.* Prevent accidental poisoning by keeping potentially harmful substances in unbreakable, spillproof containers and storing them out of your cat's reach. Don't give human medicines to your cat. Consult your veterinarian if you believe medication is necessary. He or she will prescribe the correct kind.

Medical and First-aid Supplies

Soon after you get your kitten or cat, it is important to assemble a few supplies to use in an emergency, such as:

> Rectal thermometer.
> Sterile gauze pads, particularly three by three inches and four by four inches.
> Gauze bandage: one- and two-inch-wide rolls.
> Self-adhesive bandage.
> Adhesive tape or first-aid tape.
> Cotton; cotton balls; cotton swabs.
> Hydrogen peroxide (3 percent solution) for cleansing wounds.

---

*Cats—especially kittens—are extremely sensitive to phenol and its various compounds. Many of these are found in antiseptics, disinfectants, and germicides, which are used by unsuspecting people to sanitize a cat's living quarters.

First Aid for Common Problems

Problem	Signs	Action
Animal bites	Punctures or tear in the skin. Hair matted with blood. Licking bitten parts. Swelling.	Restrain cat. If long-haired, clip hair around wound with blunt-tipped scissors. Flush wound with 3 percent solution of hydrogen peroxide. Wash thoroughly with soap and water. Apply antiseptic to superficial wound, and check frequently for signs of infection. If wound is deep or sutures necessary, see veterinarian at once.
Automobile accidents	Limping. Leg hanging, unable to support cat's weight. Burned or raw areas of skin from tires or pavement. Bleeding.	Restrain cat. Do not move cat (unless absolutely necessary) until you determine extent of injuries. 1. See that cat can breathe freely. 2. Stop bleeding with a pressure bandage. Use gauze or a clean handkerchief and apply pressure with your fingers over the wound. 3. Support broken bones with newspapers, towels, etc. 4. Keep cat warm and quiet to help prevent shock. 5. Move cat carefully if injuries are serious, and get to veterinarian at once.

First Aid for Common Problems

Problem	Signs	Action
Bleeding	From artery: bright-red blood gushes from injury. From vein: dark-red blood flows consistently from injury. From capillaries: blood seeps slowly from wound's surface.	Restrain cat. Control bleeding with pressure bandage. Place gauze dressing, clean napkin or handkerchief, or feminine napkin over wound and apply pressure with fingers or palms of hands. If bleeding does not stop, add more packing on top of original dressing and continue pressure. Use tourniquet only in life-threatening emergency if pressure methods fail. See veterinarian immediately.
Broken leg	Pain and swelling in affected area. Limping. Leg hanging, unable to support cat's weight. Bone juting though skin (in some instances).	Restrain cat. When animals break their legs, they try to lie in the position that is most comfortable, usually on the side with the broken leg on top. If bone protrudes from skin, fold towels or anything soft under the limb to prevent further damage, and cover puncture with sterile dressing to prevent infection. If bone does not pierce the skin, try to splint fracture with straight sticks, pieces of cardboard, etc., to immobilize the joint above and below the break on each side of the leg. See veterinarian immediately.

First Aid for Common Problems

Problem	Signs	Action
Choking	Gulping. Gagging. Gasping for breath. Excessive salivation. Pawing at mouth.	Restrain cat. Open mouth and try to retrieve object with your fingers or long-nosed pliers. If you cannot, use Heimlich maneuver: lay cat on its side. Place palms of your hands (one on top of the other) on cat's abdomen, just below rib cage. Press into abdomen with a sharp upward thrust to expel object. Open mouth to locate and remove object. Repeat if necessary.
Diarrhea	Frequent putrid-smelling and watery bowel movements, often streaked with blood.	Stop all food for 12 to 24 hours, but let the cat drink a little water if thirsty. Give Kaopectate or other antidiarrhea preparation. Then feed small amounts of bland food: cottage cheese, boiled rice, cooked egg, baby food. See veterinarian if problem persists more than 24 hours. Severe cases, especially when accompanied by vomiting, may require fluid therapy.

First Aid for Common Problems

Problem	Signs	Action
Electric shock (most often caused when kittens and cats chew on cords of plugged-in appliances or lamps)	Pale, bluish, and cold skin. Low temperature. Irregular heartbeat. Burns on lips and tongue. Collapse. Respiratory failure.	Do not touch cat while it is in contact with electrical current. Shut off current or unplug cord from its outlet. If this is not possible and cord is still in contact with any part of the cat's body, use a broom handle or other nonconductor of electricity to push it away. Keep cat warm and quiet to help prevent shock. Get to veterinarian immediately.
Eye problems	Depend on injury: Prominent appearance of third eyelid. Scratching eyes. Excessive blinking and tearing. Cut or bleeding lids.	Restrain cat. Eyes are very delicate and easily injured. Except for (1) small foreign bodies that you can dislodge by flushing eyes with warm water or carefully lifting out with a moistened cotton swab and (2) soap or chemical irritations, where the eyes should be flushed immediately with warm water, all injuries should be handled by a veterinarian or veterinary ophthalmologist. To prevent further injury on way to hospital, bandage and/or tape cat's front and back feet, totally covering its claws.
Frostbite	Cold, bluish, or pale skin.	Handle cat gently. Rewarm skin slowly with moist heat: hot water bottle or warm compresses. While warming, do not massage affected areas to increase circulation. See veterinarian in extreme cases.

First Aid for Common Problems

Problem	Signs	Action
Heatstroke (often caused when a cat is confined in a travel case without sufficient air in hot weather)	Heavy panting. Foaming at mouth. Dazed expression. Gasping for breath. Muscle twitching. Staggering gait. High temperature. Convulsions and collapse.	Act quickly to lower body temperature. Move cat to a cool place. Wet it all over with cool water to remove excess heat from the body. Use ice packs if water is not available. Get cat to veterinarian immediately.
Obnoxious odors (skunk, fertilizer)		The traditional "tomato juice bath" is usually ineffective. Bathe cat with shampoo and water to remove dirt and debris. Rinse well. Towel dry. Pour mixture of about 6 ounces of Massengill douche (powder or liquid) dissolved in 1 gallon warm water over damp hair. Don't rinse off. Repeat Massengill rinse if traces of odor remain.
Poison (inhaled)	Nausea and dizziness. Respiratory problems. Staggering gait. Loss of consciousness. Convulsions.	Remove cat from toxic environment to fresh air. Get to veterinarian at once for oxygen and medical treatment.

First Aid for Common Problems

Problem	Signs	Action
Poison (skin contact) from sitting, rolling, walking on toxic surfaces. These may be licked off coat and skin and ingested.	Skin reactions depend on substances, and include redness, rash, skin peeling. If poison is licked and ingested, see "Poison (swallowed)" symptoms.	Flush skin with lukewarm water to remove unabsorbed materials. Then, if substance contained: (1) an acid: rinse skin with a mixture of 3 tablespoons baking soda dissolved in 1 quart warm water; (2) an alkali: rinse with equal parts vinegar and water; or (3) paint thinners, solvents, gasoline, etc.: saturate skin with milk or vegetable oil. Shampoo several minutes later. If substance was ingested, see "Poison (swallowed)."
Poison (swallowed)	Depends on toxic substance but include: dilated pupils, trembling, shivering, vomiting, diarrhea, staggering gait, cramps, increased salivation, convulsions (sometimes), coma.	If antidote appears on package label of product ingested, follow directions. If not, call veterinarian or Poison Control Center immediately and give as much information as possible about what your cat swallowed. Depending on the poison, you will either (1) induce vomiting to remove unabsorbed portion from cat's body, or (2) if poison cannot be vomited, dilute and delay its absorption by giving milk, whipped egg whites, vegetable or mineral oil, or water. Get cat to veterinarian immediately.

First Aid for Common Problems

Problem	Signs	Action
Seizures	Excess salivation. Muscle twitching. Dazed expression. Jerking, uncontrollable movements. Loss of urinary or bowel control.	Do not restrain. Do not put any kind of medication into cat's mouth. Keep children away. Cover with a towel or blanket to keep warm. When seizure subsides, keep cat quiet and warm. If they are prolonged or recurrent, see veterinarian immediately.
Shock	Cats can go into shock after any accident or serious injury. The object of first aid is to help prevent shock from developing, or to postpone its onset. Early symptoms include pale gums, cold skin, weakness, weak and rapid pulse, and shallow and rapid breathing.	Place the cat on its side with head extended to receive sufficient oxygen. Open mouth, clean out mucus, and pull the tongue forward. Cover the cat with a blanket to keep it warm. Avoid noise that might provoke movement. See veterinarian immediately.
Vomiting	Restlessness. Increased salivation. Licking lips and frequent swallowing. Intermittent abdominal contractions.	Stop all food for 12 to 24 hours. If cat is thirsty, give small amounts of boiled, cooled water. To soothe stomach, give Pepto-Bismol or other preparation to relieve digestive upsets. When vomiting stops, feed bland food: cottage cheese, cooked egg, lean ground beef, chicken (nothing fatty), boiled rice. Consult veterinarian if problem persists more than 24 hours.

Antiseptic (Merthiolate or a tamed iodine product such as Betadine®) for minor cuts.

First aid or antibacterial skin cream.

Petroleum jelly (noncarbonated).

Plastic eyedropper or child's medicine spoon.

Emetic to induce vomiting: Give one teaspoon
hydogen peroxide (3 percent solution) every
ten to fifteen minutes until the cat vomits.

Activated charcoal tablets to absorb poisons when
specific antidote is not available.

Blunt-tipped scissors.

Antidiarrhea preparation, such as Kaopectate or
Donnagel.

Antacid liquid, such as Pepto-Bismol or milk of
bismuth.

Store all these supplies in a cardboard carton, clearly
labeled, in a location known to every family member.
Keep the telephone numbers of your veterinarian
and nearest Poison Control Center by your phone.
Information about emergency procedures obtained
by phone can help save your cat's life until you can
reach a veterinarian.

Home Nursing

Almost every cat at some period in its lifetime will
require special care after an illness, an accident, or
surgery. Many illnesses and injuries do not require
hospitalization, although long periods of convalescence at home may be necessary. The competent care,
moral support, and love and tenderness that you
provide can help speed up the recovery process
necessary to restore your cat's health. Even when
hospital confinement is called for, a great many
veterinarians believe in releasing pets as soon as

possible for home convalescence, because they know that sick animals regain their health faster in familiar surroundings, especially when they receive tender loving care from their owners. When a pet—especially a highly emotional one—is confined in a strange place, it can grieve for its loved ones, and the ensuing despondence and progressive depression can delay recovery.

In most cases you will be following a home nursing routine tailored by your veterinarian. How carefully you obey these instructions may determine how effective treatment will be. Home nursing does not require a lot of technical skill, but it does involve patience, consistency, observation, common sense, and, most importantly, loving care.

A sick or invalid cat needs a quiet and peaceful location in which to recuperate, with as little handling or excitement as possible. The most important requirement is a comfortable and clean bed placed in a warm, draft-free location. Inquisitive children, well-meaning friends, or other family pets should not be allowed to disturb the patient. The cat's sickroom should never become its prison, however, and complete isolation is unnecessary unless your cat is seriously ill or suffering from a contagious disease. Show your cat again and again that you care with soft words of affection and tender strokes of your hand.

Cleanliness is very important during convalescence, as cats are naturally fastidious creatures, especially when they cannot reach certain body parts during self-grooming or have no desire to self-groom. A gentle brushing or hand massage will make a sick cat look and feel better. A light sponging with a damp cloth will keep it fresh, especially if it vomits, or has diarrhea or urine stains on the skin or fur. Keep the bed immaculate at all times. Keep the litter tray in the convalescent area so that the cat can find it without delay. If an accident occurs in the bed, change the bedding at once.

Good nutrition is vital to a convalescent or invalid animal. The normal diet may be too irritating, and your veterinarian may recommend bland, nourishing foods that are easy to digest, such as cooked egg, cottage cheese, rice, chopped and cooked lean beef, chicken, or lamb, Cream of Wheat or oatmeal. When a cat is desperately ill, it may not want to eat but nourishment is vital. You may have to force food into its mouth, using commercially prepared baby foods or any of the bland foods already mentioned, pureed in a blender or food processor. The food can be fed by spoon or forced into the cat's mouth on your index finger. Dr. Louis L. Vine advises in the *Common Sense Book of Complete Cat Care* that "egg yolks mixed with milk and Karo syrup make a life-sustaining mixture which can be fed with an eye dropper if need be. This solution can keep a critically ill animal from dehydrating while fighting the ravages of a disease." (See "Bibliography of the Cat" in Chapter XVI.)

When your cat is sick or recovering from surgery, you may have to take its temperature or administer medications. These actions need not be an ordeal if you know the right way to proceed.

Taking Your Cat's Temperature

A cat's temperature is measured rectally—never by mouth, as the animal may bite down on the thermometer and break it. Before inserting the thermometer, shake the mercury column to below 95° F

(35° C). Lubricate the bulb with petroleum jelly. The temperature may be measured with your cat in a standing position with its hindquarters facing you, or lying on its side. Another person may have to restrain a fussy cat while you record the temperature. Hold the cat's tail in one hand and insert about half the length of the thermometer into the rectum with the other, bulb end first, and rolling it from side to side to make insertion easier. Hold the thermometer in place for about two minutes and keep the cat from moving or sitting down. Then carefully pull it out and wipe the thermometer with cotton. Roll it back and forth until you can clearly locate the end of the mercury column in its center. The normal temperature range is between 100.5° F to 102.5° F (38° C to 39° C). Any elevation over 102.5° F (39° C) should be considered as fever. The temperature may rise temporarily due to heat, excitement, or digestion of food, but one that

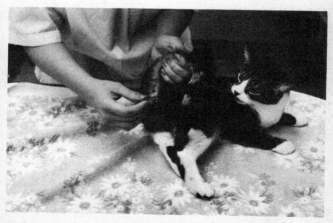

Taking the temperature.

stays lower or higher than the normal range is a sign of illness.

Giving Medications

Some cats are not very docile or cooperative when they need to be medicated internally or externally, and often retaliate by using their claws or teeth in protest. When medication *must* be given to such a cat, the owner should know how to handle the animal and protect himself from painful bites or scratches. In a few instances gentle strokes and words of reassurance will calm a cat sufficiently to permit medication. But if your cat is fussy or not very gentle, one of the following restraints may be necessary:

- If an assistant is available, have him or her grasp the cat by the skin over the back of the neck. According to Dr. Benjamin L. Hart in a column from *Feline Practice,* "This procedure produces a reflex-like type of tonic immobility and passivity." Depending on what kind of medication you will administer, the cat may then be placed down on its chest or in a sitting position on a smooth and sturdy tabletop or other elevated surface, or it can be placed on its side with the assistant's other hand grasping its back legs.
- If you are alone, wrap the cat's body, legs, and paws in a large bath towel or a blanket, leaving its head free.

Giving Pills and Capsules

Sit your cat on a firm surface, or apply the necessary restraint. Tilt the cat's head backward, putting the palm of your hand on the top of its head. Open the mouth by placing your index finger behind

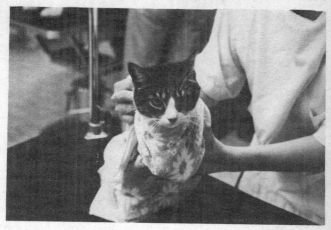

Wrap the cat's body, legs and paws in a large bath towel as a gentle restraint.

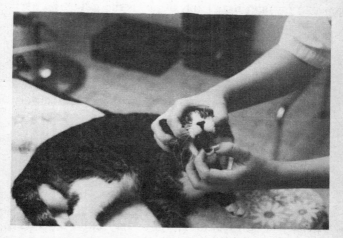

To open a cat's mouth: Place your index finger behind the fang on one side and your thumb behind the fang on the other side, and press the lips inward.

the fang on one side and your thumb behind the fang on the other side, and press the lips inward. Place the pill at the back of the tongue and give it a little downward push if you can, but be very careful. Close the mouth quickly, keeping the cat's head pointing upward, and stroke the throat until the medication is swallowed. If the cat gags or spits, however, let go of its head so it can eject the pill. If your cat is fussy, or if you don't place the pill far enough back on the tongue, it probably will spit it out and you'll have to repeat the procedure. Try coating the pill with butter or margarine, or covering it with cheese, fish, sardine, or some other snack that the cat finds appetizing.

Giving a pill or capsule to a cat with a bad disposition can be dangerous because you could be badly bitten. The best solution is to use a pill gun, a long syringe-like device specially designed for cats, with a plunger that safely deposits the pill at the back of the tongue without your fingers going into the mouth. If all else fails, try crumbling the tablet or emptying the contents into the cat's food and mixing it thoroughly, but be sure your cat eats its entire ration to get the medication's benefits. This method is recommended as a last resort because it is almost impossible to deceive a cat's keen sense of taste.

Giving Liquid Medicine

If the medicine is pleasant-tasting, see if your cat will lick it off a spoon. If not, a liquid medicine should be given in (1) a plastic medicine dropper, (2) a spillproof spoon made for giving liquids to infants, or (3) a syringe (with the needle removed). Do not open the cat's mouth and try to pour the liquid down the throat. Instead, pour or squirt a small amount of liquid between the teeth, let the cat swallow, then repeat the procedure until the required amount has been given.

Giving Ointments and Gels

It may be necessary to give your cat medication in the form of ointments or gels which have the consistency of jelly. If the medication comes in a tube, it can be squeezed into the corner of the cat's mouth. You can also put the required amount of medication on the nose or on one of the front paws and the cat will lick it off.

Medicating the Ears

The first step in medicating the ears is to carefully wipe out all traces of wax, dirt, or old medication with cotton before inserting fresh eardrops or ointment. Clean the outer ear tenderly, and then around the opening to the canal. Do not probe deeply. Insert the prescribed liquid or ointment into the ear opening. Most ear ointments are packaged in long-nozzled tubes. If your cat is fussy, be sure to have someone control it against sudden movement so the nozzle tip won't injure the ear. Steady the head with one hand to keep your cat from shaking and discharging the medication, while you use the other hand to gently massage the base of each ear, to spread the liquid or ointment to the deepest parts. As soon as you release your hold on the head, the cat will shake. Don't worry. This is a natural reaction to protect the delicate ear canal.

Medicating the Eyes

Eyedrops are best applied with your cat's head tilted slightly upward. Use one hand to steady the head as you drop the medication into the inner corner of each eye. Blot any excess solution at the eye corners with cotton or a cotton swab. Do not rub ove the eyeball with cotton; it can be easily scratched or irritated.

To apply eye ointment, gently pull the cat's lower lid away from the eyeball with your thumb. Squeeze a little ointment into the lower lid, release your thumb and let it go back into place. The ointment will spread each time your cat opens and closes its eyes.

Elizabethan Collar

Should you have to prevent your cat from biting, licking, or scratching any part of its body (especially if there are stitches closing an incision), make an "Elizabethan collar" with a stiff paper plate or by cutting a piece of cardboard into a circle. Then cut a V shape from the outside edge to the center, and a circle in the center large enough for the cat's neck, so that the device resembles the following shape:

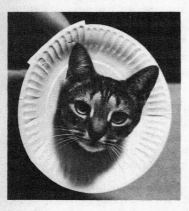

A paper plate makes a good temporary Elizabethan collar.

Place the collar around the cat's r eck and draw the edges together. Fasten with staples or Scotch tape. The outside edge of the Elizabethan collar should face forward.

VII The Nature of the Beast:
Behavior and Training

Long may you love your pensioner Mouse,
Though one of a tribe that torment the house;
Nor dislike for her cruel sport the Cat,
That deadly foe of both mouse and rat.
Remember she follows the law of her kind;
And Instinct is neither wayward nor blind.

—William Wordsworth

Cats seem to have been less affected by domestication than dogs. They can be loving and affectionate pets that delight in the comforts of regular meals and an agreeable home, yet they still retain the inborn hunting instincts of their early ancestors, and could survive without humans if they had to.

Dogs are social animals that conform to "pack" behavioral patterns. Pack relationships are based on a descending pecking order where there is a pack leader that *always* dominates, establishes organization, disciplines the rest, and maintains group order. Fighting is greatly reduced in fixed dominance hierarchies; conflicts are usually resolved by threats from the leader and submissive behavior from the dog of lower rank. The same pack behavior governs the dog's relationships with humans. People become pack members as if they were dogs. Dogs are highly motivated by and dependent on their leaders or masters, and this makes them very trainable. When they are disciplined or punished by their masters, they exhibit submissive behavior just as they would to the leader dog of the pack.

Cats, on the other hand, do not form fixed dominance hierarchies. Aside from the interplay between a mother and her kittens, or brief encounters during mating season, much time is spent avoiding one another. The rituals of scent-marking also help to reduce close contact between cats. In fact, all members of the cat family, with the exception of the lion, are loners. Lions live in social groups known as prides, and are the only felids to hunt in packs. Cats, therefore, do not respond to people as if they were pack leaders or members. It is futile to try to dominate or punish a cat as you would a dog. Rather than assuming a submissive posture, the cat will always try to escape or fight.

This does not mean that cats are totally asocial, however. Although there are no *fixed* hierarchies of dominant cat, second cat, and so on down the line, cats often form what animal behaviorists call *relative* dominance hierarchies that are related to time and place. One cat may be domineering at mealtime, for instance, while another one rules over the sleeping quarters. Neighborhood cats may form a sort of hierarchy, but this will never be as specific a dominance/subordination relationship as it would be among dogs. Cats can develop enduring social relationships with other animals as well as people. Cats that live from kittenhood with other cats or dogs can become very affectionate and protective toward these companions, and the longer the animals live together, the stronger the relationship becomes. Cats also can mourn the loss of a feline, a canine, and a human companion.

Another interesting phase of feline behavior is the "party," or social gathering without hostility, that usually takes place in the early evening in some neutral area. Paul Leyhausen, the eminent German zoologist, describes these friendly meetings in *Cat Behavior: The Predatory and Social Behavior of Domestic and Wild Cats* (see "Bibliography of the Cat" in Chapter XVI):

> Males and females come to a meeting place adjacent to or situated within the fringe of their territories and just sit around. . . . They sit, not far apart, some individuals are even in actual contact, sometimes licking and grooming each other. There is very little sound, the faces are friendly and only occasionally an ear flattens or a small hiss or growl is heard when one animal closes in too much on a shy member of the gathering.

Leyhausen writes that the gatherings would last for several hours before the participants retired to their respective sleeping quarters.

We know that experiences in the early part of an animal's life can profoundly affect its behavior as an adult. Scientific studies show that there are critical phases of puppy development where early rearing practices will produce either maladjusted dogs or those of the highest capacities later in life. Although many behaviorists feel that feline actions are innate and such critical socialization periods do not exist for cats, early human contact can influence a cat's behavior as an adult. The touching or stroking of baby kittens, for instance, is very important for their emotional and physical growth. This implies not that nonhandled kittens will grow up to be sickly, but that handling stimulation in infancy produces healthier, vivacious, and more manageable adult cats.

Predatory Behavior

"The cat," according to Claire Necker in her marvelous work *The Natural History of Cats* (see "Bibliography of the Cat" in Chapter XVI), "is a carnivore, a machine exquisitely constructed for killing. . . . Both its mind and body are geared for efficient hunting; the method employed is inborn and not deliberate bloodlust or cruelty."

Predatory behavior begins in the nest. Paul Leyhausen says that a kitten's first prey-catching movement, a tentative forward grope with one paw, is made as early as three weeks of age. Mother encourages play and hunting actions, and as the kittens watch her behavior they learn how to chase, stalk, pounce, hold, and even bite prey. Their movements are clumsy at first, but after much interaction with the littermates six-week-old kittens are agile and dexterous and know a great deal about predation. Although predatory behavior is inherited, experts say it can also be influenced by early experiences. Mother, if given the opportunity, may bring killed or injured prey to the nest, or the kittens may accompany her on a hunting trip. These events often determine whether or not kittens will grow up to be good hunters. If they are removed before mother teaches them how to hunt, or if they never receive this early experience, they are less likely to become real predators.

Domestic cats prey upon mice, rats, squirrels, moles, chipmunks, and other small animals, flies, butterflies, crickets, grasshoppers, moths, frogs, toads, lizards, and birds, which they may eat or occasionally bring home to their owners. Cats can efficiently stalk and kill animals as large as themselves, but usually they do not attack anything larger than rats or pigeons.

Both domestic and wild cats follow a definite pattern when hunting. When the prey is located, the cat silently stalks and approaches it by running swiftly in a crouching position with its stomach close to the ground. When the cat nears the prey, it will hide under some type of cover and assume a watching position with its body flat against the ground, its head and ears pointing forward, and whiskers fanned out. If the distance is too great, the cat will make another swift and stalking run to come within striking distance of the prey. Now the cat freezes and prepares for the final pounce. Its hind legs move slightly backward and begin to step up and down. The hindquarters raise up and swing from side to side, while the tip of the tail quivers with growing intensity. The cat suddenly springs forward and grasps its victim with the claws of one or both forepaws. As the claws pin down the prey, the cat bites into the nape of its neck. The dagger-like teeth sever the victim's spinal cord and death usually is instantaneous. If the prey is too large to kill on the first attempt, the cat may punch violently with its paws to stun the victim, and then seize the nape of its neck and apply the killing bite. Sometimes the cat will release small prey without killing the victim, only to stalk, pounce, hold, and shake it many times before the final kill.

Territory

Domestic cats, like feral and wild cats, are territorial creatures. In the wild, cats select and establish their territories in proportion to the number of other cats and the amount of food and shelter in a given area. They will defend their territories, when necessary, to keep other cats from killing their prey, to protect their young, and during the mating season.

Domestic cats do not always choose their territories; they are often selected instead by their owners. Each cat, however, will have its home base or "first-order home," a term used by Paul Leyhausen. This is usually a room or a favorite corner of a room in the house in which the cat lives. Around the home base—in the rest of the house or the yard—are areas that the cat likes to use for napping, playing, sunbathing, and surveillance. The extent of the home range depends on the age, the temperament, and especially whether the cat is a male, a female, or neutered. Females and neuters seem to feel more content within a limited area of their home or yard, which they will spiritedly protect. The home range of tomcats, conversely, may be many times larger, especially during the mating season. Beyond the cat's limited home base, according to Leyhausen, is a range connected by an elaborate network of pathways leading to more or less regularly visited areas for hunting, courting, contests and fighting, and other activities. While there will be more than one path to each of these places, the areas between the passageways are seldom used.

In most cases the boundaries of the territories are firmly established. Within them a stranger must be prepared to challenge the resident cat; outside the boundaries, the intruder will be overlooked. A cat's aggressiveness in defending its territory may not be too obvious in a single-cat home. But when there are two or more cats, the territorial imperative becomes more discernible as each determines its first-order home and learns to share other areas with other individuals. A confrontation on the border of a territory will never be as severe as when one cat invades the territory of another. The resident cat will usually try to intimidate the stranger by hissing and screaming vocal threats, baring its fangs, and assuming offensive body positions. But if these postures do not scare off the intruder, a noisy and ritualized battle will take place.

Scent-marking and Communication

A cat's olfactory senses are considerably different than ours. Not only can cats smell things that humans cannot detect, but once a territory has been claimed, they perform the ritual of scent-marking to define it and reveal their presence to other cats. The distinctive messages that a cat leaves behind tell other cats much information about the individual.

Urine Spraying

Urine spraying is done primarily by entire male cats, although the custom is occasionally seen in females and neuters. Males spend much of their time marking the boundaries of their home territory by spraying objects such as trees, shrubs, fences, mail-boxes, porches, the sides of houses, automobile tires, and so forth. The cat backs up to an object, holds its tail erect, quivers, and then sprays a steam of urine at a height suitable for sniffing. A tomcat's urine contains a fatty ingredient that leaves a repugnant odor that endures through even the most inclement weather. Its mark communicates the tom's presence to other males in the area. It is, as many authors have put it, the male's calling card, announcing, "This is my territory." When a strange male wanders into another male's area, he can tell how recently the marking occurred.

Cats usually spray during certain times of the day and often when they are agitated or emotionally troubled, such as at the arrival of a new baby or pet in the family, or changes in the territory. Spraying also increases during the breeding season, possibly because marking is helpful in attracting sexually receptive queens to a male's territory. Entire males that are kept indoors will probably spray your furniture and other household objects. (This problem is discussed later in this chapter, and again under "Spraying and Neutering" in Chapter VIII.)

Rubbing

Rubbing is another type of scent-marking. The cat has ample scent glands around its lips, on the chin, on either side of its forehead between the eye and the ear, and along its tail. These glands are situated in places that cats like to rub, and this action is a form of marking favorite individuals, other animals, and inanimate objects such as chairs and other furniture, and doorways. During the rubbing process the cat transfers to the person or object glandular secretions that humans cannot smell but other cats can detect. Animal behaviorists also say that cats sometimes use rubbing as a form of greeting.

Tree or Wood Scratching

Scratching trees or wood is a territorial marking process that leaves visual as well as olfactory evidence of a cat's presence. The animal may scratch a horizontal or vertical piece of soft wood or the bark of a tree with its forepaws. This action not only conditions the extension and retraction ability of the claws, but it also helps remove loose and worn outer sheathes of the claws on the forelegs.* At the same time, secretions from sweat glands in the cat's foot probably give the object a particular scent. When a cat claws furniture or objects indoors, it is engaging in a form of territory marking, and the longer an article is scratched, the more important it becomes and the more difficult the habit is to break.

The Flehmen Reaction

Cats have a keen sense of smell, which is sometimes enhanced by the Jacobson's or vomeronasal organ, a small sac (near the nasal passage) with a duct that connects to the roof of the mouth. This organ is present in cats, horses, and certain other animals but not in man. The vomeronasal organ is lined with olfactory cells that are connected to two different parts of the hypothalamus in the cat's brain, relating to appetite motivation and sexual behavior.

Cats make a peculiar facial expression called the "flehmen reaction" when the Jacobson's organ is stimulated.† When a cat flehms, it stretches its neck,

---

*A cat removes the worn-down outer sheathes on its hind paws with its teeth.

†*Flehmen* is a German word for which there is no English translation.

opens its mouth slightly, and lifts its upper lip. As the animal inhales it apparently retains traces of the odor on its tongue, which is then exposed to the Jacobson's organ when the tongue touches the roof of the mouth. The flehmen reaction is most often observed in tomcats when they respond to sex pheromones in the urine and vaginal secretions from queens in heat, but it may also be noticed in both males and females (including spayed and neutered cats) when they respond to catnip and certain other odors.

Communication: Body and Vocal Language

People often misunderstand cats and see them as enigmatic creatures because of their sensitive and cunning behavior. Cats make charming pets, and learning to interpret their lavish repertoire of body and vocal language will enhance your relationship with them.

Body Language

Cats use their faces, eyes, ears, whiskers, bodies, paws, tail, and fur to express their feelings. They can show you in very specific ways if they are happy and contented or angry, so with a little careful observation you can learn to interpret these body movements and determine your cat's emotional state.

Cats have various facial expressions in which the eyes and the ears play an important role. When a cat is happy and contented, it will sit with its face relaxed, ears upright, and its eyes partly closed or with the eye pupils narrowed to a slit. A cat that is being petted and spoken to will keep its eyes in this manner while purring and turning up the corners of its mouth in a sort of smile. The eye pupils of an angry cat, or one facing an opponent, will dilate, its ears will flatten sideways, and its mouth will open to express a warning.

The tail is an expressive communicator of feline moods. A tail held very straight and high can be a form of greeting or a sign of pleasure in being stroked. When a cat holds its tail erect, it can also mean "I'm hungry" as it looks forward to a meal. A tail arched over the back or into an inverted-U shape means the cat is merry and playful. Cats sometimes gently swish their tail when you talk to them or when they are pleased, but the lashing or beating of a cat's tail from side to side has a different meaning and indicates tension or anger.

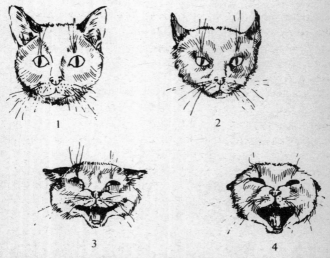

When a cat is threatened, its face changes from (1) a normal alert expression to (2) one of annoyance and increasing anger; (3) its ears begin to flatten sideways and its mouth opens to hiss or growl a defensive threat; (4) eventually the ears become completely flattened, the pupils dilate, and the mouth opens wide so that all the teeth are exposed.

Cats use various body postures to tell other cats or individuals whether or not they can come nearer. Rolling over and exposing the abdomen is felinese for "I want to play." During the breeding season it may also mean "I want to mate." Contentment or relaxation is expressed by several positions, such as lying stretched out on one side or sitting with the paws deftly folded underneath and the tail curled around the body. The classic "Halloween cat" silhouette is a defensive threat posture to avoid fighting. The animal stands with its legs erect, back arched, and tail held to one side. It turns sideways and every hair on its body and tail stands straight out to make it seem larger in size and more menacing looking. The posture is further enhanced by the facial expression: dilated eyes, teeth bared, whiskers held close to the skin, and ears flattened back.

An offensive threat posture indicates that a cat is fearless and likely to attack. It faces its assailant head on, making direct eye contact, in a straightforward stance. Its whiskers fan straight out, and its ears are flattened back. The tail lashes from side to side. The two cats hiss and scream at each other, and they

On the defensive: The "Halloween" cat silhouette is a defensive posture to avoid fighting. The cat stands with its legs erect, back arched, and tail held to one side or close to the ground. The hairs on its body and tail will stand straight out to make the cat seem larger in size and more menacing looking.

On the offensive: A cat that is likely to attack will face its opponent head on, making direct eye contact, in a straightforward stance. Its whiskers fan out, and its ears begin to flatten backward. The tail is held erect, and will lash from side to side.

maintain this posture until ritualized fighting begins, or one becomes intimidated and capitulates.

Vocal Communication

Cats also use many sounds to express themselves vocally. These are grouped into three patterns—murmurs, vowels, and strained-intensity sounds—based on how they are produced.

The murmur patterns are sounds a cat makes while its mouth is closed, and include purring and the dulcet vocalizations that express greetings or acknowledgment. The vowel patterns include different sounds, such as "Meow" and its many variations, that are employed by a cat to coax, demand, complain, inform, and express surprise. The sounds are started while the cat's mouth is open and finished when it is closed, and they are used for communicating with other cats and with humans. Most of the chatty sounds made by Siamese are classified as vowel patterns. The strained-intensity sounds are made with the mouth open, and express intense anger or emotion. These include growling, snarling, hissing, spitting, screaming, and the ritual mating cry, and cats make these sounds when they are frightened, angered, mating, fighting, or in pain.

Each cat will have its own particular vocabulary, the size of which will vary greatly depending on breed, sex, and temperament. Siamese, for example, are known to be excessively talkative, while other breeds may "say" very little. Cats carry on conversations with their owners, their kittens, and other cats. But undoubtedly vocal communication reaches its pinnacle during the mating season. Many females become very noisy when they go into heat and "call" loudly to inform the opposite sex that they are ready to mate, while the males howl and caterwaul at night.

Leash Training/Cat Walking

Cats of any age and breed can learn to walk on a leash, although the ideal time to begin is during kittenhood.* Perhaps a few comments about what can be accomplished in leash training are in order. Walking a cat is a different process entirely from walking a dog. Cat owners should not expect to make those invigorating jaunts that help keep both dogs and their owners in good physical condition. Most dogs eagerly await their daily outings, to heed nature's call outdoors, and to follow the directions of their leader. Walking a cat is not the same, but more like a mutual concession. Rather than you leading your cat, you both decide in which direction you will go. And cats will seldom urinate or defecate outdoors; they would rather use a litter pan.

---

*Siamese seem to be more leash-trainable than others.

It is important to begin with the proper training/ walking equipment. A kitten or an adult cat should wear a harness, not a collar that it could slip out of. The best choice is a lightweight harness shaped like a figure eight or a figure H, about three eighths of an inch wide. The correct styles for cats fasten under the chest, placing the pulling force on the shoulders instead of the neck. Do not purchase a small dog harness; it will not fit properly or be flexible enough. Harnesses are sold according to girth measurement, so you must measure around your cat for the correct size. You will also need a leash made of comfortable material, such as nylon, canvas, or soft leather. The leash should also be about three eighths of an inch wide, with a small but sturdy snap. Examine the different harness and leash styles at your pet supplies dealer to determine which will be comfortable for both you and your cat. The equipment and training procedure can frighten even the most self-assured cat, and boundless patience, sensitivity, and composure are necessary at all times.

The training should commence indoors. Lay the harness near your cat and let it examine and perhaps push the device with a paw. When the cat is convinced that the harness is not dangerous, try to put it on. A few cats will accept a harness right away, but the average puss will roll on the floor and devise ingenious ways of getting out of it. Once the harness is fastened, praise your cat and stay close by. Let the cat wear the harness for twenty- to thirty-minute periods several times a day, then remove it, praise the cat, and have a little play period.

As soon as your cat becomes accustomed to wearing the harness, snap on the leash and let puss drag it around the room. Don't pick up the leash in your hand or try to guide the cat in any way for the first few times, but stay nearby to see that it doesn't get tangled in something and become injured. After a few sessions hold the leash loosely in your hand and follow the cat around the room. The next step is to try to lead the cat where *you* want to go. Puss will definitely balk, pull backward, lie down and roll over, and probably turn somersaults to assert its independence. Be patient and gentle; bend down and give your cat a few loving caresses. If your cat will "Come" on call, give that command in your most enticing voice while you give the leash a gentle forward pull. Tempting the cat with a favorite food treat might help too.

When things go well, the next step is to go outdoors. Take frequent short walks and be sensitive to your cat's feelings. You might want to take along a cat carrier for the first few outings in case puss should become frightened by traffic noises or dogs off leash. Not all cats will learn to walk outside on leash. But watching those that do rambling on, smelling flowers and blades of grass, or catching flies, you will agree the training is worth the effort.

Training Your Cat to "Come"

Cats are often characterized as being untrainable and distant because they use their natural independence to disguise their remarkable intelligence. When an owner expects bad manners and contrariness from a cat, quite often that is exactly what he or she will get. Cats can learn, and the extent of their training depends greatly on the loving and positive attitudes of their owners. You can train your cat to respond to certain vocal commands by taking advantage of its natural response tendencies and by offering rewards.

The most basic command to teach a cat is to "Come" when called. Training ideally should begin during kittenhood, for young animals are very receptive to learning. Cats of any age can be trained, however. It just takes a little longer to train an adult cat because it has been doing things its own way for a long time. The easiest way to make your cat respond to the word *Come* is at feeding time. As soon as a meal is ready to serve, call the cat to "Come," and get its attention, if necessary, by tapping a spoon on the side of the dish. When the cat comes, praise it lavishly, then offer the food. This will develop a response pattern that associates "Come" with praise and food.

As soon as your cat comes for meals, the next step is to command it to "Come" for other reasons. Since the response is patterned for praise and food, try standing a few feet away from the cat in a room other than the kitchen. Call the cat to "Come," and when it does, praise it lavishly and feed it a special tidbit. Walk to the opposite side of the room and repeat the procedure. When the cat obeys, praise it lavishly once more, and offer a food treat. The treat should always be a choice morsel that the cat really craves, offered in *small* amounts. The idea is to get the cat to come to you, not to make it obese. Jo and Paul Loeb, authors of *You Can Train Your Cat* (see "Bibliography of the Cat" in Chapter XVI), advise "since this is a command that, to have any meaning or effectiveness, must be obeyed by your cat when he is at a distance, you must get your cat's attention by calling his name before telling him to come. Therefore, before teaching the command make certain that your pet knows his name by repeating it often while you are playing with him. Then, when teaching him the command, call his name just once, say 'come,' and give him a hand command by making a large beckoning gesture toward you, usually with your right hand. At the same time hold a special treat such as an appetizing morsel of food in your other hand and tempt him with it." Never call your cat to "Come" and then discipline it. Kitty must always associate this command with a pleasant experience.

Discipline/"No!"

It was previously mentioned that cats often become ill-mannered and destructive because their owners believe they can't be trained or reprimanded. Cats *can* be trained and *can* be disciplined, and the best time to start is as soon as a new kitten or cat moves into your home, before undesirable behavior patterns are developed.

Every cat can learn bad habits. Correcting or eliminating them is called negative training, because you are teaching the animal what you *don't* want it to do. Just as you praise a cat when it does something right, so you must discipline it when it misbehaves. And to make a reprimand effective, the cat must be caught in the act, because it will not feel guilty about or understand discipline for a misdeed that occurred in the past. Never strike your cat. That's punishment, not discipline, and it is useless to try to punish or dominate a cat as you would a dog. Dogs are pack animals, remember, and they will display submissive behavior to anyone who takes a dominant role in the pack. Cats are not social animals like dogs, and they do not form dominant-subordinate relationships. Dr.

Benjamin L. Hart, in a column from *Feline Practice,* comments that "in handling animals such as dogs, horses, and cattle, physical or verbal punishment, or the threat of punishment is often an effective training procedure, along with reinforcing the dominance-subordination relationship between man and animal. With cats, such punishment is almost always ineffective with training because it innately evokes a tendency for the cat to fight back or escape rather than to conform to the wishes of the person delivering the punishment."

When you catch your cat misbehaving—chewing houseplants, clawing furniture, or jumping on kitchen counters, for instance—voice your disapproval immediately with a firm "No." Cats dislike loud noises, and the vocal reprimand should be coupled with a loud handclap or the smacking of a folded newspaper or magazine across your palm. Should kitty persist, keep a plant-mister or water pistol in readiness, and reinforce your vocal reprimand with a few squirts (not in the cat's face, however). Another discipline for persistent offenders recommended by many animal behaviorists is to pick up the cat and support its body with one hand (or arm) while you hold the scruff of its neck with the other. Shake the animal once or twice (never violently) as you voice your displeasure with a firm "No." The object of these actions is to produce a response pattern, such as, "When I chew houseplants, or when I scratch furniture, I get frightened by a generous squirt or a loud noise, so chewing houseplants or clawing furniture is a naughty deed." Praise your cat lavishly when it obeys and reward it with a food treat.

Behavior Problems

Some common problems—such as urinating or defecating away from the litter tray, clawing furniture and drapes, and chewing potentially dangerous houseplants—and their possible solutions are discussed in Chapter III. Other seemingly "incurable" problems can be solved too, with a little corrective training. Here are some additional suggestions to supplement the disciplinary actions already recommended:

JUMPING ON FURNITURE.   Inflate several balloons and anchor them to the chairs or sofas you don't want your cat to sit on. The sound of popping balloons should discourage your cat from jumping on the furniture.

CHRONIC CLAWING.   Along with the scratch post positioning and training recommended in Chapter III, anchor a few inflated balloons to the area that's being clawed.

JUMPING ON KITCHEN COUNTERS.   A well-aimed squirt of the plant-mister works wonders if you can catch puss in the act, otherwise try stacking aluminum baking pans on the counter, in such a way that they will tumble down when your cat jumps up. The clatter should be a deterrent.

RAIDING TRASH CANS/WASTEBASKETS.   Inflated balloons once again are the best deterrents. Tape them where the cat's claws will cause them to burst and frighten it.

CHEWING WIRES.   Coat electric wires or other chewable objects with Tabasco sauce or Bitter Apple (the latter can be purchased at most pet stores).

WOOL CHEWING.   Chewing or sucking on woolen blankets, sweaters, and socks is a problem that

Siamese may develop around the time of puberty. Some behaviorists feel it is caused by early weaning, others say it may be the result of boredom or insecurity. There is no successful corrective training, other than to remove all wool items. Some cats outgrow their craving for wool, others never do. Try to interest the cat in stimulating toys or possibly the addition of a companion cat to the household.

URINE SPRAYING.   Spraying is one of several behavioral changes that occurs in male cats after puberty. It is, as mentioned earlier in this chapter, a form of scent-marking where the cat backs up to a vertical surface, lifts its tail, and squirts a stream of urine on the object. Inside the house, this can be on your furniture, walls, or drapes. Some females exhibit the same behavioral pattern and spray as well. In addition to scent-marking its territory, a cat may spray because it is jealous or resentful, such as when a new baby or another pet comes into the household, when it has been punished, or when it doesn't get enough attention. It's impossible to say if this is a learned response that the cat knows will bring attention, or a natural emotional response. Corrective measures involve determining the exact cause of the spraying. Injections of progesterone-type hormones have been effective in dealing with difficult cases of spraying, but these should only be used on the advice of your veterinarian. Neutering will stop the spraying habit in about 90 percent of male cats. (This subject is discussed under "Spaying and Neutering" in Chapter VIII.)

Aggression and Biting

The stalking and play-biting of kittens in their education of the art of defense and offense is charming, but as kittens grow up their baby canine teeth are replaced by dagger-like fangs. Those cute little play bites can accidentally or intentionally turn into the real thing.

Kittens may bite accidentally in play or deliberately when they are teething and there's no call for discipline. Adult cats often bite too, for diverse reasons. They may give their owners "love bites" after being stroked or groomed. It's common for a cat to show affection by gently taking hold of a hand or a wrist and keeping its mouth attached for a few seconds. Petting certain sensitive body parts—the stomach, for instance—sometimes evokes a reaction in which a cat will wrap its legs around your arms and put its teeth into your flesh. Every cat owner should be prepared to receive a little nip every once in a while, but when play-biting turns into pain-biting, a cat must be disciplined. Immediately after your cat bites, say "No" firmly and in a loud voice, and gently tap its nose with your finger. If this doesn't eventually stop the biting, show your displeasure a little more forcefully by picking up the cat and supporting its weight with one hand (or arm) and grasping the skin over the back of its neck with the other. Shake the cat a few times while you say "No" very sharply. Stronger physical reprimands will not work. With a little perseverance and tenderness, most cats will soon get your message. If these reprimands do not bring results, however, have your cat examined by a veterinarian to determine if there is a physical cause for the biting.

The cat that hides under the bed or a chair and dashes out to attack your legs is more than likely asserting its pent-up hunting instincts. To discourage this habit, the "victim" should grab hold of the cat as soon as it rushes out, and say "No" firmly while he or she taps the cat's nose with a finger. The best solution may be to redirect the cat's play to furry objects that can be held between the paws or in the mouth, tossed into the air, pounced upon, and "killed," to satisfy kitty's natural hunting abilities.

Cats also fight other cats for many reasons, including competition for queens in season, the presence of a stranger in their home territory, and to protect their young. A cat's long and dagger-like canine teeth can puncture the skin and cause extensive damage to the tissues underneath. Because cats have a great deal of bacteria in their mouths, their bites are painful and likely to cause severe infection. Punctures from cat teeth may not look very serious on the surface and may heal in a day or so, but bacteria are left behind in the deepest part of the wound, which can cause an abscess.* Abscesses can go inward or outward, and when they extend to deeper tissue and go unnoticed by the cat's owners, the infection can enter the bloodstream and cause septicemia. Deep punctures on the tail or legs can cause a bone infection. Any bite wound from a cat (on another cat, a dog, or a human being) should be cleansed immediately and thoroughly with hot running water and soap. The victim should receive an injection of antibiotics from a veterinarian or a physician as soon as possible.

---

*Bite wounds from fighting are the most common causes of abscesses in the cat (see Chapter VI).

VIII   To Breed or Not to Breed

No matter how much the cats fight, there always seem to be plenty of kittens.

—Abraham Lincoln

The decision to breed your cat requires a great deal of thought. Raising a litter of kittens sounds like tremendous fun, but the delivery and care of a litter is both time-consuming and expensive. And very few, if any, cat breeders make a profit from selling the kittens they raise. Then there is the matter of finding suitable homes for the kittens. By the time they reach six to eight weeks of age, you'll be so attached to them that you can't sell them to just anyone. You must be sure that each kitten receives love and the best of care from its responsible new owner. Unless you are a breeder who comes into contact with prospective buyers at cat shows or through magazine or word-of-mouth advertising, finding homes for kittens isn't easy. There is an overabundance of cats and dogs throughout the world, and the animal control figures are monstrous. The Humane Society of the United

States estimates that at least fifteen million cats and dogs are euthanized in animal shelters every year because there are not enough homes for them. *The Kansas City Times and Star* reports that "many shelters dispose of *all* female cats brought in because their chances of adoption are so slight." And these statements do not include the millions of cats that are abandoned or become lost to roam the streets in all sorts of weather, to end up in laboratories, to starve to death, or to die under the wheel of an automobile.

All animals—including cats—are naturally inclined to reproduce, but none has the automatic privilege to do so at the expense of mankind. Who must assume the responsibility for our terrible overpopulation problem? The professional breeders are not the guilty parties. They are painfully aware of the population explosion and carefully plan their breedings so that they do not flood society with unspayed and unneutered cats. The culprits are more often the cat owners whose unaltered pets are allowed to roam free and breed indiscriminately. To those innocents who think one or two random breedings are insignificant, Pet Pride of New York, a humane organization, once charted the mating habits of two uncontrolled breeding cats plus all their kittens and all their kittens' kittens. If none were ever neutered or spayed and produced two litters per year over a period of ten years, the total would reach 80,399,780!

People often think it would be "educational" for the children or "psychologically beneficial" for the family cat to give birth to a litter. There is little to support the belief that breeding a female cat is healthful or psychologically advantageous, or that every female should experience the "miracle" of delivering and nursing a litter of kittens. And to breed a random-bred or mixed-breed cat is inhumane. Through the knowledge of genetics it may be possible to predict the outcome of certain breedings of pure-breed cats with a degree of mathematical accuracy, but it is impossible to predict that mixed-breed kittens will resemble either parent.

Spaying and Neutering

If you do not intend to breed your cat after it reaches sexual maturity, you should consider having it surgically altered. Spaying and neutering (or castrating) are technical words that describe the surgery performed by a veterinarian to remove the sexual organs. Female cats are spayed, that is, have their ovaries and uterus removed, and male cats are neutered or castrated, that is, their testicles are removed. Both spaying and neutering are irreversible procedures, and males and females are not able to breed afterward. Such animals cannot compete for Championship or Grand Championship titles at cat shows, but they are eligible to seek Premier and Grand Premier titles, the equivalent designations for altered cats.

The only permanent solution to recurring heat periods or unwanted pregnancies in a female cat is spaying or ovario-hysterectomy. The best time to spay is between six and seven months of age, before the cat has experienced her first heat period. The operation can be performed with satisfactory results at any age, but the longer you postpone it, the more serious it becomes. Younger animals, too, tend to heal quicker than older ones. While spaying is considered major surgery, it is a relatively routine procedure that most experienced veterinarians can do in less than fifteen minutes. The operation involves anesthesia, an abdominal incision and sutures, and hospitalization for a day or two. After the cat returns home, she should be kept indoors and her activities restrained until the sutures are removed.

The best time to neuter or castrate a male cat is between eight to nine months of age, or before he becomes sexually mature. The operation can be performed at any age, but like the spaying of the female, the earlier it is done, the better. The relatively simple procedure to remove the testicles involves anesthesia, no abdominal incision, and perhaps overnight hospitalization. The cost of spaying or neutering can vary from $50 to $150 depending on several factors (the operation is usually less expensive for males than for females, for instance), but in many cities low-cost spay/neuter clinics are available where the fee may be as low as $25.

Spaying and neutering does not adversely affect a cat's personality, but the operations do usually make cats of both sexes less noisy and aggressive, more affectionate, playful, and contented. Males are less likely to roam and get into fights over queens in heat or become injured in traffic accidents. Castration prevents or suppresses the obnoxious habit of urine spraying, too. Neutering will stop the spraying habit in about 90 percent of male cats, and when the operation is performed before sexual maturity, the cat may never begin to spray. Altered cats of both sexes usually live longer and healthier lives. Unspayed females tend to develop uterine infections such as pyometra, which may require surgery. Spaying will eliminate the possibilities of uterine and ovarian disease, and greatly reduce the risk of breast tumors and mammary cancer. Spayed and neutered cats do not experience sexual desires, and loss of sexual capacity will not make a cat insecure.

The Knowledgeable Breeder

Should the information mentioned previously not be discouraging, you should consider only breeding healthy, good-looking pedigreed cats, of good temperament and free from hereditary faults, that conform favorably to their breed standards. Selective mating of this kind will improve a breed with each generation by producing kittens that are better than their parents.

The key to successful breeding is knowledge. Everyone who wants to succeed in his or her chosen field must prepare by study and experience, and cat breeders are no exception. Read everything you can about the art of breeding cats and about your chosen breed. Attend cat shows, join a local cat club, get to know other breeders, and do everything you can to increase your knowledge. Before a mating takes place, it is imperative that you understand the subject of genetics, especially as it relates to your breed. Books about genetics, breeding, and reproduction are listed in the bibliography in Chapter XVI. Read them carefully and refer to them often.

Getting Started

Let's assume you are a novice with no experience in breeding cats. You'll need some basic information about when cats reach sexual maturity, the queen's reproductive cycle, the mating of a male and female cat, care during pregnancy, and the delivery and rearing of the kittens.*

Both male and female cats show an unrestrained and lively interest in procreation at an early age. The appearance of the first heat period in the female usually is related to her ability to conceive. It usually occurs between the ages of seven to nine months, depending on the time of year and the cat's breed. Most female cats come into season early in their first spring. The onset of puberty, or sexual maturity, can vary considerably, however. Burmese, Siamese, and other oriental breeds have been known to come in season as early as three to five months of age, while Persians may reach fifteen to eighteen months before the first signs of heat appear. Environmental factors also can influence the queen's reproductive cycle. It has been discovered that young females exposed to hot weather, increasing daylight, tomcats, and other cycling queens generally show the first signs of estrus before similar females not subjected to these influences.

Although many young toms are sexually precocious by five months of age, males usually reach sexual maturity between nine and twelve months, after spermatozoa enter their seminal tubules.

The Healthy Queen

Healthy kittens begin with a healthy mother. When you breed your female, she should be in good physical and psychological condition. She should be in good flesh—not too thin or too fat—to ensure an easy delivery. Have your cat examined by a veterina-

---

*An *entire* adult female cat (or one that has not been spayed) is referred to as a queen.

rian at least a month before any mating is anticipated. Weight problems, nutritional deficiencies, worms, external parasites, skin problems, runny eyes or nose, and other complications should be diagnosed and corrected before the queen is mated. See that all her vaccinations against the major feline infectious diseases are current.

The Reproductive Cycle of the Queen

Female cats are seasonally polyestrus animals, which means that they experience many heat periods. The number of periods and their occurrence depends on the time of year and the nature of each cat. In North America the breeding season generally begins in January or February and extends through late summer. Most cats do not cycle from October through the early winter, although some will cycle year-round. A heat period lasts about four days if a tomcat is present and breeds the female. But if the queen is not bred, the heat period lasts at least ten days and recurs at approximately fourteen- to twenty-one-day intervals. Some females are constantly in heat during breeding season if they are not mated. The queen's reproductive cycle is divided into four phases:

ANESTRUS.   The early fall/winter period in which there is no estrus activity. The queen is not interested in males or in any aspect of mating during this stage. If a stud male makes sexual advances, she will hiss and claw at him.

PROESTRUS.   This is the preliminary phase between the resting period, or anestrus, and the time when mating will be permitted. Proestrus lasts from one to three days and causes sudden behavioral changes in the queen. She will become extremely friendly and affectionate, and start rubbing continuously against objects, especially with her cheeks and neck. The rubbing advances to rolling, and the queen will stretch and rhythmically open and close her claws. She may permit a male to approach and lick her head or sniff her vulva, but attempts to grab her by the neck or mount her will provoke her anger.

ESTRUS.   This is the stage of true heat, or when the queen will permit mating. She continues to rub and roll, and begins "calling" to the male in her distinct mating cry. *Calling*, in fact, is a word used to describe female cats that have come into heat and are ready for breeding. When a stud male approaches, the queen will assume the mating position: front part of her body crouched low to the floor, rear slightly elevated with tail flipped to one side. There may be a slight reddish discharge to the vulva. Ovulation does not take place unless the queen is aroused through copulation, and this is the reason for constant heat periods during the breeding season when a female is not mated. The vagina may be artificially stimulated to induce ovulation and shorten the heat period, but this should only be done with your veterinarian's supervision.

METESTRUS.   This stage follows estrus and lasts about twenty-four hours. The queen will still tolerate the stud male's advances, but when he tries to mate, she will attack him. At the close of this phase the queen returns to anestrus.

These signs of heat, incidentally, do not appear in spayed females.

Arranging the Breeding

If your queen is a pedigreed cat and you plan to register her kittens, the choice of a stud male requires a great deal of research and consideration. He should be chosen well in advance of mating time. It is wise to select an experienced stud (especially if your female has never been mated) whose pedigree complements that of your queen, and whose virtues surpass her faults so that the offspring will be as good or better than their parents.

The owner of a distinguished stud will want to know all about your queen—her health, her temperament, and her pedigree, for instance. You will be asked to produce a health certificate and proof of current vaccinations, and probably a certificate showing that your queen is free from feline leukemia virus (FeLV). You may, of course, ask the owner of the stud for similar certificates.

The stud's owner receives some type of payment for his services. It can be a cash fee payable at mating time (the male's bloodlines, consistency of previous litters, and show record, among other factors, determine the fee), or perhaps the owner will agree to waive the fee and take pick of the litter. To protect both parties, record all the facts in an informal contract to be signed by each owner. The contract should include: (1) the names, addresses, and telephone numbers of the owners of the queen and the stud; (2) the names and registration numbers of the cats being mated; (3) the date of breeding; (4) terms of mating—cash fee or kitten; (5) boarding fee if the queen will stay at the cattery for several days; and (6) provisions for a repeat service. When a cash fee is paid, the owner of the queen may wish to make arrangements for a repeat breeding at no charge if she does not conceive. It's always better to settle details in advance before problems arise and tempers flare. An informal, signed agreement protects both parties against misunderstandings.

It is nearly impossible to determine exactly when a queen will come into heat, but at the first signs of proestrus, you should phone the owner of the stud and inform him or her that your queen is ready for breeding. If the stud lives a great distance away and you have to ship the queen by air, make the travel arrangements promptly and confirm them with the stud's owner to be sure that she will be collected promptly upon arrival. When a queen has to travel long distances, she may stop being in heat by the time she reaches her destination and have to board there until she begins to call again. Most professional breeders insist on receiving a queen as soon as she shows signs of proestrus. When she is confined near the stud male a day or so before the mating; she can adjust to her new surroundings and flirt a bit with her intended. If you can deliver your queen for breeding in person, do so, keeping her in a sturdy cat carrier and not in your arms. Even the most demure female may become unhinged at the whiff of a stud male and try to escape.

Territory is most important to the tomcat's sexual behavior, and for this reason the queen goes to the male in most instances for breeding, because he is apt to perform better and feel more secure in familiar surroundings. Indeed, many toms will not breed in a strange place.

The Breeding Takes Place

When the queen and the stud meet in the breeding area, an elaborate courtship takes place that can last up to several minutes. Although each tom has his own way of courting a queen, generally there is a pattern to the proceedings. The male usually begins by circling the queen and then approaching her. If she backs off, he may cry out to her. The queen may roll on her back, or the pair may investigate each other through mutual smelling. The stud may lick the queen's face and then try to inspect her vulva. During estrus the female produces sex pheromones in her urine and vaginal discharge, which indicates to the male that she is sexually receptive. All these actions stimulate the queen, and she soon assumes the mating position—body bent low to the ground with hind-quarters slightly elevated, hind legs apart, and tail swung to one side—while the male prepares to mount her.

When the male mounts the queen, he holds her by the scruff of her neck with his powerful jaws to keep her from escaping and to help maintain his balance.

The actual mating begins when the stud seizes and holds the queen by the scruff of her neck. The male's teeth seldom penetrate her skin, although he holds the queen to keep her from escaping, more or less, and to maintain his balance. The stud mounts the queen and encircles her body with his front legs and then his hind legs, and begins to make thrusting motions while his penis becomes erect. The queen, simultaneously, steps or treads with her hind legs to adjust her position to facilitate insertion. After a forceful thrust by the stud, insertion and ejaculation occur, and the queen utters a shrill scream.* After the lively and noisy courting the acts of insertion, ejaculation, and withdrawal take less than fifteen seconds. As the male withdraws his penis and the queen screams, her eyes begin to dilate and she pulls ahead, turns toward the tom, and spits and scratches at him. An experienced stud gets out of her way quickly.

The queen begins to lick her vulva and to roll rhythmically on the floor. Within fifteen to ninety minutes, depending on the queen, she will allow the stud to breed her for the second time. It has been noted that experienced pairs may breed as often as ten times per hour. A minimum of three observed matings are suggested to assure the chances of conception.

Infertility

Cats are generally very fertile, but if the breeding proves unsuccessful, your queen might be infertile.

---

*The queen's cry and ensuing hostility toward the male are said to be caused by the barblike spines on the penis that stimulate her vagina and cause ovulation. Cats are induced ovulators; this means ovulation is induced by mating, and that a queen will not ovulate unless mating occurs.

Infertility in the female cat can be caused by infection, inadequate nutrition, hormone imbalances, physical or metabolic disorders, uterine abnormalities, or psychological or environmental problems. The queen should receive a complete physical examination from a veterinarian to determine the cause. Often a particular mating of a queen and a stud proves incompatible. If your veterinarian cannot find the cause of your queen's infertility, try mating her to another stud.

False Pregnancy

Although false pregnancy is uncommon in cats, it does occur occasionally after sterile matings. The signs and degree of pseudopregnancy vary from a slight swelling of the mammary glands to an increase in weight, an enlarged abdomen, and breasts filled with milk due to an abnormal secretion of the hormone progesterone. If the signs are mild, the condition usually lasts for about a week or so, but if the symptoms are severe and last longer, take your female to a veterinarian. He or she can prescribe something to slacken the milk flow and reduce the breast swellings, and may suggest hormone treatment. If there is a recurrence in future heat cycles, your veterinarian may suggest spaying to stop the problem.

Fetal Reabsorption

A queen will occasionally show positive signs of pregnancy and then suddenly appear not to be pregnant at all. If the pregnancy is interrupted before the fifth week of gestation, it is possible for the dead fetuses to be absorbed by the uterus back into

309 Cats: Breeds, Care, and Behavior

the queen's body. You may notice a slight vaginal discharge at the time of reabsorption, and the queen will come into heat within a few days. Feline leukemia virus (FeLV) is one of the most common causes of fetal reabsorption.

Prenatal Care

After mating, keep your queen on her normal routine, diet, and amount of food for the next three weeks. The first signs of pregnancy usually occur around the third week, when the nipples enlarge and turn pink, and the hair surrounding them recedes slightly. Should you wish to have professional confirmation of pregnancy, have the queen examined by a veterinarian around the twenty-eighth day after mating. A veterinarian can carefully palpate the abdomen at this time and determine the presence of fetuses, which should feel like walnut-sized balls.

You must provide the queen with nutritious food during pregnancy, as well as added vitamins and minerals, and this is a good time to ask the veterinarian's advice about diet and supplements. Pregnancy and lactation are critical periods when a queen requires increased levels of vitamins, minerals, and energy. If she does not receive adequate nourishment for herself and the developing kittens, the queen will deplete her own body reserves. The queen's appetite will increase, and around the fourth week you should gradually increase her food intake. Foods that contain high protein levels—fish, meat, poultry, cooked eggs, cheese—and milk are especially nutritious. During the last weeks of pregnancy, as the queen's uterus expands, she may not be able to eat large meals.

Divide her food intake into several smaller meals each day.

Between the fifth to sixth weeks the queen will become noticeably swollen. Exercise and play are essential during pregnancy until the time of delivery, but do avoid strenuous activities like letting the queen dash on or off furniture or jump from high places. Any fall could cause her to miscarry.

Do not give drugs to the queen unless you have been instructed to do so by your veterinarian. Many drugs are potentially dangerous to the unborn kittens, *especially* griseofulvin (an antibiotic used to treat ringworm), which is known to cause severe deformities. Should the queen become infested with fleas or ear mites, seek your veterinarian's advice about the proper insecticides to use and the correct method of application. Do not put anything on the coat that can be licked off to cause illness. Groom the queen every day to remove dead hair and to prevent tangles, and pay special attention to the areas she now cannot reach.

The gestation period from the time of mating to the delivery of the kittens is about sixty-three days. It is possible though for a queen to deliver her kittens as early as the sixtieth day or as late as the seventieth day if she is not suffering in other respects. In the last week of pregnancy the kittens may be observed moving inside the queen when she lies in a relaxed position.

Preparing for the Delivery

While you wait for the kittens to arrive, use the last weeks of pregnancy to prepare for the big event. The queen will become restless and start searching

through all the dark and secluded areas of your
house for a place to give birth to her kittens. This is
an ideal time to prepare the maternity box in which
she will deliver her young. The box should be roomy
enough for the queen to lie down, stretch out all four
legs, and nurse the kittens comfortably, but not so
large that the kittens can spread out over too great an
area. A suitable choice is a large cardboard carton
with sides high enough to keep out drafts and a
hinged lid on top. (A hinged lid provides seclusion
for the queen but gives you access from the top.) Cut
down one side of the box to allow the queen to enter
and exit without difficulty, but leave a ledge to retain
the kittens. Place the maternity box in a warm but
ventilated area, away from noise, small children,
other animals, and the family's normal traffic pattern.

Let the queen become familiar with the maternity
box a week or two before the kittens are due, add a
blanket or some soft towels, and perhaps a treat or
two and let her sleep inside. Keep drawers and
cupboard or closet doors closed at this time. A few
days before delivery she will start rearranging the
bedding in her nest. Allow her to do this, but when
actual labor begins, remove the blanket or towels and
put down newspapers or other porous materials to
absorb the blood and other liquids discharged during
the delivery. Some breeders frown on the use of
newspapers because they feel that the inks used in
printing them could be mildly toxic if licked in
sufficient quantities. You may choose to use white
tissue paper instead. The following supplies should
be on hand near the maternity box:

- Rectal thermometer.
- Supply of freshly laundered hand towels.

- Newspapers or other porous material to change the maternity box after the delivery.
- Petroleum or lubricating jelly.
- Small forceps.
- Dental floss or white nylon thread.
- Blunt-tipped scissors.
- Antiseptic safe for cats.
- Absorbent cotton.
- Paper towels.
- Plastic trash bag (for cleaning up).
- Notebook and pen to jot down whelping details or danger signs. These are important to report to your veterinarian in an emergency.

It's also wise to have a few Borden's small animal nursing bottles and nipples handy plus a feline milk substitute, such as Borden's KMR (Kitten Milk Replacer).

Notify the veterinarian during the end of the eighth week that delivery is expected soon, and check to see if he or she will be on call. During the last week gently wash the queen's abdomen and vulva with warm water and mild soap, then rinse and dry these areas thoroughly. If she has long hair, carefully scissor or clip the coat from around the breasts and vulva. Delivery will be more sanitary by doing this, and the kittens will be able to locate their mother's teats and nurse without difficulty. Pat the trimmed areas with a little vegetable oil suitable for eating to prevent the skin from becoming irritated.

Signs of Labor

Knowing the signs of the first-stage of labor will help you prepare for the delivery. The queen will become extremely restless and she will scratch furiously and rearrange the bedding in her maternity box. She may lick herself constantly. Her teats will become erect, and if they are gently squeezed, beads of milk may appear. The queen probably will refuse to eat, and her body temperature (normally in the range of 100.5° to 102.5° F, or 38° to 39.2° C) will drop to about 99° F or 37.5° C. When it stays at this lower level without fluctuating, the queen should give birth within twenty-four hours.

The queen will urinate frequently; in fact, she will interrupt her normal activities many times during the day to rush to the litter tray. Her vulva will become swollen and soft, and there will be a mucous discharge from the vagina, colorless at first and then blood-tinged, an indication that the cervix is dilating to prepare for the delivery of the kittens. Some females become overly distraught at this time, crying repeatedly and following their owners constantly. Do not allow the queen to go outside during the first-stage of labor, as she could steal away to some damp and secluded area to deliver her kittens.

The Normal Delivery Process

When delivery is imminent, the queen will become increasingly agitated. She will pant, lick her vulva, and strain as if she were trying to have a bowel movement. As she lies on her side you will be able to see and feel the abdominal contractions. These force the fetuses down the uterine horns and into the birth canal. Once they are in the canal, the queen helps to expel the fetuses by pushing along with the contractions. Eventually a slippery and almost transparent, fluid-filled sac containing the first fetus will appear at the vulva. It may be drawn back into the queen a few times and take several contractions to be expelled. Normally a kitten is presented head first, but some are delivered buttocks (a breech birth) or hind legs first. If the queen has difficulty expelling a kitten, try to assist her. Spread petroleum jelly or lubricating jelly around the opening of the vulva, then grasp the partly exposed membrane with a hand towel or handkerchief. With each contraction gently but firmly pull it downward and outward. Do not squeeze the kitten; pull carefully, not forcefully, until it is delivered.

The queen should automatically tear open the sac with her teeth and sever the umbilical cord. Should she not do so within thirty seconds—and this sometimes happens with inexperienced queens—break open the membrane carefully with your fingers,

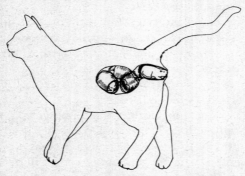

The unborn kittens lie in the two horns of the queen's uterus. Each is developed in its own placenta, a transparent fluid-filled sac which is attached to the queen by a umbilical cord. During labor, the kittens methodically move down the birth canal as the cervix dilates. In the illustration, a kitten is ready to be born. Kittens emerge headfirst in a normal delivery, but occasionally they are born hindquarters first; this is called breech birth.

uncovering the head first to keep the newborn kitten from suffocating. Wipe away any fluids from the kitten's mouth and nose. If the placenta is still attached, clamp the umbilical cord near its center with the forceps, then tie the cord with dental floss or white nylon thread about an inch or so from the kitten's abdomen (take care not to stretch the cord from the kitten and cause an umbilical hernia). Cut the cord in front of the knotted thread with sterilized blunt-tipped scissors. Swab the severed edge with antiseptic, then remove the forceps. Once tied, the rest of the cord will shrivel up and fall off within a few days.

Massage the newborn kitten with a terry hand towel, then place it near its mother. She will lick it until it is clean and dry. Don't be alarmed that she licks vigorously; she's just encouraging the kitten's respiratory and circulatory systems to function. A healthy kitten will soon find its mother's teats and begin to nurse. If it does not, gently squeeze a little milk from one of the breasts, then put the kitten's mouth around it. If the kitten does not breathe easily or looks weak and lifeless, keep rubbing it vigorously to stimulate breathing and circulation. Should its lungs sound like they are filled with fluid, hold the kitten upside down in the palms of your hands (firmly supporting its neck and body), raise your arms overhead, and swing them downward. This action usually helps to drain fluids from the chest and clear the breathing passages.

The series of events previously described will be repeated with the birth of each kitten. The time between the delivery of each one may range from ten or fifteen minutes to one hour in a normal delivery.

An average litter usually contains four kittens, and the normal delivery time takes about two to four hours. Between each birth process offer the queen a drink of water or warm milk (no milk if it causes diarrhea), pat her gently, and tell her in your most charming voice that her kittens are simply beautiful!

The afterbirths are normally expelled with the fluid-filled sac, or just after a kitten is born, or before the birth of the next kitten. There will be one afterbirth for each kitten; count them carefully to be sure that every one is expelled from the uterus. The queen will try to eat each afterbirth once a kitten is delivered. It is not necessary to let her eat every one, as this often causes diarrhea and vomiting. Eating one or two will be sufficient.

Danger Signs

Although it is unusual for a queen to experience difficult birth, call your veterinarian *immediately* if any of the following problems exist:

1. The queen experiences prolonged labor or strains arduously for more than one hour without results. This can indicate (a) an abnormal presentation; (b) two kittens blocking the birth canal; or (c) kittens too large to pass through the birth canal.
2. The contractions weaken or stop completely. The queen appears to tire before a kitten is born. This indicates uterine inertia.
3. The queen cries in agony as she strains to expel a kitten.
4. The queen keeps straining and you notice a bubble appearing and disappearing at the vulva for a long time.

5. The queen expels a greenish, foul-smelling discharge. This may indicate a detached placenta or decomposed fetus.
6. Part of a kitten is delivered and the queen is unable to expel the rest, even with your assistance.
7. Profuse bleeding after delivery.
8. The queen runs a high temperature after delivery.
9. The kittens are restless and cry constantly.
10. The queen has no milk.
11. Heavy, dark, and foul-smelling vaginal discharge several days after delivery.
12. The queen's teats are enlarged or discolored, or she produces off-color milk.

Postnatal Care

After the last kitten is delivered, the queen may want to go to her litter tray to relieve herself. If she refuses to leave the kittens, have someone take her to the tray while you remove the soiled linings from the maternity box and put down a new supply. The queen may be hungry after the delivery. Feed her a little bland food and offer her a drink.

Just after delivery check frequently to see that the queen is producing enough milk to feed her kittens. Her first milk, a watery secretion called "colostrum," is richer in protein and fat than her later milk. For the first twenty-four hours after birth newborn kittens receive antibodies from their mother's colostrum that grant them immunity from certain infectious diseases, such as feline panleukopenia, for several weeks. If the queen has no milk, your veterinarian can give her a hormone injection to encourage it to flow.

The queen may show a slight vaginal discharge for several days after kittening. A blood-tinged discharge for seven to ten days after delivery is normal; it should decrease gradually, become clear, and then stop altogether. But if you notice a heavy, foul-smelling, dark-colored discharge or elevated temperature, inform your veterinarian as soon as possible, as an afterbirth may have been retained or the uterus may be infected. A retained kitten or a placental membrane or uterine infection can cause serious problems when ignored.

Feed the queen as much soft and bland food as she desires for the first day or two, plus fresh, clean water, then return to her regular diet, supplemented by the high-protein foods added during pregnancy. Feed her as much as she wants to eat during the nursing period. She should also continue to receive a vitamin-mineral supplement.

Postnatal Complications

Agalactia

Insufficient milk production is rare in the cat but sometimes, especially after the first litter, the queen is unable to produce milk. This condition can be inherited, or it can be caused by nervousness, abnormalities of the teats, or an imbalance of hormones. It may be corrected after a veterinarian injects the queen with the hormone oxytocin to stimulate the production of milk. The milk should start flowing within twenty-four hours. Until it does (or if the injection is ineffective), you may have to bottle feed the kittens.

Galactosis

Galactosis is a condition in which the queen's breasts become engorged with milk and quite painful after the birth of the kittens. It generally occurs in queens heavy with milk but not enough kittens to empty the breasts regularly. An excessive amount of milk may lead to mastitis. Treatment includes hormones to decrease milk production, massage to alleviate pain, and hand milking to reduce excess accumulation.

Mastitis

Mastitis is a painful inflammation of one or more mammary glands caused by an infection in the queen. The affected breasts become painful and swollen and feel hot to the touch. They often appear red or purplish in color, and the milk secreted by them, discolored or blood-tinged. Other symptoms may be evident: fever (often as high as 105° F), diarrhea, anorexia, constipation, and reluctance to nurse the kittens. Warm compresses will help to relieve the pain, and antibiotic treatment by a veterinarian will be necessary. The kittens should be removed from nursing from the queen and bottle fed until the veterinarian feels she can resume feeding them.

Metritis

Metritis is a severe bacterial infection of the uterus caused by prolonged or difficult labor, retained afterbirth or fetal tissue, or the entrance of bacteria through instruments or internal manipulation. Symptoms of metritis include listlessness, dehydration with excessive thirst, vomiting, anorexia, and fever, but the most obvious danger sign is a dark red, foul-smelling, purulent vaginal discharge. Metritis can be fatal, and immediate veterinary attention is necessary. The queen's milk may be toxic and her kittens should be removed from nursing on her and raised by hand.

Eclampsia or Lactation Tetany

Another serious postnatal complication that requires *immediate* veterinary attention is eclampsia or lactation tetany. It can occur in the last two weeks of pregnancy but it is most likely to develop within the first three weeks after delivery, when the queen is lactating heavily to feed her litter. Eclampsia is a metabolic problem in which the blood calcium level drops below normal. Its exact cause is unknown. The first signs are nervousness and restlessness, fever, and staggering gait. As the condition progresses uncontrollable muscle-twitching and stiffness develop in the queen's head and legs. If untreated, the muscle spasms become more prolonged, and the queen may experience convulsions, or collapse and fall into a coma.

Caring for the Kittens

During the first fourteen days there is little to do except to keep the queen supplied with nutritious food and fresh water. Check mother daily to see that her abdominal and rectal areas are clean, that no breasts are discolored or caked with milk, and that the kittens are not scratching her teats. If mother has long hair, you may need to sponge, dry, and comb the hair on her underparts to keep it from becoming sticky and matted while the kittens are nursing.

Mother will spend nearly all her time caring for the kittens and keeping the maternity box tidy, but you must check frequently to see that each kitten is nursing properly and growing as fast as the others, and that no problems are developing. Normal healthy kittens sleep soundly between nursings and twitch and jerk in their sleep. They have no problems crawling toward or locating mother, and their sucking instincts are strong and vigorous during nursings. Their little tummies are full, and their stools are firm and yellow. Normal kittens seldom cry. Their bodies are warm and coats shiny and smooth to the touch. By contrast, sick kittens cry persistently and crawl aimlessly around the maternity box. Their reflexes are poor, and while nursing, their sucking instincts are weak. Their bodies are cold and clammy to the touch, and coats are dull and harsh. They have hollow tummies and are frequently bothered with watery diarrhea.

The most important factor for newborn kittens is warmth. Their body temperatures are lower than normal for the first two weeks of life. Neonatal kittens and puppies have no shivering reflex for the first few days of life. If they do not have an external source of heat (in addition to their mother's warmth), their body temperatures can drop and they become chilled and die. Since infant kittens cannot sustain their body temperatures, they must be maintained in an environment that will do it for them for the first week. Don't overheat, though. Keep the temperature of the maternity box and surrounding area at around 85° to 90° F (29.5° to 32.2° C) for that period. The heat source can be room temperature, or an overhead heating unit, such as an infrared lamp, that can be raised or lowered. After the first week reduce the temperature by five degrees weekly, or until it reaches 70° F (21.5° C) by the fourth and subsequent weeks.

Weigh the kittens frequently on a food scale with accurate measurements for grams, ounces, and pounds.* If they are healthy, each should gain about one-half ounce per day during the first week. Be sure the kittens nurse from all the mother's teats, especially those that are swollen with milk, otherwise some of the breasts (especially the lower two) may become painfully inflamed and mother may be reluctant to let them nurse. At the end of the first week (and weekly thereafter) trim the sharp points from the kittens' nails to keep them from scratching mother's teats. Check the kittens daily for cleanliness. Mother usually licks them clean, and as she does this in the genital area each kitten is stimulated to urinate and defecate. By the sixth to the tenth day, depending on the breed, the kittens' eyes will open. You should gently wipe away any mucus discharge in the eye corners during this time with a cotton ball moistened with warm water.

Don't hesitate to pick up and fondle the kittens occasionally. Scientists have found that the events that take place in the first weeks of an animal's life can dramatically influence its behavior as an adult. A little fondling of newborn kittens—even a few days after birth—results in friendlier, healthier, less hostile and more adaptable animals. Be cautious, though, about admitting too many visitors to the nursery area. Some mothers become terribly upset when strangers view or handle their kittens, and they may try to harm the visitors or even the litter. If the queen feels nervous or insecure, she may even move her kittens, one by one, to another place, or she may attempt to destroy them!

During the second week of life the ears open and

---

*Most food scales have trays to comfortably hold each kitten as it is being weighed.

become erect, and the kittens begin to hear. They also learn to crawl, and soon after start to toddle around the maternity box. If you have not already sexed the kittens, this is an ideal time to do it. Carefully hold each kitten with its rear toward you, look under the tail and you will notice two small openings. The opening at the top that is closest to the tail is the anus and is the same in both males and females. The lower opening is the external sex organ and is different. In the female it is the vulva, or a tiny vertical slit directly below the anus. In fact, the area looks like the small letter *i*, in which the anus is the dot and the vulva the letter. In the male, it is a tiny circle, farther apart from the anus than the slit in the female, which conceals the tip of the penis. Examine a few kittens together and it shouldn't be too difficult to determine their sex.

Long-haired kittens should receive a little daily grooming starting around the age of four weeks so

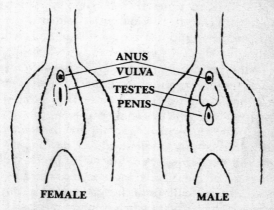

ANUS
VULVA
TESTES
PENIS

FEMALE   MALE

SEXING A CAT

they learn to accept this procedure when it becomes more time-consuming in later life. If you put a small litter tray in or near the maternity box, the kittens will instinctively learn to use it, often with a little motivation from mother.

Self-play begins at about two weeks, where each kitten will try to swat at moving objects. As muscle coordination develops the play progresses to pawing and occasional biting between littermates. By the fifth week the kittens will be leaping, stalking, arching their backs, chasing mother's tail and bedeviling her in other ways, and exploring their surroundings.

Around the fourth week mother begins to ignore the kittens for longer periods, and this is a good time to start weaning them. The weaning diet may consist of baby cereals, strained baby meat, ground beef, chicken or beef liver, salmon, sardines, canned cat food (liquify all meats or canned food in a blender), or Borden's Kitten Weaning Formula mixed with Borden's KMR or water to a soupy consistency. Put the food in a flat dish or pie pan, hold it up to the kittens' mouths, and try to get them to lick it by spreading a little of the mixture around their lips. Try putting the pan inside the maternity box eventually. If you have never enjoyed the experience of weaning baby animals, you're in for some fun. A few will instinctively try to lap up the mixture, but the rest will sit in it, walk through it, and try to investigate the inviting and soupy compound. Don't panic. The kittens will learn to eat, and they will enjoy their food. Begin with one meal a day; increase it to two and then to three and so forth, until they are eating about two cereal/milk meals and two fish or meat meals per day. As soon as they are eating well, of course, thicken the consistency of their food. Don't forget to ask your veterinarian for recommendations about a proper vitamin-mineral supplement. Provide water, milk, or KMR at all times as soon as weaning begins. Keep mother out of the maternity box for longer periods of time, and by the sixth week the kittens should be eating on their own. They can then eat a variety of foods including dry, canned, or semimoist cat food. Gradually decrease the queen's food intake to her normal prepregnancy maintenance level and her milk should dry of its own accord. If she still produces ample amounts of milk, however, consult your veterinarian.

A responsible breeder who is concerned about the future of the kittens will teach them how to use a scratching post at this time. He or she will continue to fondle the kittens and play with them frequently. Even though mother will teach them all about stalking and pouncing on prey, you can enhance the kitten's natural hunting instincts by providing stimulating toys. Check with your veterinarian about early immunization against feline panleukopenia, rhinotracheitis, and calicivirus. No two kittens (even from the same litter) are alike regarding immunity. Each acquires a different level of protection from its mother's colostrum immediately after birth, and each loses that protection at a different rate. Generally speaking, by about seven to eight weeks of age half the litter still possess some maternal immunity while the others do not, and there is no way to distinguish the protected from the unprotected. Permanent vaccinations should begin at eight weeks. (More information about the illnesses for which immunization is necessary will be found in Chapter VI, "Keeping

Your Cat Healthy.") When the kittens go to their new homes, don't forget to furnish the new owners with a written schedule listing the type of food being given, feeding times, immunization schedule, and other pertinent health facts, and include the name and address of your veterinarian.

The Care of Orphan or Rejected Kittens

It is sometimes possible to locate another queen with milk that will accept orphan or rejected kittens. If you cannot find a foster mother, however, you must hand-rear them. Raising a litter of orphan or rejected kittens is a demanding experience. Kittens that have lost their mother, are rejected by her because of certain psychological problems, or those isolated from her because of breast problems ranging from infected milk to no milk at all, need the following attention:

- Warm, draft-free surroundings. The mother's body heat helps to keep her kittens warm. When she is not available, a uniform environment must be maintained to prevent chilling, the most common cause of death in orphan kittens. This can be done through room temperature and overhead infrared lamp or heating pad with thermostat set on "Low." Follow the temperature requirements mentioned above under "Caring for the Kittens." If you use a heating pad, enclose it inside a towel and seal it carefully to keep the kittens from crawling in between and smothering. Cover only part of the maternity box bottom with the pad to let the kittens crawl off if they are hot.

- Uninterrupted sleep and no unnecessary handling. Except for feeding and cleaning, don't disturb them.

- Hand cleaning. Rub over the kittens with a dampened washcloth and dry them thoroughly. If the overhead lamp or heating pad causes dry skin, rub in a little baby oil. When the eyes open, the corners should be gently wiped with a cotton ball soaked in warm water.

- Temporary immunity if the kittens did not receive their mother's colostrum. Check with your veterinarian.

Feeding Orphan or Rejected Kittens

When it is necessary to hand-feed the kittens, you need a formula that meets their nutritional requirements. Feline milk has a higher protein content than other milks produced by domestic animals or humans. For this reason cow's milk, dog's milk substitutes, or premixed human baby formulas are not nutritionally balanced for kittens. Near-perfect equivalents, though, are the liquid kitten milk substitutes, such as Borden's KMR (Kitten Milk Replacer), a correct blend of proteins, fats, carbohydrates, and vitamins and minerals. Should you not have a supply of KMR or similar product on hand, the following will serve as a temporary substitute until you get some from your veterinarian or pet store:

Formula #1:   ½ cup whole cow's milk
                   1 hard-boiled egg
                   1 teaspoon powdered calcium carbonate (buy at pharmacy or health food store)

Formula #2:   8 ounces canned evaporated cow's
                        milk
                    1 egg yolk

Mix both formulas in an electric blender, refrigerate,
then shake well before using. Along with the homemade formula the kittens should also receive a liquid
vitamin-mineral supplement.

You will also need Borden's small animal nursing
bottle and nipple or a doll's bottle with nipple in
working condition. Some people like to use an eyedropper to feed very young kittens, but this can be
somewhat dangerous. Just be careful that you don't
drop too much milk into a kitten's mouth and cause it
to choke. The calorie content and suggested amount
of formula to feed per pound of body weight will
appear on the Kitten Milk Replacer label. Divide this
amount into about six equal feedings per day. Should
you use a homemade formula temporarily, ask your
veterinarian about the correct amount to feed. Bring
the formula to room temperature or slightly warmer.
Fill the bottle(s), then turn each upside down to see if
the milk comes out properly. It should trickle slowly
from the opening. If the milk is not flowing sufficiently, enlarge the nipple hole with a heated needle.

Sit down, fold a towel into thirds, and place it on
top of a table or in your lap. Put a kitten down, with
its paws resting on the towel so it has a textured
surface to grab onto and knead as if it were nursing
on its mother. Open the kitten's mouth with your
finger to make sure its paper-thin tongue is in normal
position and not sticking to the roof of its mouth.
Insert the nipple and hold the bottle up (but not too
erect) to keep the kitten from sucking too much air.

Once healthy, hungry kittens taste milk, they usually nurse enthusiastically. If the kitten is too weak to feed on its stomach, hold it upright in the palm of your hand at about a 45-degree angle. Don't let the kitten drink too quickly. Milk bubbling from the nose or mouth is a sign that formula is being consumed too quickly.

After the feeding, burp each kitten like a baby, holding it against your chest and rubbing or patting its back. For the first seven to ten days of a kitten's life, you will have to stimulate it to urinate and defecate after feeding if its mother is not available. Dampen a cotton ball slightly with warm water and rub over the abdomen and the area under its tail.

The kitten should learn to lap as soon as possible. The best way to determine if the formula is meeting the kitten's needs is by consistent weight gain and the color and amount of stools and urine. Stools should be firm and yellowish, never soft, watery, or discolored. Expect four to six bowel movements when a kitten is fed four to six times a day. Urine should be clear to pale yellow and never amber or orange. Consult your veterinarian as soon as possible when problems arise, especially if you notice abnormal color or consistency of the urine or stool.

IX   The Aging Cat

> *Life will go on forever,*
> *With all that a cat can wish;*
> *Warmth, and the glad procession*
> *Of fish and milk and fish.*
> —Alexander Gray,
> *On a Cat Ageing*

Pets, like vintage wine, seem to improve with age. Their youthful high spirits may disappear, but they are replaced by affection, companionship, and mutual trust that develop through the years. Of all small domestic animals, cats are the longest-lived. Their life expectancy has increased dramatically as a result of today's superior nutrition and veterinary care. The average life span ranges from fourteen to eighteen years. Many cats live to be past twenty, and a few have even reached their thirties.

There are no sirens to herald the onset of old age. Senescence is a gradual process, and its signs are not always apparent. Some cats, in fact, stay healthy and spry until their late teens. Feline senior citizens can be comfortable and happy in their later years if they receive proper attention and care from their owners. Frequent home examinations are highly important. You should know by now what is normal behavior for your cat, and *any* unusual or abnormal condition or actions should be reported to your veterinarian at once. You'll save your elderly friend a great deal of pain and suffering by having it examined regularly by a veterinarian. Regular checkups are important for cats of all ages, but they are especially significant for aging felines. Along with good health care, an older cat needs to feel secure and loved and wanted. Like older people, they are extremely sensitive to physical and emotional stress. Take extra time to stroke your old friend lovingly and speak affectionately, and try not to disrupt the normal pattern of its life.

When a Cat Is Considered Old

It was once believed that one year in the life of a cat or dog was equivalent to seven years of a human life. Another schedule has been published recently by the Gaines Research Center in which a year-old pet is roughly thought to be the equivalent of a fifteen-year-old human. After two years of age the pet/human aging process levels off at about a ratio of one to four:

Pet's Age	Man's Age	Pet's Age	Man's Age
6 months	10 years	10 years	56 years
8 months	13 years	12 years	64 years
12 months	15 years	14 years	72 years
2 years	24 years	16 years	80 years
4 years	32 years	18 years	88 years
6 years	40 years	20 years	96 years
8 years	48 years	21 years	100 years

Changes in the Older Cat

As a cat grows older its body cells change gradually
and become less functional. The aging process varies
with each individual animal, although a number of
signs are common in all cats. The aging cat gradually
becomes less active and less interested in its surroundings. It will sleep more, play and exercise more
modestly, and perhaps become touchy or quick-
tempered about things that it previously tolerated.
Hearing and eyesight may become less acute. Although cataracts are less common in cats than in dogs,
they may develop, or you may notice a bluish haze
inside your cat's eyes from a condition known as
nuclear sclerosis. Loose or infected teeth, tartar
buildup, or gum disease may cause problems in the
mouth. The skin glands become sluggish. The hair
begins to gray, become thin, and lose its sheen. The
abdominal muscles lose their tone and strength. An
older cat will walk, lie down, and get up slowly.

The body metabolism slackens and the vital organs
begin to function less efficiently. Kidney function
becomes greatly reduced, and almost every old cat
experiences some degree of kidney failure. Older
males become susceptible to urinary tract obstructions. Cardiac diseases—while not as common in cats
as in dogs—do occur, especially congestive heart
failure. Older cats are more susceptible to anemia.
They are also prone to skin tumors, oral tumors, and
mammary tumors (in unspayed females). Some of
these are benign, while others may be cancerous. The
most serious and common type of cancer found in
elderly cats is lymphosarcoma, a disease connected
with the feline leukemia virus (FeLV). Other malig-
nancies of the skin, bones, intestines, liver, lungs, and

pancreas may occur in old age. Pyometra, a condition in which the uterus becomes filled with pus, is often seen in older unspayed females. Symptoms include a distended and painful abdomen, sticky and offensive-smelling yellowish vaginal discharge, loss of appetite, and increased thirst accompanied by vomiting after drinking. If the cervix is closed, the discharge cannot be emitted and death may result from toxemia. Immediate surgery is necessary in either case. Other problems frequently experienced in old age are constipation, diarrhea, diabetes, arthritis, respiratory problems, digestive disturbances, and liver disease.

Care of the Older Cat

The management of a geriatric cat, apart from heeding your veterinarian's advice, consists of common sense, observation, and a great deal of emotional understanding. Good nutrition is vital. Feed your cat a balanced diet with the correct amounts of proteins, fats, and vitamins and minerals necessary for old age. Even if you have carefully controlled your cat's weight throughout its lifetime, now it is essential to guard against obesity or its reverse, progressive weight loss. Should your cat's sense of smell and taste begin to diminish, try adding snippets of strong-smelling food that the cat loves on top of its regular ration. Consult your veterinarian about any dietary problems; great progress has been made in the field of nutrition for geriatric animals. Be sure fresh drinking water is available at all times.

Keep your cat well-groomed. Regular combing and brushing stimulates the skin, gives the hair a healthier appearance, and removes the dead coat before it can be ingested by the cat and form into hairballs. An old cat may not be able to keep itself fastidiously clean, and a little extra attention with your comb, a damp sponge, or coat cleaner will maintain its dignity. Examine the mouth frequently. Have tartar accumulations removed and infected teeth pulled promptly. Trim the nails often. Above all, keep vaccinations up-to-date.

It is wrong to think that older pets should not exercise. Most cats (except those with serious physical problems) will benefit greatly from exercise, and many forms can be enjoyed by animal and owner together. Walks on harness and leash may be slower and shorter than they once were, and playtime may not be as energetic, but these are wonderful ways to keep your cat in shape both mentally and physically. Don't expose your cat to weather extremes. If it goes outside to an exercise area, don't leave the cat there very long in hot or cold weather. Keep it off damp surfaces that can aggravate arthritis. And if the cat has the freedom of the yard, walk through to see that no low obstructions could trap or injure it, and protect it from being unsupervised near a swimming pool.

As a cat grows older, as with an elderly person, it becomes rather fixed in its habits and less adaptable to change. The cat enjoys certain things—meals, play, naps in warm and sunny places, for instance—at definite times of the day. Make every effort to maintain that schedule and to avoid stressful situations, for this will add to your cat's security. Keep the food and water pans in the same location. Cats with impaired hearing or sight can manage quite well as long as they stay in familiar surroundings. When the hearing is less acute, the touch of your hand will help ease your cat's discomfort and make it more self-assured. If the eyesight is failing, keep all fragile or sharp objects out of the cat's path and avoid moving the furniture to different places. Such cats should always remain indoors, away from the dangers of automobiles and other animals.

When your cat requires medication, see that it is given promptly according to directions. While arthritis does not seem to affect cats as severely as it does dogs, your veterinarian can prescribe pain-relieving medication should arthritis become a problem. The medication will not cure the condition, but it can help to relieve the pain and stiffness and make your cat more comfortable. Should bladder control weaken, your cat will need to use its litter tray more often. A concerned owner will place extra trays at strategic locations in a multistory household. But even then "accidents" may happen in various parts of your home away from the litter pan. Don't scold or punish your cat for an accident that may now be beyond its control. Be understanding, and try to make litter trays more accessible.

When the End Comes

Death may come at home comfortably and quietly from natural causes, but when a cat is terminally ill, you may have to consider the possibility of euthanasia. The decision to end the life of a beloved pet is one that should be made by the entire family, for obvious reasons. All members of the family are affected, but children are particularly vulnerable because it may be the first time they have to deal with loss. What happens during this crisis can influence their reactions to future bereavement. It is important for the entire family to discuss their feelings and their grief as openly as possible. Herbert A. Nieburg and Arlene C. Fischer deal with the death of beloved pets in their poignant work *Pet Loss*.* They mention that

> people who have strong ties to their pets are often deeply affected by grief, which can temporarily overshadow other aspects of their lives. Crying and feeling lonely or depressed are natural ways of responding to the death of a cat or dog that has shared one's daily life. There is a classic definition by grief therapist Colin Murray Parkes of grief as an emotional and behavioral reaction that is set in motion when a love tie is broken. A "love tie" accurately describes the relationship between many people and their pets: the loss deprives the owner of love as well as other basic needs and pleasures.

Seek the guidance of your veterinarian, too, for he or she can best advise if the cat is suffering with no hope of relief. When you are positive that you cannot do more for your beloved cat, when its serenity is replaced by suffering and it can no longer enjoy life, euthanasia is the dignified and humane solution. When a decision is made to euthanize a cat, it can be done in a veterinary hospital or, possibly, in your home. The cat will be less apprehensive when its owner stays close by during the procedure, if this is permitted. Veterinarians use a swift and humane method to euthanize pets. The animal is given a lethal

---

*Herbert A. Nieburg, and Arlene C. Fischer, *Pet Loss* (New York: Harper & Row, 1982).

injection that literally puts it to sleep in seconds. There is no pain and no suffering.

Disposal of the Body

The disposal of the body is another matter that should be discussed with your veterinarian, for regulations and facilities vary from one locality to another. You may wish to bury your cat in your garden, but some city ordinances prohibit the burial of animals on residential property. You may choose cremation and/ or burial of the cat or its ashes in a pet cemetery. Thousands of establishments in the United States and Canada offer crematory or burial services for animals. They are listed in the classified section of the telephone directory under "Pet Cemeteries and Crematories." The average cat funeral costs around $75 but can run into the thousands, depending on the size and location of the burial plot, the cost of the casket, and the size and design of the marker. It costs from $25 to $75 to have a cat cremated, which includes the return of the ashes in a container (the more elaborate the container, the higher the price). These prices usually include removal of the cat's body from the hospital or your home to the cemetery. It is not necessary to spend a lot of money. Most veterinarians will dispose of the remains if you wish. Local humane organizations and health authorities also provide free or low-cost disposal facilities, usually by cremation.

Another Companion?

When the tears have stopped flowing and you realize you are lonely without the companionship of a cat, perhaps you will think of sharing your life with another. No animal can ever be exactly like, or take the place of another. But if you carefully select a worthy successor, and give it love, understanding, and the best of care, and allow it to make its own place in your life, that would be a lovely tribute to the memory of your departed friend.

X All About Cat Shows and the Cat Fancy

The smallest feline is a masterpiece.
—Leonardo da Vinci

Today, with more leisure time available than ever before, people from all walks of life have become interested in showing their pets. The number of cat shows and the scores of entries in them have increased dramatically in the last ten years. Showing cats is one of the few exciting hobbies that can bring great satisfaction to the young, the middle-aged, and the elderly. It is truly a competitive activity that the entire family can enjoy.

The First Cat Shows and Cat Fancy Organizations

The first organized cat show was staged at the Crystal Palace in London on July 13, 1871. It was planned by Mr. Harrison Weir (1824-1906), who devised the first standards by which breeds could be judged, and who commented about the event: "There lay the cats in their different pens, making no sound save now and then a homely purring, as from time to time they lapped the nice new milk provided for them. Yes, there they were, big cats, very big cats, middling-sized cats, and small cats, cats of all colors and markings, and beautiful pure white Persian cats."* The 160 short-haired and long-haired feline competitors created such a sensation that other shows followed in rapid succession, and the exhibition of pedigreed cats became quite popular. The pastime of exhibiting cats was regarded with favor by the English elite because their animal-loving monarch, Queen Victoria (who owned a pair of blue Persians), attended cat shows regularly in the company of her son, the Prince of Wales (later Edward VII). The royal twosome often presented the show trophies, and the prince gave inscribed photographs of himself to the winners.

The first cat fancy club to be organized and to institute a stud book and registry of cats was the National Cat Club formed in 1887 with Harrison Weir as president. Eleven years later a competitive organization called The Cat Club was established, and it, too, operated a cat registry. The two groups existed together until 1910, when they consented to merge into one organized structure that was called the Governing Council of the Cat Fancy. Other clubs sprang up through the years and became associated with the council. Today more than sixty clubs are affiliated with the GCCF, which oversees all cat fancy activities in the United Kingdom.

The first shows in the United States were exhibitions of Maine Coon cats that were staged in New England in the 1860s. One of the first all-breed

*Harrison W. Weir, *Our Cats and All About Them* (Tunbridge Wells, England: R. Clements, 1899).

expositions took place at Bunnell's Museum in New York in March 1881, a show that drew much attention from the press. But the exhibition of pedigreed cats became popular after the first "professional" show was held at Madison Square Garden in New York in May 1895. One hundred and seventy-five cats were shown, and the title of Best Cat was awarded to a tabby Maine Coon (the popular breed of the day) named Leo. It is recorded that Leo went on to win top honors at shows in Boston in 1897, 1898, and 1899, and was defeated by his son in 1900. The first American club, The Beresford Cat Club (named after Lady Beresford, founder of The Cat Club in England) was formed in Chicago in 1897. Some of the Beresford Club members founded the American Cat Association (ACA), the first American governing body, in 1904, and this was followed by the formation of the Cat Fanciers' Association (CFA) in 1906.

Modern Cat Shows and the Present-day Fancy

A little more than a century after the first show at the Crystal Palace, the cat fancy is well organized throughout the world. In each country where the breeding and showing of cats is organized, there are one or more governing bodies that (depending on the organization) have a number of local cat clubs under their jurisdiction, register pedigreed kittens and cats, recognize new varieties and breeds of cats, license cat shows, award championship certificates, approve show judges, and promote the welfare of cats. These associations do not usually stage the shows themselves but grant licenses to affiliated regional clubs to organize them.

There are nine governing bodies in North Ameri-

ca: American Cat Association (ACA), American Cat
Council (ACC), American Cat Fanciers Association
(ACFA), Canadian Cat Association (CCA), Cat Fan-
ciers' Association (CFA), Cat Fanciers' Federation
(CFF), Crown Cat Fanciers Federation (CROWN),
The International Cat Association (TICA), and
United Cat Federation (UCF). The Cat Fanciers'
Association is the largest and most influential organi-
zation, with over 600 member clubs in the United
States, Canada, and Japan. CFA has registered more
than 650,000 cats as well as more than 17,000
individual cattery names. The addresses of the North
American registering bodies will be found in Chapter
XVI, "Reference Material." All of these can be a real
source of information to the novice who wants to
learn more about pedigreed cats or cat shows.

The single registering body in Great Britain, the
Governing Council of the Cat Fancy (GCCF), is made
up of delegates from affiliated cat clubs throughout
the United Kingdom. There are three show categories in the UK: (1) Championship shows, governed
by GCCF rules and regulations, at which Challenge
Certificates (CCs) are awarded to winners of the open
classes considered worthy by the judges. Premier
Certificates are awarded to winners of the Open
Neuter classes; (2) Sanctioned shows, also governed
by GCCF rules and regulations, but where no Challenge Certificates are awarded; and (3) Exemption
shows, where standards are basically the same but less
stringent. Shows in the last category are ideal for
beginners, who can gain experience and learn show
procedures in a relaxed atmosphere. To earn a
Championship in the United Kingdom, a cat must
win Challenge Certificates at three shows under three

different judges. Premier Certificates must be won under three different judges for a neutered cat to achieve the title of Premier. To become a Grand Champion, a Champion cat must win three Grand Challenge Certificates from three separate judges. The titles have to be approved by the GCCF.

Although there are several small independent organizations in Europe which stage shows, the preeminent registering body is the Fédération Internationale Féline de l'Europe (FIFE), which controls cat clubs in twelve European countries: Austria, Belgium, Czechoslovakia, Denmark, Finland, France, Germany, Italy, the Netherlands, Norway, Sweden, and Switzerland. FIFE shows are all championship events at which cats are judged on a scale ranging from 45 to 100 points. A *Certificat d'Aptitude au Championnat* (CAC) is awarded to the winner (that earns at least 93 points) of the Open class for both sexes of each breed. A *Certificat d'Aptitude de Premier* (CAP) is awarded to the winners (that earn at least 93 points) of the Open Neuter classes of each breed. To become a European champion, a cat must win CACs at three shows under three different judges. CAPs likewise have to be earned under three different judges for a neutered cat to achieve Premier status. Once a cat earns its championship, it may compete in the Champion class, where a *Certificat d'Aptitude au Championnat International de Beauté* (CACIB) is awarded to the winner (that earns at least 95 points) for both sexes of each breed. To become an International Champion in Europe, a cat must win CACIBs under three different judges, and at least one of these has to be awarded in a separate country. International Champions of record may then compete in the

International Champion classes, where a *Certificat d'Aptitude au Grand Championnat International* (CAGCI) is awarded to the winners. Three CAGCIs qualify a cat to assume the title of Grand Champion International, the highest European award. There are registering bodies also in South Africa, Australia, and New Zealand.

Cat shows throughout the world are methodically organized and staged according to rules and regulations of the clubs that sponsor them. They are not the same, however, in every country. The breeds that are recognized, the breed standards, the show classes, and the manner of judging vary according to the policies of the licensing governing body.

Shows usually take place on weekends, and the size of the country frequently influences how they are scheduled. Many North American shows are two-day events, which are an advantage to exhibitors who travel great distances. Several shows, sponsored by two or more clubs in a given area, may take place on successive days at the same location. One of these may be an all-breed show, another may be restricted to one breed, a third might be a longhair specialty, while a fourth could be a shorthair specialty, and so forth. So many associations license shows in North America that it is possible to show cats practically every weekend. In the United Kingdom, South Africa, Australia, and New Zealand, most cat shows are one-day affairs. Two- and three-day shows are customary on the European continent, the longer events usually being international shows that attract exhibitors from other countries.

Shows can range in size from fewer than one hundred cats to large championship events with entries well over five hundred. The largest show in the world is that of the National Cat Club held every December in London, at which more than two thousand cats are entered. In the United States the shows of the Empire Cat Club in New York and the Santa Monica Cat Club in California are among the largest and most prestigious. The Felikat show in Amsterdam, Holland, and the Paris Cat Club show in France, are two of Europe's most important events. Persians constitute the largest classes at North American, British, and European shows. Next in order of popularity in this country are Himalayans, Siamese, Abyssinians, and Burmese.

Showing in the United States and Canada

You already know that there are several governing bodies in North America. Some of these are active from coast to coast and throughout Canada, while other associations are strong in certain parts of the United States and Canada. The largest registering body, as previously mentioned, is the Cat Fanciers' Association, whose activities are international in scope. Each association has a number of local clubs within its jurisdiction, composed of members who show and breed cats and are interested in promoting the welfare of all cats. Remember, the registering bodies do not stage shows themselves but grant licenses to regional clubs to hold them. And it is the dedicated members of the local clubs who make cat shows a reality. They work hard to make the show a success so that the profits can be donated to shelters and humane societies, to low-cost spay and neuter clinics, and to organizations that sponsor studies into the diseases and health problems of cats.

Getting Started in the Show World

You have much to learn if you are a novice to the cat fancy. Even though you have purchased a top-quality animal, you must learn how to get and keep your cat in show condition. Physically and mentally preparing an animal for show takes lots of time and effort. It is not something you do the day before exhibition. It does mean, however, providing your cat with optimum nutrition and the best health care, grooming, and handling from kittenhood.

Study and work hard to learn as much as you can about your breed. Breed books, books on general care, and cat magazines all contain valuable information for the cat fancy newcomer. Consider joining a local cat club to learn more about your particular breed or cats in general. Membership in a local club truly benefits an amateur, for the club's roster is usually composed of judges, breeders, and seasoned exhibitors. There is another pleasant benefit to be derived from being a club member: You have an opportunity to meet and socialize with people who share a love of cats.

The next step is to attend a few cat shows as a spectator, to watch how the exhibitors prepare their cats for judging, to observe the judging, and to become familiar with what will happen when your cat goes into the ring. To determine forthcoming shows in your area, contact your local cat club or consult the "Show Calender" section of *Cat Fancy* magazine or the "To Show and Go" column of *CATS Magazine,** which

---

*These magazines are usually available at newsstands and pet stores. To subscribe, see "Cat Magazines, Periodicals, and Yearbooks" in Chapter XVI.

list shows throughout the country by date, state, city, and location. The name, address, and phone number of a show's Entry Clerk will also appear, and from him or her you can learn the show hours and judging schedule.

Cat show judging is composed of three categories: Championship classes for registered entire (not altered) cats of recognized breeds; Non-Championship classes for pure-breed kittens from four to eight months of age, Household Pets, and others; and Premiership classes for registered spayed or neutered pure-breed cats. The entire cats are competing for wins leading to Championships and Grand Championships, while the altered cats compete for wins leading to Premier and Grand Premier titles. Purebreds are judged by a written standard that describes the ideal specimen of each breed, point by point, and is composed of sections defining a cat's general appearance, head, skull, nose, muzzle, chin, jaw, ears, eyes, neck, body, legs, paws, tail, coat, and colors, plus any points to be penalized or disqualified. The sections are assigned a certain point value, the total being 100. The reader acquires a word picture of each breed by putting the sections together. Written words are sometimes interpreted differently by people who read them, however, and this is one reason why the same cats do not win at every show.

The accepted breeds and the show rules and regulations vary slightly from association to association. The only sure way to know what is accepted is to write to the association sponsoring shows in your area and purchase a copy of their standards and show rules.

Advice for New Exhibitors

Let's suppose you are ready to show your cat. Here are some helpful hints to make your first show less intimidating.

Your decision to enter a show must be made well in advance. Entries for most shows close about four weeks before the actual show date to permit the Show Committee to set the entries in order, have the catalog printed, and arranging the caging areas. Once you have selected a particular show, write or call the Entry Clerk to receive an entry form and information flyer or Premium List. The flyer will specify (in addition to the date and location) the show hours, the judges for each breed, the classes that may be entered, the cost of entries, cage fees, health precautions, special disqualifications, the names of the Show Committee and official veterinarians, all other show regulations, and the entry closing date, together with the name and address of the person to whom entries should be sent. The flyer will also contain a list of sensibly priced motels and hotels located near the show site that will accept cats. If you plan to arrive the night before, reserve your room early because most of the listed motels fill up quickly.

Completing the Entry Form

Study the entry form carefully before you fill it out, for even the slightest error could cause your cat to be disqualified. Enter your cat's name, registration and association numbers, breed, sex, color, eye color, birth date, the names of its sire and dam, and the breeder's name. Much of this information appears on your registration certificate and should be copied verbatim.

The entry form will contain a space for you to indicate the class in which you are entering your cat. Classes are divided by breed, sex, and color. This part may be confusing for a novice, so don't be afraid to ask for help from a seasoned exhibitor friend or to check with the Entry Clerk. The following is a short description of the regular Championship classes:

Novice Class. For cats over eight months of age that have never won a first-place ribbon at a show licensed by the sponsoring association. At CFA shows the Novice classes were eliminated in 1978 and such cats must now be entered in the Open class.

Open Class. For cats over eight months of age that have won a first place blue ribbon in a sanctioned show but are not yet recognized Champions.

Champion Class. For cats that are recognized Champions according to the association's rules but are not yet confirmed Grand Champions.

Grand Champion Class. For cats that have earned by wins and points the title of Grand Champion according to the rules of the association.

The Premiership classes for spayed and neutered cats are the same as the regular Championship classes, except that these cats compete for Premier and Grand Premier titles.

The Non-Championship classes include:

Kitten Class. For kittens over four months of age and under eight months of age on the opening day of the show.

Household Pet Class. Competition is open to domestic cats of unknown origin or unregistered lineage. The number of cats competing in the Household

Pet class has increased substantially over the past few years. Many people feel that this is an opportunity to gain experience at showing before buying a purebred. Many seasoned exhibitors of pedigreed cats, in fact, got started by showing a household pet. The experience was such fun that they were bitten by the "show bug" and invested in a purebred. Household pets can be shown as kittens from four to eight months of age, and after that time they compete as adults. They may be any size, color, or physical appearance, but they must not be declawed. The deliberate breeding of mixed-breed cats is viewed with disfavor by most of the cat fancy, and many associations require household pets to be altered after eight months of age. There is no written standard for household pets, and their judging may vary slightly depending on the association. They are judged primarily on condition and grooming, although cleanliness, personality, and beauty play a part in the judge's decision. Beauty clearly is in the eye of the beholder in this class, for one never knows what might appeal to a certain judge, and that's what makes the Household Pet competition so popular and thoroughly enjoyable.

AOV (Any Other Variety) Class. For cats that are suitable by their lineage to be shown in the regular championship class, but for which there are no acceptable breed or color classes.

Provisional Breed Class. For breeds that have been granted provisional status in an association. This means that although judges have a chance to evaluate a new breed and grade cats according to a provisional standard, the breed is not yet in championship competition. This is the last important step, however, before a breed is advanced to championship status in an association.

Cats may also be entered "For Exhibition Only" and "For Sale," and these entries are not examined by the judges.

You will also notice space on the entry form to indicate your cage requirements and benching instructions, among others. Be sure to enter your name, address, and telephone number. Glance over the form to be sure all details are correct, then sign and date your entry. Mail the form with a check for the entry fees to the clerk before the closing date of the show.

When your entry is accepted, you will receive a confirmation before the show date, which will also acknowledge your cage requirements and special benching instructions. The exhibitor's card will list your cat's name, breed, and the classes in which it is entered, along with its identification number for the day. This will be your cat's benching number and its identification number in the show catalog. Be sure to take this information along with you to the show.

Preparing Your Cat

As soon as your entry is accepted, you must start preparing your cat for show. Every cat should be free of dead hair and dirt, and the longhairs must not be tangled or matted. If the coat is dirty, it should be bathed or dry-cleaned. Most exhibitors prefer to shampoo their cats several days before a show, to allow the natural oils to return to the fur. Chapter V, "The Well-groomed Cat," describes the necessary grooming tools and techniques for both shorthairs and longhairs. Clip the claws, if necessary, so that no one will be scratched. Examine the ears for signs of parasites or inflammation, and clean away any dirt or excess wax with a cotton ball moistened with warm water. Attend to the hair under the eyes if it is tear-stained. To be admitted to the show, your cat's inoculations must be current and the cat itself should look sparkling clean and exhibit no evidence of skin disease, external parasites, ear mites, or contagious disease.

Other Preparations

You will also want to prepare your cat's show cage in advance. The cages at most shows are decorated with drapes around three sides, plus a cushion or mat, litter box, toys, and other trappings that match or contrast with the cat's coat color. Here you can be

Russian Blues in a miniature room with brocade drapes and make-believe chandeliers.

as conservative as you please, or express your most creative decorating concepts. Most shows give awards for the best-decorated cages, and it's not unusual to see them transformed into miniature rooms for the cats, complete with wall-to-wall carpeting, bunk beds, various pieces of furniture, make-believe television consoles, and lighting fixtures! The entry form will include the size of the show cages to be used (these are somewhat uniform among associations) so that you can prepare the drape in advance. Don't forget a covering for the floor of the cage—a towel, fluffy bath mat, or piece of rug will do nicely.

Start making a list of items you must take to the show. You'll be amazed at how many articles you add as the big day approaches. Begin with grooming equipment and supplies, such as combs, brushes, nail trimmer, cornstarch or grooming powder, antistatic greaseless coat dressing, eye-stain remover, cotton balls, Q-Tips, chamois or silk scarf, and other items to make your cat look its best. The greater part of the grooming is always done at home before the show, but the seasoned exhibitor always carries a tack box of equipment and supplies for last-minute touch-ups or emergencies. Plan to take a portable grooming table if you own longhairs. Don't forget a few bath towels, paper towels, nontoxic cage disinfectant, premoistened towelettes (to clean and refresh yourself), and a roll of masking tape for broken wires on cages. Most shows provide disposable litter boxes and food and water dishes, but you may want to take along your own to make the cat feel at home. Some shows offer free food, but you are wise to take along your cat's regular food and bottles of your own water to avoid digestive upsets. And don't forget a few of your cat's favorite toys.

The Day of the Show

On the day of the show allow sufficient time to arrive at the show site, unload your equipment, check in, set up your cage, and prepare your cat in a comfortable and relaxed manner. If you rush about nervously, your cat may be a bit ruffled by judging time. Wear comfortable clothes and especially sensible shoes, as you will be standing on your feet a great deal throughout the day. If you are showing more than one cat, each should be transported to the show in a separate carrier, clearly labeled with your name and address.

When you arrive at the show, your cat will be examined by a veterinarian to determine that it is healthy. After you check in, the Entry Clerk will direct you to the correct benching area. Your cage will bear the identification number previously assigned to your cat when its entry was confirmed. If your cat is number 150, for instance, it will be listed under that number in the catalog and identified by that number in the benching area as well as in the judging ring. Numbers are always used to identify both cats and dogs at shows so the judges do not know the identities of the entries.

Disinfect your cage before you hang the drapes and arrange the inside. When everything (including the litter box) is in place, take your cat out of the carrier and place it inside the cage, where the familiar smells should have a comfortable effect. Spectators will undoubtedly stroll by to look at and inquire about your cat. This can be a delightful experience, but if it's kitty's first show, discourage strangers from poking fingers inside the cage.

Check the judging schedule to determine when your cat will be judged. Cats are usually judged four times by different judges, and the Show Committee carefully arranges the classes so that no cat is scheduled in more than one ring at a time. Take ample time to groom your cat and add the last minute touch-ups. During judging you will hear numbers called over the loudspeaker system. It is the exhibitor's responsibility to observe the progress in the judging rings and listen for judging calls. Most shows have a three-call restriction; if you don't take some action after the third call, the judging will begin without you.

The Judging Ring

When you hear your number being called, carry your cat promptly to the ring and put it inside the cage marked with your identification number. Do not

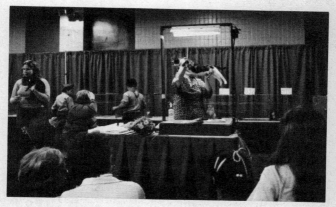

A judging ring at the Empire Cat Club Show, New York City.

talk to the judge. Leave the ring and go to the spectators' area at ringside to watch the judging.

The judge will take each cat out of its judging cage and put it on a table where he or she will thoroughly hand-examine the cat's conformation, muscle tone, skin, and coat texture and then assess its color. The judge will then place the cat back in its judging cage, wash his or her hands, and disinfect the table before handling and examining the next entry.

Let's pretend that you have entered a CFA show, and briefly explain how cats are judged. The judge starts with the Open classes. He or she examines all the Open males in a color class of a particular breed (White Persians, Black Persians, Seal Point Siamese, and so forth) and awards a first-place (blue), second-place (red), and third-place (yellow) ribbon. The cat that gets first place will also receive a red, white, and blue Winner's ribbon if the judge feels that he is worthy of becoming a Champion. As soon as the judge finishes looking over the males, the same procedure is repeated for the Open females in the color class of the same breed, ending with the awarding of a Winner's ribbon if the judge feels the first-place female is worthy of becoming a champion. The judge then examines the male Champions and awards first- through third-place ribbons to the best three males in the color class. The same procedure is repeated for the female Champions in the color class. The male and female Grand Champions are then judged in the same manner. When the total entry in the color class has been examined, the judge reviews them all and awards Best of Color Class (black) and Second Best of Color Class (white) ribbons.

Some breeds of cats are a single color (Bombays are

always brown, Korats are always blue, and so forth), while in others the color classes are arranged by the popularity of a particular breed. There are many white or black Persians and Seal-Point Siamese, so there are separate color classes for white Persians and black Persians, and for Seal-Point Siamese, for instance, but in other, less popular, breeds all the colors may be shown together in the same class.

After all the color classes in a breed have been judged, the judge will award a Best of Breed or Division (brown), Second Best of Breed or Division (orange), and Best Champion of Breed or Division (purple) ribbons. The word *division* applies solely to Persians. There are so many that they are separated into solid, smoke, shaded, tabby, and particolor divisions. Thus there will be a Best Abyssinian Champion or a Best Burmese Champion, but no Best Persian Champion and instead a Best Smoke Persian Champion, Best Tabby Persian Champion, and so on.

After the judge examines and assesses all the cats, he or she begins final judging to select the top cats in the show. Requirements differ slightly as to how a cat becomes a Champion or Grand Champion, and it is suggested that you consult the show rules of the various associations for more information. Four to six winner's ribbons awarded by three different judges are required by most associations (a cat needs six to become a CFA Champion). The title of Grand Champion is achieved by defeating other champions of the same or different breeds, for which a cat is awarded a certain number of points. As few as 15 points are necessary to reach Grand status in some small associations, while most breeds must accumulate 200 points to become a Grand Champion in CFA. The requirements for Premier are generally the same as for Champion, but in the CFA, 150 points instead of 200 are necessary for Grand Premier. The points are converted into Grand Ribbons.

XI All About the Traveling Cat

Sooner or later you will come up against the problems of holidays and travelling. Most cats welcome a change of surroundings, and provided you carry it in a cosy travel basket and attend to its normal needs, you will probably have little trouble. Some cats, however, hate all forms of travel, and if yours is one of these, do not attempt to take it with you.

　　　　—John R. Gilbert,
　　　　　　Cats, Cats, Cats, Cats, Cats, Cats

If you are planning a vacation, you must decide what to do with your cat. Will the cat accompany you on the trip, will it be cared for at home, or go to a boarding cattery? Traveling with a cat can be a delightful experience, although possibly a little ticklish at first until things run smoothly. Long journeys can cause great psychological and physical stress. Cats that are not used to traveling sometimes become unsettled when they leave places that they consider to be their territory. Every cat has a regular daily routine. Away from home that normal procedure changes, and new surroundings, unfamiliar people, changing climate, or different food and water can upset your cat. Here are some points to ponder before deciding to take along your four-legged friend:

Is your cat a good traveler?   Any trip will be more pleasant when your cat is:
- In good health.   Kittens, nervous cats, very old cats, and those in poor health may not adjust comfortably to travel.
- Well behaved in a car or plane.
- Seldom or never affected by motion sickness.
- Not in heat or pregnant.
- Not destructive.

   If you can't answer a majority of these questions positively, consider boarding your cat in a cattery or leaving it in the care of a reliable friend or pet sitter.

What time of year will you travel?   Spring and fall are ideal times to travel with pets. Travel in oppressive heat or extreme cold is not a good idea. If you do drive in hot weather, however, provide adequate ventilation inside the car, as prolonged exposure to high temperatures can cause heatstroke in cats. Those with very short, depressed noses, heavy coats, or heart or kidney problems, as well as kittens and geriatric or obese cats are especially susceptible to heat prostration. When confined in poorly ventilated enclosures in hot weather, where interior temperatures soar within minutes, such as a closed car parked in direct sunlight or a cramped carrying case, cats are subject to suffocation and death!

Where will you go?   Cats are welcome almost everywhere in the world. Travel within the United

States (except Hawaii, where pets are quarantined 120 days) presents few difficulties. Motels, hotels, mobile-home parks, and campgrounds throughout the country accept cats, and commercially prepared food, supplies, and veterinary care are available even in the smallest of towns. If you're planning a visit to a foreign country, check with that nation's embassy in Washington, D.C., or its nearest consulate weeks in advance to learn if your cat will be permitted to enter and precisely what documents are required. Most foreign countries require a health certificate and proof of rabies vaccinations. A few countries (including the Soviet Union) do not admit cats; others quarantine them for periods ranging from ten days to six months (included in the latter are United Kingdom countries and some Caribbean islands). Other nations require import permits or licenses, which must be obtained in advance. These must often be validated by a state USDA veterinarian, and then legalized by the country's consulate. It's sometimes difficult to find a variety of prepared cat foods in most foreign countries; plan to take a supply of dry or canned food and bottled water to last the trip. When you do travel abroad with a pet, however, there's no need to worry about a language barrier. Fanciers are the same the world over, and nothing encourages conversation or performs introductions between strangers faster than a cat or dog!

Advance Preparations

If you definitely decide to take your cat along with you, some advance planning will help to assure a safe and comfortable journey.

1. Medical Requirements.   Visit your veterinarian several weeks before your trip to be sure that your cat has all necessary vaccinations. Most American states require a health certificate and proof of rabies vaccination. If your cat travels with you in your car, you probably will never be asked for these certificates, but if you are traveling by plane or shipping the cat via air cargo, you will have to produce these papers before the airline will accept your pet. Mention the trip to your veterinarian; he'll probably offer some good advice on keeping your cat healthy en route.

2. Be able to identify your cat.   The value of positive identification is discussed in Chapter XII. Should your cat become lost or stolen, this information can help locate it.

3. If you travel by air, reserve space for your cat in the passenger section or baggage compartment of the plane in advance.

4. Purchase a well-ventilated carrying case for the cat, large enough for it to stand up or stretch out in. Many types of cat carriers are available, from corrugated cardboard (inexpensive) to light-weight molded plastic crates (expensive) approved by airlines for shipping pets. The type you choose should depend on how often you expect to use the carrier and the method of transportation. Your cat's comfort and safety are of prime importance. After you purchase a

carrier, it's a good idea to precondition your cat to it weeks before the trip. Place the carrier in a conspicuous place, open the door (or lid), and let him go in and out at will for a few days. Then put a cushion or a favorite toy inside. Eventually put the cat inside and close the door (or lid) while you stay close by for reassurance. A few weeks of positive reinforcement and the carrier will be your cat's security blanket away from home.

5. Cats usually do not become carsick as often as dogs, but if your cat is a frightened or nervous traveler, ask your veterinarian to prescribe a tranquilizer. Try the medication at home several days before you depart for effectiveness and/or possible side effects.

6. Plan an itinerary. Get a written confirmation that your chosen vacation spot (resort hotel, motel, campground, national park, mobile-home park and so forth) will accept your cat. Many popular tourist attractions, including Disneyland in California and Disney World and Cypress Gardens in Florida, provide boarding at reasonable rates for tourists' pets. They will water and feed your cat or dog, and even keep it overnight. If you stop at motels along the way, make reservations in advance. Nationwide chains that accept pets include Days Inns, Econo-Travel Motor Hotels, Hilton, Holiday Inns, Howard Johnson's, Marriott, Motel 6, Quality Inns, Ramada Inns, Rodeway Inns, and Sheraton. Other chains, including Best Western, Hyatt, Radisson, Treadway Inns, and Western International, accept pets at some but not all

locations. Most of these have toll-free reservation numbers, and one call is all that is necessary to learn if a particular location accepts cats and to make a reservation. (Dial 800-555-1212 to learn any toll-free number.)

Directories and Guidebooks

Directories and guidebooks listing additional hotels and motels, campgrounds, trailer parks, and national parks that accept pets include:

Touring With Towser.   A 64-page directory of motels and hotels in the United States and Canada. Although the book is directed to dog people, it's just as helpful to cat owners. Send $1.25 to Gaines TWT, P. O. Box 1007, Kankakee, Illinois 60901.

Country Inns of America.   Separate editions for Upper New England, Lower New England, New York and Mid-Atlantic, and California. Published by Holt, Rinehart & Winston.

Rand McNally Campground and Trailer Park Guide.   A complete camping directory including information for over 19,000 public and private parks in the United States, Canada, and Mexico.

Rand McNally Campgrounds and Trailer Parks.   Separate editions for the East, Northeast, Southeast, Midwest, and West.

Rand McNally National Park Guide.

Mobil Travel Guides.   Separate editions for the Northeast, Southeast, Middle Atlantic, Great Lakes, Northwest and Great Plains, Southwest and South Central, and California and Western States.

Sunset Western Campsites.

AAA Regional Guidebooks and *AAA Camping and Trailer-ing*. Published by the American Automobile Association and available at no charge to AAA members.

To learn which national parks accept pets, you can also contact the United States Department of Parks or state park services. Visitors to Canada can obtain a great deal of tourist information at no cost. The Department of Travel and Tourism of each province publishes a directory of hotels, motels, and resorts, listing their addresses, rates, services, and if they accept pets.

The Traveling Cat Owner's Responsibilities

Your obligations to your cat and to other people are as important while you are away as they are at home. Respecting these common-sense rules of etiquette will make your cat welcome all over the world.

- Don't leave your cat alone in a strange room for long periods of time. Even the meekest of cats can become noisy or destructive when it is lonely or frightened.
- Unless your cat is confined in a travel carrier when you go out, place a "Do Not Disturb" sign on the door or confine the cat in the bathroom, with a clearly lettered notice on the door of the cat's presence. Speak to the maid if you can, and advise her whether it is safe or not for her to enter your room.
- Question the maid about the use of disinfectants for cleaning the room. Many common commercial disinfectants are extremely poisonous to cats

and should not be sprayed or mopped about the room, especially around the cat's litter tray.

- Keep the hotel/motel room clean. Bring along a supply of medium (or eight-gallon-capacity) polyethylene garbage bags. Line the wastebaskets with them before you dispose of empty cat food cans or change the litter. Dispose of the bags daily.

- Pack an old towel or bath mat to lay under the litter tray. When your cat tracks litter out of the tray, keep the room cleaner by shaking it back into the box.

- If your cat is leash-trained, ask the manager or bell captain where it can be walked. Stay away from gardens, swimming pools, or the beach. Don't take the cat into the restaurant, cocktail lounge, or recreational areas.

- Campgrounds, mobile-home parks, and national parks maintain strict pet laws. Become familiar with and observe them. They were devised for your cat's safety and protection as well as a courtesy to others.

Travel by Motor Vehicle

A cat's first ride in a car or recreational vehicle can be a disaster. Too often cats become frightened by the new experience of being confined inside a moving object, the speeding up or slowing down of the vehicle, or the noise. Under any circumstances it is a serious mistake to wait until vacation time and discover these problems exist. The first rule of road travel, therefore, is to let your cat gain experience in gradual stages, so that when you do take a long trip, it will be a seasoned traveler.

Devise a safe way of taking your cat to and from the vehicle. The best solutions are to (a) wear a collar or harness on the cat with leash securely attached and held firmly in your hand, or (b) put the cat in a carrier. Never carry an unleashed cat in your arms. A loud noise can frighten the cat (especially if it lives indoors), and it can jump out of your arms and escape.

Once inside the vehicle, the next consideration is the cat's safety. Never allow your cat to roam about a car at will, especially if it's nervous or frightened. Unrestrained cats are a constant danger. Should you have to brake to a sudden halt, your cat could be thrown off the seat and seriously injured. Worse yet, its hyperactivity—such as jumping into the driver's lap, or crawling under the dashboard and squeezing around the driver's feet, or touching the brake or accelerator—could cause an accident in which family members would suffer. Keep your cat under control by wearing a collar and leash and sitting it in someone's lap, or by using a roomy cat carrier. A carrier generally is the best solution because the cat should feel more secure if it has been preconditioned to the travel case. If your cat cries or tries to scratch the carrier as you drive, ignore it. Turn on the radio or pop a cassette in the tape deck and hope it will calm down. Talking to the cat, letting it out of the carrier, or tapping on the case's side will most likely only make it worse when it learns how to get your attention. Wear a collar on your cat while it's inside the carrier, then you can snap on the leash as soon as you open the door or lid.

Begin the cat's training with short drives. Drive through the neighborhood, to the market, or to drop off or collect school children. Each time you stop, be absolutely sure that your cat is leashed and held firmly, or inside a carrier, before you open a window or a door. An overnight trip in a recreational vehicle should be a prerequisite to a long-distance journey. After a few drives your cat should adjust easily to a variety of experiences on the road, its fears and anxieties should pass, and it should tolerate, if not totally enjoy, riding. But if your cat turns out to be one of the few that cannot ride without becoming frightened or nauseated, don't despair. Ask your veterinarian to prescribe a tranquilizer or motion-sickness preparation, depending on the problem.

For more information, write to the ASPCA and request a copy of their bulletin entitled *Ten Easy Steps to Remember When Traveling with Your Pet by Car* (see "Free and Low Cost Literature for Cat Owners" in Chapter XIV).

Your Cat's Luggage

Don't forget to take along supplies and favorite things to make your cat's trip more comfortable, such as:

- Collar or harness (with identification securely attached) and leash.
- Favorite toys.
- A favorite cushion, rug, or blanket.
- Cat food (plus spoon and can opener, if necessary). Pack enough food for the entire trip, to avoid changes in diet. Feeding new food can cause digestive upsets and result in vomiting and diarrhea.
- Drinking water. Pack a container of water from

home. Changes in water can also cause digestive upsets.

- Food and water bowls.
- Paper towels and pet deodorant to clean unexpected accidents.
- Flea/tick preventatives. These are absolutely necessary if you are traveling in hot, humid weather. Wearing a flea collar on your cat, or spraying it lightly upon arrival in a hotel room, will help keep off any fleas or ticks deposited by previous feline guests.
- Litter tray (disposable cardboard litter boxes are ideal for travel).
- Supply of kitty litter.
- Kitty scoop.
- Plastic trash bags.
- Instant dry shampoo for cats.
- Comb or brush.
- Necessary medications.
- Premoistened towelettes (for cleaning your hands after attending to the cat).

Points to Observe En Route

1. Feed the cat a light diet about six hours before the trip and give only small sips of water to drink before starting out.
2. Provide adequate ventilation if your car is not air-conditioned, and ensure sufficient space. If the cat stays inside a carrier, don't wedge it between luggage that restricts air flow or space. Keep luggage secure against unexpected shifting during sudden stops.
3. Never put your cat in the trunk of your car. It

could suffocate or die from carbon-monoxide poisoning.

4. Stop frequently to let the cat exercise or use its litter box. A good location for a disposable litter tray is under the dashboard on the passenger's side in a sedan, or in the back of a station wagon. If you store the tray in the trunk of your car and must get out to fetch it, pull into a remote section of a rest area or parking lot, away from traffic, if possible. Be sure a leash is hooked onto your cat's collar and securely held in your hand before opening the door and letting the cat out.

5. If you must leave your cat alone in the car, park in the shade whenever possible. Open the windows slightly for ventilation, but not enough for the cat to escape if it's loose in the car. Check the car often in hot weather, and *hurry back.*

Travel By Bus and Train

Greyhound, Trailways, and other interstate bus lines will not accept pets except Seeing Eye dogs. Amtrak, which provides nationwide rail service, once accepted cats in both the passenger and baggage compartments, but discontinued that policy early in 1977 when a new U.S. government statute laid down stringent rules for space requirements and temperature regulation. Some smaller railroads do permit cats, but they almost always have to ride in the baggage sections which have no temperature controls.

Travel By Plane

Cats travel either as baggage or air cargo on United States and foreign airlines. When a cat travels with its owner, it is considered excess baggage and rides either in the passenger section or baggage compartment, where it will be unloaded with other baggage at the airport. When a cat travels alone, it goes as air cargo and arrives at the freight terminal for pickup.

Traveling By Air With Your Cat

Most airline companies permit one pet in the First Class section and another one in the Tourist section per flight. The pet must be small enough to fit into a carrier about twelve inches square that is stored under the seat. After takeoff, depending on the flight attendants, you might be able to hold your cat in your lap for short periods if it is well-behaved. If the airline does not allow pets in the passenger sections, your cat must travel as excess baggage. In either case, make reservations well in advance. Although each airline has specific rules about pets traveling in the cabin or baggage areas, a general outline of what is involved is explained in a TWA booklet entitled *Consumer Information About Air Travel with Pets*. The twelve-page booklet can be obtained at TWA ticket counters or most travel agencies at no charge.

Several details should be attended to before you depart. The first is to see that the cat's medical records and vaccinations are current. If the cat will travel in the cabin, you probably will be able to purchase an inexpensive carrying case that fits under the seat from the airline. If it will travel in the baggage compartment, the cat should go in a sturdy shipping crate which you supply, or possibly rent or buy from the airline (See "Shipping Your Cat as Air Cargo" for more information about shipping crates.). The advantage of owning your own crate, as previously mentioned, is that you can precondition your cat before the trip. On the day of departure, give your cat a light meal about six hours before the trip, then give only small sips of water to drink before starting out.

Consult "Your Cat's Luggage" and pack all the necessary essentials you will need for the trip. When you arrive at the airport, don't let the attendant at the check-in counter send the crate through the conveyor system. Tip someone, if necessary, to carry the crate to the baggage area.

Shipping Your Cat as Air Cargo

When a cat travels alone on a plane, shipping methods differ, and a comfortable trip depends considerably on advance preparations made by the shipper (you).

Pets shipped on airlines and other interstate public carriers are protected by federal laws designed to reduce the stress and suffering caused by the rigors of long-distance shipments. Most of the rules affect commercial shippers, dealers, and laboratories regulated by the U.S. Department of Agriculture, but pet owners are affected too. Some of the rules involving personal pets include:

Age: Cats and dogs must be at least eight weeks old and must have been weaned for at least five days.

Temperature: Government regulations prohibit the shipment of cats and dogs in temperatures below or above certain degrees.

Cages: Cages or other shipping containers must meet stringent standards for size, ventilation, strength, sanitation, and handling. They must be:

- Large enough for the animal to stand up, turn around, and lie down with normal posture and body movements.
- Strong enough to withstand shipping, free of interior protrusions that could cause injury, and with adequate access to the animal.
- Constructed with a solid, leakproof bottom, and provided with litter or absorbent material unless a wire or other nonskid floor separates the animal from the bottom.
- Ventilated adequately on at least two opposite sides so that the air flows through both the upper and lower parts of the walls. There must be projecting rims or knobs on the outside to keep ventilation from being blocked by adjacent cargo.
- Fitted with handles or grips for proper handling, and marked LIVE ANIMAL with arrows indicating the upright position.

Other regulations cover food and water during long trips, scheduling, and medical requirements. A copy of the Federal regulations covering animal shipments may be obtained by writing Animal Care, APHIS, U.S. Department of Agriculture, Hyattsville, Maryland 20782.

Crates come in a variety of materials: fiberboard, wire, lightweight plastic, wood, and metal. Cardboard and fiberboard are not suitable for air cargo shipment. Wire crates may be used for car travel because they offer good ventilation in warm weather, but they are not suggested for air cargo shipment. The most popular type of shipping carrier, approved by many domestic and foreign airlines, is made of lightweight molded plastic. When not used for transportation, the lower half of the carrier can be detached and used as a bed.

Your shipping carrier should have ample ventilation holes on each side, high enough to let in fresh air and keep your cat from being exposed to a draft. There should be no openings on the top of the crate, as fragments can fall through. The door should have close-set vertical metal bars to allow your cat to look out but not escape. This is an important feature because an animal may become frightened if it cannot see outside. The door latch should be sturdy and constructed in a way that your cat cannot open it.

Advance preparation can facilitate the handling of a cat en route and help to reduce the physical and psychological stress of the trip. Follow this step-by-step procedure:

- Secure a health certificate and proof of rabies vaccination (if necessary) in advance.
- Make reservations as soon as possible. Many airlines limit the number of pets to be shipped on one flight.
- Plan the flight carefully. Book a direct flight from point of origin to point of destination. If that isn't possible, select the flight with the least number of stops or transfers. Avoid shipping in hot weather, but if you must, book an evening flight. The quality of service varies from airport to airport, unfortunately, and some pets in shipping crates have been left sitting in the sun, rain, and snow between flights. Certain large airports, such as Kennedy in New York and International in Los Angeles, provide kennel facilities staffed by trained personnel to care for pets during long stopovers.

- If you ship to a foreign country, don't schedule the cat to arrive at its destination on a national holiday or over a weekend. Customs offices will be closed and your cat may have to wait several days (in its shipping crate perhaps) to be allowed to enter.
- Check the shipping crate several days before the trip to see that everything is in good condition.
- Place shredded newspaper in the bottom of the carrier to absorb urine and to insulate against the cold.
- Add a favorite toy to make the cat feel more secure.
- Mark the top and sides of the crate prominently with the following: LIVE CAT—DO NOT PLACE IN SAME COMPARTMENT AS DRY ICE. (Fumes from dry ice used to preserve perishables in transit can be deadly.) Attach clearly printed labels with the consignee's name, address, and telephone number, plus your name, address, and telephone number as the shipper. Use a pen that doesn't smear or run in damp weather. Arrows should indicate the top of the crate.
- Place health certificates and other documents inside a heavy manila envelope marked IMPORTANT PAPERS, and securely attach it to the top of the crate.
- If the trip will be long, include dry food in a Ziploc plastic bag along with feeding instructions.
- See that the carrier contains a water dish that can be filled without opening the door. Don't fill the dish before the trip. The water will only spill and your cat may become wet and chilled.
- See that an identification tag and, when applica-

ble, rabies tag and current license are securely attached to the cat's collar.

- Feed a light meal about six hours before departure. Give a small amount of water to drink before you put the cat inside the carrier.
- Tranquilize only by veterinarian's advice.
- Purchase travel insurance for the cat. The value of a household pet is generally the purchase price paid, but a cat used for breeding or a show Champion is worth considerably more.
- Arrive at the airport well in advance of scheduled departure time.
- Stay at the airport until the plane takes off, if possible.
- If you don't stay until departure, leave your name and telephone number with the agent and ask to be notified if the flight is delayed or canceled.
- Advise the consignee of the carrier's name, flight number, freight bill number, airport, and scheduled time of arrival.

If you are receiving a cat:

- Check with the airline to determine the exact time of arrival.
- Ask the freight agent to have the cat taken off the plane as soon as possible.
- Do not let the cat out of its carrier until you arrive at home.
- Notify the sender that the cat has arrived safely.
- Offer food and water at home.
- Check the cat carefully for the next few days. If anything seems abnormal, consult a veterinarian.

Pet Shipping Services

Several agencies throughout the country offer door-to-door pet shipping services. These are almost always listed under "Pet Transporting" in the classified section of the telephone directory. Some firms that offer nationwide and international services include:

Flying Fur Pet Travel Service, 133-50 41st Avenue, Flushing, New York 11355. Regional offices: Miami, St. Petersburg, Buffalo, Syracuse, Akron, New Orleans, Houston, Salt Lake City, Omaha, San Francisco, San Jose, Oakland, Van Nuys, and San Diego.

World-Wide Pet Transport, 96-01 Metropolitan Avenue, Forest Hills, N.Y. 11375.

Each company will send a brochure upon request. The American Boarding Kennels Association (ABKA) offers a *Pet Shipping Directory* of businesses which provide pick up and delivery of pets at the nation's major airports. The directory also includes shipping tips, the USDA requirements for shipping crates, and state health requirements for traveling cats. For more information, contact the American Boarding Kennels Association, 311 North Union Boulevard, Colorado Springs, Colorado 80909.

Guidelines for Choosing a Cat Sitter or Boarding Cattery

If your cat will not travel along, you are faced with two alternatives: to leave it in someone's care or to board it at a cattery. The former may be a reliable friend, a relative, or professional pet sitter who will either take your cat into his or her home, or live in your home while you are away. Professional cat sitters usually charge modest fees when they board cats in their own homes, and a higher rate when they live in your home. There are many ways to locate a reliable cat sitter: through recommendations of friends, your veterinarian or professional groomer; by contacting senior citizens' organizations or college employment bureaus; and by consulting the classified telephone directory under "Pet Exercising and Feeding Services."

Interview each prospective sitter thoroughly; ask for references and check them carefully, especially when a stranger will be living in your home. Once you choose someone, it's best to work out financial arrangements in advance and put them in writing. Don't devise an elaborate agreement, merely something short that protects both parties against misunderstandings.

If your cat goes to the sitter's home, he or she will probably require proof of vaccination and perhaps a health certificate from your veterinarian. Take along the cat's food and water bowls, litter tray, bed or basket, and some favorite toys to make it feel at home. Some sitters will ask you to bring a supply of food; others will ask about your cat's diet and buy the food themselves. The sitter may also ask for a small cash advance to cover the cost of veterinary treatment and medications, should they become necessary.

When the sitter stays at your house, he or she should arrive at least a day or two in advance. Ideally, you should acquaint the sitter with your cat's eating, exercising and sleeping habits, and any temperament peculiarities while you are still at home. Tell the sitter about any medical problems the cat may have, and explain how to deal with them. If the cat is receiving regular medication, you may have to demonstrate how to administer it. Point out where all the necessary supplies are kept, and specify any plants, knick-knacks, antiques, or rooms that the cat should stay away from. Write down all pertinent information, and discuss everything with the sitter before you leave. You may wish to arrange for other services, such as collecting mail, answering the phone, or watering plants. Provide an ample supply of cat food and litter. Leave some cash to cover the cost of veterinary treatment or medications, should they become necessary. Write down the phone number of your veterinarian (also his address), the Poison Control Center, and the police and fire departments. In fact, if your cat is receiving medical treatment for any problem, inform the veterinarian that you are going away and that a sitter will be caring for the cat. Leave a copy of your itinerary and where you can be reached at all times in case of an emergency. If you are unreachable, provide the name, address, and phone number of a relative or friend.

The second choice is to board your cat at a cattery (an establishment dealing exclusively with cats) or a kennel (a place handling both dogs and cats). You can locate such businesses in the classified telephone directory or by asking for recommendations from your veterinarian, local cat club, humane organization, or from friends who have favorably boarded cats (word of mouth is wonderful advertising). Humane groups may not wish to recommend specific boarding facilities, but they can often point you in the right direction.

There are ethical professional catteries and kennels

in cities and the suburbs and country today, but finding the right one requires some effort for there is little standardization throughout the country. Commercial boarding catteries and kennels are licensed and regulated by state laws in most areas, but the enforcement varies greatly. Some states are strict while others are casual about regulations. The best method is to visit several establishments, take a guided tour, and then decide. Be wary, incidentally, of places that refuse to show you their facilities. Phone for an appointment. When you arrive, look carefully at the following:

Construction:　Is the cattery or kennel well built or a structural hazard?

Sanitation:　Once inside, use your nose and your eyes. Suffocating, offensive odors indicate unsatisfactory sanitation. Are the sleeping quarters and exercise areas clean? Of course, you expect to see feces in litter trays, but one glance will tell you whether it's been piling up. Does every cat have a bed, a litter tray, and food and water bowls? Does every cat have fresh drinking water? A totally indoor cattery should have substantial air circulation to disperse airborne germs, or some accommodation to let in fresh air and sunshine.

Comfort:　Every cat should have ample room to move about. Kennels that accept cats should have adequate facilities for handling them and should not keep them in dog enclosures. Every cat in an indoor/outdoor cattery should have its own cubicle and exercise area. Each should be completely enclosed and as escape-proof as possible. The cats should be isolated from other animals; the sounds or sight of other pets can be upsetting.

Maintenance: Are there enough employees to care for the number of cats boarded? Do the attendants seem cheerful and handle their charges with care? Or are there one or two employees who seem testy and fatigued? Too few employees might indicate a lack of attention to the boarding pets.

Diet: Does the cattery or kennel feed one specific diet or a variety of commercially prepared foods? Do they stock the brand your cat is currently eating? If not, can you supply your own food at your expense? Weight loss is a common problem of boarding animals. They miss their owners and pick at their food or may not eat anything for days. A dietary change is not wise at this time. How many times a day are the cats fed? Is the feeding schedule compatible with your cat's routine?

Medications: Will the cattery or kennel assume the responsibility of giving necessary medications on schedule?

Veterinary care: Does the cattery/kennel have a working relationship with a veterinarian in case of accident or sickness?

Health: For the safety of your cat and other boarders, the cattery/kennel should demand proof that vaccinations are current. Be sure your cat is immunized for the feline upper respiratory diseases. Unfortunately, these can be very contagious in boarding establishments.

Grooming: Does the cattery/kennel groom regularly?

Are the cats clean and tangle-free when they go home?

Rates: Are the boarding charges commensurate with other reliable area facilities? Be cautious of any place that offers special discounts or excessively low rates to get business.

As soon as you select a cattery or kennel, reserve boarding space in advance, especially during the summer months or on weekends or holidays. If your cat has never been away from home overnight, being sent to a boarding facility can seem a frightening experience. Find out whether you can bring along any of the cat's personal belongings. Its basket or bed, a toy or two, or a favorite blanket will make the adjustment easier. Before you leave, prepare an information sheet for the cattery listing any special feeding instructions; necessary medications; the name, address, and phone number of your veterinarian; your itinerary, and where you can be reached in an emergency. Don't forget to attach identification securely to your cat's collar. Inform the cattery when you will return and call for your cat. If you extend your stay, notify the boarding establishment at once.

XII Vital Information for Cat Lovers

The real martyrdom of cats is that of strays in towns. To what extent are these the victims of human selfishness? There are the cats put out on the streets because their owners are going on holiday; there are those who, kept with their mother—just for her milk— are abandoned when they grow up: all those cats who, weary of hiding all day, of avoiding cars, dogs, and brutal people, come together instinctively to find refuge in the meager thickets of public parks, behind fences in empty lots or houses under construction. Then, with the coming of winter, how ever do they bear the cold, rain and hunger?

—Fernand Méry,
Her Majesty the Cat

How to Protect Your Cat

Millions of cats and dogs are lost or stolen every year, and experts estimate that 70 percent of all missing pets are never found by or returned to their rightful owners. Anyone who has ever lost a pet knows the heartbreak of trying to find it. You blame

yourself for not taking adequate precautions to protect the pet, and worry about what will become of the
companion that has known only affection all its life.
Death is possibly easier to acknowledge than the
agony of worrying if a lost pet is cold and hungry, if it
is caught in a trap or other enclosure, if it is lying
injured somewhere, or if it has been mutilated by a
vehicle or a cat- or dog-hater.

Stolen Pets

The stealing of pets is a serious problem in the
United States. Every day in every community professional pet thieves operate individually or in teams.
And often cat and dog owners make a pet thief's job
easy. They are totally unaware that such people exist
and don't realize that the market for stolen pets is
profitable and that the well-cared-for family pet is an
easy victim.

Pets are stolen for many reasons. If an animal is
valuable, thieves might kidnap it to demand ransom.
After the ransom is paid, the pet usually is returned
to its owner. Some thieves steal cats and dogs and
make it seem as though the pets escaped by themselves. Then when advertisements appear in the "Lost
and Found" column of the local newspapers, the
thieves call and claim the rewards.

Stolen pedigreed cats and dogs are frequently
transferred from one city to another with falsified
papers, then resold to new owners or bred at every
opportunity for the money to be made. Many animals
are sold at auctions and end up in research laboratories. Cruel "bunchers" (ruthless middlemen who
gather pets from various sources) travel through
towns in vans, looking for pure-breed cats and dogs.
Females in season are often brought along to entice

males. Children are often questioned as to the where-abouts of strays, or they are encouraged to pick up strays and deliver them to bunchers for a small fee. Once the buncher collects his quota, the pets are taken to a remote location where they are half-starved and kept under filthy conditions. Here some are sold and others go to auctions or trade days where their buyers' names are seldom recorded. As ownership changes hands everyone gets their percentage, as long as the poor animal survives!

HOW TO PROTECT YOUR CAT FROM BECOMING LOST OR STOLEN.   The majority of pets are lost because of human carelessness. With a little common sense you can keep your cat as safe as possible by observing the following precautions:

1. *A cat should never be allowed to go outside alone.* As the number of vehicles on highways and other city and suburban hazards increases, it is no longer safe for a cat to roam free, even in most rural areas. Today very few cats that are allowed out of their homes on their own ever live out their natural lives. If you want to take your cat outside, put it in a carrying case, or train it to walk on a leash (Chapter VII). Even holding an unleashed cat in your arms outdoors can be unsafe. The cat can be terrified by other animals or powerful sounds and leap from your arms and run away.

2. Put screens in every window to prevent your cat from falling or jumping out.

3. Cats are incredibly adept at slipping out doors as you close them. Any time an entranceway is opened and closed, check to see that your cat is inside. This is important too if you live in a city

apartment building. When a cat sneaks out of an apartment door, it can become lost in the stair-wells or trapped in laundry or trash rooms. If the cat is found by a pet-hating tenant, doorman, or porter, or if it slips outside to the street, it could mean death.

4. Most cats adore crawling into empty grocery bags, heavy-duty trash bags, department store boxes and cartons. Don't throw away any con-tainer before checking to see if your cat is inside.

5. Don't leave your cat alone in a car, even when it is inside a carrying case. Pet thieves canvass shopping malls and parking lots searching for pets in cars, and they are ingenious at opening locked doors.

6. If your cat will not be used for breeding, have it spayed or castrated. Altered animals are less likely to stray.

7. Be able to identify your cat positively. Should it be stolen and the thief later apprehended, you may have to prove that you are the cat's legal owner.

IDENTIFYING YOUR CAT.   One of the most important factors in providing safety for a lost cat is identifica-tion. These are ways to identify your cat:

IDENTIFICATION CHART AND SNAPSHOTS.   It was sug-gested in Chapter III that you file your cat's important papers (pedigree; health and vaccination certificates) in a single place. Add to that file *now* a complete written description of your cat and other facts (scars, tattoos) to help trace and identify it should it become lost. Take clear color snapshots: a closeup of the head and a profile view of the body. Photograph each side if they are differently marked. Have extra photographs printed, and file them with your cat's important papers. Replace kitten photographs as soon as your cat matures.

COLLAR/IDENTIFICATION TAG. If your cat does slip outside occasionally or go wandering, the right kind of collar with a securely attached identification tag can save its life. Most experts recommend an elasticized or "break away" collar to minimize the danger of strangulation should the cat get snagged on something. (Chapter III contains more information about cat collars.) Some type of identification—either an engraved metal tag or a tiny metal tube with an identification form to be filled in with pen—clearly stating your name, address, and telephone number should be fastened to the collar. If your cat wears only a flea collar, print your name, address, and phone number directly on the collar with permanent ink. (Do remember, though, that flea collars are not elasticized.)

LICENSE. Cat licensing regulations are in effect in several cities throughout the United States. If cats are not licensed in your area, and your pet is a real vagabond, consider buying a dog license, unusual as it may seem. States that license animals keep records, and this is a potential source of identification if your cat gets lost. Record the license number with your cat's personal papers, and when the license is renewed, make a note of the new number immediately.

TATTOOING. If a lost cat is found by a sympathetic person or an animal shelter, an identification tag and license will hasten its return. But an identification chart, snapshots, tags, and licenses are sometimes not enough. Professional pet thieves can remove tags and dispose of them. And as soon as a cat loses its tag and license, it loses its identity. The only positive means of identification is a tattoo. The process can be done quickly (it takes about three minutes) and painlessly (it requires no anesthesia) with an electric needle by a veterinarian, authorized tattoo registry agent, or through humane societies, 4-H clubs or other groups that sponsor tattoo clinics. It is permanent and lasts for the life of the cat. No dealer or research establishment will accept a tattooed animal; they are subject to heavy fines if a stolen pet can be positively identified.

As soon as your cat is tattooed, the number should be recorded with a national registration organization. The oldest established registry in the United States is the National Dog Registry. Founded in 1966, NDR is endorsed and used by the Humane Society of the United States, Guiding Eyes for the Blind, various state conservation councils, as well as thousands of individual dog and cat owners. NDR does not actually do the tattooing but refers cat owners to nearby authorized agents who, for a fee, tattoo an owner's nine-digit Social Security number inside a cat's ear or on its inner right thigh. After the cat is tattooed, NDR registers the number, and notifies the owner as soon as a lost cat is located (anywhere in the United States) by an animal shelter, police, individual, or other source. The registry is open 24 hours a day, 365 days a year. For more information contact National Dog Registry at 227 Stebbins Road, Carmel, New York 10512, or call (914) 277-4485.

Another national registry that tattoos cats is I.D. Pet, P.O. Box 2244, Noroton Heights, Connecticut

06820. I.D. Pet also refers owners to nearby authorized agents who tattoo cats with a series of letters and numbers beginning with the prefix *X*. Each cat is assigned a specific number. After the cat is tattooed, I.D. Pet registers the number and furnishes the owner with a collar tag that states on one side *Please call I.D. Pet. Toll-free 800-243-9147. Connecticut: call collect: 1-327-3157.* On the other side the tag reads: *Warning! I am tattoo registered. If found, phone collect.* Animals that have been previously tattooed with American Kennel Club, Cat Fanciers' Association, or Social Security numbers and family names are also eligible for registration.

If Your Cat Disappears

Should your cat disappear, *act immediately*. The first twenty-four hours are the most critical. Don't wait for the cat to find its way home, for it may be unable to do so. Stay calm and collected! Confusion will only slow down your efforts to locate the cat. Here's what to do:

1. Notify the tattoo registry if your cat is tattooed.
2. Thoroughly search the area where your cat was lost. While cats usually don't wander as far away as do dogs, you'll have to be more thorough, because cats tend to hide in the tiniest of places and even climb up into them. Call your cat's name frequently. Unlike most dogs, however, a frightened cat may not come when you call its name. But it might meow in response to your voice, so be attentive. Talk to your neighbors and ask them to look out for your cat and to carefully search their basements, garages, and other places of concealment.

3. Notify every animal shelter in your area and give them a full description of your cat. Follow up phone calls with visits to the shelters every day. Don't rely on employees. Go look for yourself. Shelters and humane societies have various holding periods for strays, but most large organizations in big cities have fast turnovers. They either place animals for adoption or euthanize them within forty-eight hours to five days to make room for incoming pets.

4. Notify veterinarians. Leave full particulars and ask them to phone you if your cat is brought in for treatment.

5. Notify local police and those in nearby communities.

6. Notify local radio stations. Many will announce lost (and found) animals.

7. Place an ad in the "Lost and Found" or "Lost Pet" column of your local newspaper. Include a complete description of the cat. Offer a "substantial" reward, but don't indicate the amount. Check all "Lost and Found" columns regularly.

8. Make a LOST CAT poster:

   a. Paste a clear photograph or pen-and-ink drawing of your cat in the center of a sheet of paper.

   b. Print LOST CAT in large letters across the top of the page.

   c. Print REWARD prominently on the poster.

   d. Write a brief description of your cat: breed, sex, age, color, and markings.

   e. Clearly print your telephone number. Include the number of a dependable relative or friend who will receive calls at all times.

   f. Take the poster to a photocopy or duplicating center and have dozens of copies made.

9. Place the posters immediately in the following locations:

- Animal shelters.
- Police stations.
- Veterinarians' offices.
- School bulletin boards.
- Supermarkets and other area stores.
- Post offices.
- Bus stations.
- Lampposts (the New York ASPCA recommends that you poster six blocks in each direction from where the cat was lost; that you place the posters at eye level, and make them large enough to be seen by passing cars). Check the postered areas frequently and replace any that have been removed.

10. Walk, bicycle, or drive streets, parks, and the countryside. Take along snapshots and talk to children, postmen, delivery people, highway workers, sanitation men, and others. Give them posters and ask them to be on the lookout for your cat.

11. Have an announcement made in school assemblies. Children are wonderfully sympathetic when an animal is lost, and they will gladly join in the search.

12. Leave food outside in case your cat returns while you are away.

13. If you are traveling and lose your cat, contact

the police department or sheriff's office in rural areas to locate the nearest animal control agency or dog warden. If there is no animal organization, give the police full particulars and tell them where you are staying. In urban areas notify the nearest animal shelter, humane society, or ASPCA.

14. Don't become discouraged and give up. Cats are often found several weeks or even months after they are lost.

15. If you think your cat is being held for ransom, call the police at once. Should you receive a telephone call from a person who demands a ransom for the cat, try to remain level-headed. If you have to pay ransom, do it only when the cat is given in return. Remember as much as possible about the kidnapper's physical description. Jot down the license number of his or her car, then call the police.

16. When you find your cat, pay attention to the conditions that allowed it to escape and correct them immediately.

Moving with Your Cat

Each year more than forty million Americans move to new homes. Those who own pets sometimes forget that changes in life-styles and locations can greatly affect their animals. Pets are creatures of habit, and a change in surroundings can cause great apprehension. A cat or a dog doesn't know why it is being uprooted from a secure environment, and you can't sit down and explain things. Therefore, if you are changing your residence, try to anticipate the move's adverse results on your cat. Help it adapt to the changes with a little preplanning and special attention.

Short Distance Moves

Short distance moves are easiest to cope with. If you are moving a few blocks away or across town, it's best to keep your cat out of the house on moving day to protect it from the subsequent confusion. Doors and windows will certainly be left open, clearing the way for your cat to escape. A cat can also crawl into an empty carton or hide in newspapers or tissue paper during unpacking, and be carried outside to the trash. The ideal solution is to board the cat for a day or two at a cattery, or with a reliable friend.

If boarding is not possible and the cat accompanies you to the new residence on moving day, confine it (with litter tray) temporarily in the bathroom or other safe place. Tape a sign on the door indicating that the cat is inside, so no movers will accidentally enter and let it escape. Pack a "cat box" to be opened as soon as the movers leave. The presence of its favorite toys on the floor, its food and water bowls in the kitchen, and its bed in a new bedroom will help reassure your cat that this strange place is home.

Once you are settled, keep your cat inside the house or apartment for a few weeks and don't let it run free. Pets in new surroundings become quickly disoriented and are more likely to wander off and get lost. They often try to go back to their old home. If the cat is leash-trained, take short walks outside to let him become familiar with the new surroundings. Change the address and phone number on the identification tag immediately so your cat is protected. A move to a new home is an especially crucial time for a cat to wear correct identification. Remember:

Your new neighbors don't know your cat by sight and can't be helpful in identifying it. Question the neighbors about dogs and cats in the area that could be potential adversaries. Don't take your cat outside until you are positive it won't meet a canine or feline attacker.

Long Distance Moves

Long distance moves to other states or foreign countries require a great deal of advance planning. If you are relocating to another state, the cat will have to go there by plane or car. If the cat travels by plane: (1) Plan to ship it a few days before you move. Arrange in advance for someone from a cattery, boarding kennel, or veterinary hospital to pick up the cat at the airport and board it until you arrive. Contact the American Animal Hospital Association or the American Boarding Kennels Association (consult "Useful Addresses" under Chapter XVI) for area recommendations; or (2) Move to the new location first, then have a pet forwarding service or trusted friend send your cat to you. *Never* ship a cat by plane while you are en route and can't take charge of arrangements.

If you travel by car, determine beforehand which hotels and motels accept pets, and make advance reservations. Directories listing such motels and hotels are listed in Chapter XI. If you move to a foreign country, check with its consulate months in advance about rules and regulations governing the entry of pets. Most countries require a health certificate and rabies vaccination, and some nations quarantine pets for periods of from two weeks to six months at the owner's expense.

A few weeks before your move, have the cat

examined by a veterinarian. Most states also require a health certificate and proof of rabies vaccination (see Chapter XI) and your veterinarian can attend to these matters and give you the cat's medical records for future reference. Make long distance moving more comfortable and less traumatic for your cat by taking along the items and familiar possessions listed under "Your Cat's Luggage" in Chapter XI.

Traveling to the New Home

Place your cat inside a carrying case, and give the case adequate space and ventilation in the car. Don't crowd the case between luggage or cartons that restrict air flow as well as space. Luggage and cartons should be protected from unexpected shifting in case of sudden stops. Take along a litter tray (small treated cardboard boxes designed to be discarded after a short time are ideal for travel) and a supply of litter. Stop regularly to let the cat use the tray. If your cat will exercise on grass, do not open the car door until a leash is attached to its collar or harness and held securely in your hand.

When you arrive at your new home, try to spend as much time as possible on the first day reassuring your cat. Remember, its favorite toys and familiar possessions will make an unfamiliar house seem like home. If you do have to leave your cat alone, be sure there are no hazards around that might cause problems. Make a big fuss over the cat as soon as you return. With a little understanding and special attention your cat will soon feel secure in new surroundings.

Cats and Landlords, Condominiums, and Cooperative Apartments

The subject of moving with a cat cannot be complete without mentioning the potential problems of apartment tenants or owners of condominium or cooperative apartments.

Landlords seem to be objecting more and more to cats and dogs. They often refuse to rent to individuals or families with pets, even when the prospective tenant owns a cat that never sees the outdoors. Pets can be destructive, and some landlords do have bona fide complaints, but generally it is the thoughtless cat and dog owners who cause so many problems for others.

Read your lease carefully before you sign it, to determine if there is a no-pet clause or any other restrictions. If none are listed, don't take a rental agent's word that pets are allowed. They might tell you anything to get you to rent an apartment! If you have nothing in writing and move into an apartment with your cat, the landlord can later serve you with a thirty-day notice that pets are not permitted. Should you ignore the warning, next you will receive a three-day notice stating that you must give up the cat or be evicted. If you can't find a home for the cat, you may have to give it to an animal shelter where the possibility of adoption is slight. Even if the landlord previously acknowledged and allowed your cat, he can evict you any time he wants to with no-pet restrictions. In New York and other cities with rent control or stabilization regulations, a speedy change of tenants can be quite lucrative because the landlord can raise the rent with each new leaseholder.

What to do? Obtain a written statement permitting

you to keep your cat in the apartment. If the landlord asks for a security deposit against your cat's possible destructiveness, pay it. Be a concerned cat owner. Consider the rights of others, and observe pet ordinances. If you are unfairly forced out of your apartment, call the local housing authority to locate a city agency that can help. Dealing with city agencies can be a frustrating experience, but keep trying until you get specific results. Contact local humane groups and ask if there are sympathetic pet-owner organizations that can help. If there is a tenants' association in your building, meet with the other dog and cat owners, and join together and fight to keep your pets and your apartments!

The question of pets in condominiums and co-operative apartments is another controversial subject. Get a copy of the association's regulations and by-laws as soon as you contemplate purchasing a condominium or cooperative apartment. Read them carefully to determine if there are any pet restrictions. As previously suggested, don't accept the word of a real estate agent. Visit the building and check things out yourself. Talk to the person responsible for maintaining the grounds. Speak to as many apartment owners as possible. Without confiding that you own a cat, question them about pet problems or restrictions. Their comments will quickly make you aware of any complications. When you do move in, attend board meetings regularly. Contact other pet owners in the complex and form a united group to express your views on unreasonable cat or dog restrictions.

If You Have to Part with Your Cat

It is agonizing to discover that you can no longer keep your cat, but the thoughts of where it will go and what will happen to it are even more heartbreaking. Every cat, especially one that has given you years of devotion and companionship, deserves to live a long and happy life in a loving home. Giving up a pet is a mournful experience, especially if you must do it against your will. Your primary concern is the animal's welfare. To make the best choice for your particular cat, examine the following possibilities and determine how each would affect your pet:

1. Give the cat to a reliable neighbor, relative, or friend.
2. Advertise for a new owner in your local newspaper, or by posting notices on bulletin boards in veterinary hospitals and grooming salons. Notify cat clubs, humane organizations, and local private animal adoption agencies.
3. Place the cat in a shelter that will try to find a new owner or, if it is not adopted, will keep it for the rest of its life. The majority of humane organizations, operating on limited budgets and space, euthanize a large percentage of the animals referred to them, simply because there are more unwanted pets than potential pet owners. Some shelters put animals to sleep immediately if they are "unadoptable" because of injury, illness, age, or behavior problems. Others place animals for adoption for a certain time period, then euthanize them if they do not find homes. But there are shelters throughout the United States that will not destroy pets unless they are incurably ill, and will care for them as long as

they live. These are usually filled to capacity, however, and accept new pets only when resident animals die or are adopted.

4. Have the cat euthanized by a veterinarian or humane society. Euthanasia is an emotional and controversial subject. But in the case of ill-tempered, debilitated, or elderly cats that have little chance of being adopted, it might be a more humane solution than life in an institution or with a new owner who could be abusive.

The ideal solution would be to find a new owner for the cat. You know its habits and personality, and are best qualified to locate a compatible person who will treat it well. Interview prospective new owners, to be sure they really want your cat. Don't be afraid to ask questions. Here are some important points to cover:

- Why does the person or family want a cat?
- Has the person previously owned a cat? What happened to it?
- Are there children in the family? What are their ages? (An important consideration, especially if your cat is not used to living with children or coping with toddlers.)
- If the prospective owner(s) live in an apartment or rented home, will the cat cause problems with the landlord?
- Does the prospective owner understand the responsibility of animal care?
- Can the new owner afford the costs of food and veterinary care?
- Will someone be home with the cat every day, or will it be left alone a great deal?

When you find the right new owners, give them your cat's collar or harness, leash, food and water bowls, toys, bed, and carrying case. There's nothing like a few familiar possessions to make an animal adjust faster to a new home. Visit the new owners several weeks after they acquire the cat. Knowing that all is well may be the best medicine for your low spirits.

Above all, don't abandon your cat. There are laws against abandonment in every state, yet thousands of animals are turned loose every day to roam at will. There is always an increase in the number of pets abandoned by vacationers in the summer. One wonders how any person who cared for a cat all summer long could dump it along a roadside and speed away when the holiday is ended. The majority of people who abandon pets say they do it because the animal stands a better chance of finding a new home. *Very few abandoned cats find new homes.* They wander the streets instead, frightened and hungry; they are often hit by cars and die a slow and miserable death; or they end up in research laboratories. Perhaps the "lucky" ones are picked up by animal control organizations and euthanized. Inevitably, most abandoned pets will die, quickly if they are fortunate, agonizingly if they are not. Tree House Animal Foundation, a Chicago-based humane group reports that there are more than 100 million stray cats and dogs currently living (and dying) in the United States. "The vast majority of these animals unneutered and unspayed, compound the stray population by approximately 5,000 puppy and kitten births per hour! And, an estimated 20 million strays are euthanized each year in animal control facilities (the cost: $320 million) and disease, accidents and malnutrition also play a role in decreasing their number. Still, that 100 million figure grows by about 5-percent each year."

XIII The Cat and the Arts

I do not think the cat can be over-estimated. He suggests so much grace, power, beauty, motion, mysticism. I do not wonder that many writers loved cats. I am only surprised that all do not.

—Carl Van Vechten,
The Tiger in the House

The cat and the arts is a fascinating subject. The earliest reproductions of the domestic cat date back to ancient Egypt. Through the centuries we encounter the cat on canvas; in bronze, wood, stone, marble, terra-cotta, ivory, jade, and porcelain; and in engravings, drawings, and prints. We see the cat on stamps, coins, tombs, and even in churches. It appears in cartoons and often assumes a satirical role. The cat cuts a figure in mythology, folklore and legend, advertising, proverbs and sayings, and has received a great deal of recognition from the world's great writers.

The Cat in Literature

Literature is filled with references to cats in prose and verse. To devote a short section to the many fictional cats, or to the real felines whose names or prankish adventures have been immortalized by their famous masters is frustrating, for where does one begin or end, and which cats should be included?

One of the earliest testimonials to the domestic cat in English literature is an eighth-century poem entitled Pangur Ban, composed by an Irish monastery student. The poet, owner of the cat, describes their mutual interests:

> I and Pangur Ban, my cat,
> 'Tis a like task we are at;
> Hunting mice is his delight,
> Hunting words I sit all night.

Geoffrey Chaucer (1340?-1400), the English poet, used "The Maunciple's Tale" (one of the *Canterbury Tales*) to illustrate the cat's natural predilection for the mouse. He reveals that even the most well-nourished puss will abandon mouth-watering treats and every comfort for a mouse:

> Lat take a cat, and fostre hym wel with milk
> And tendre flessche, and make his couche of silk,
> And lat hym see a mous go by the wal;
> Anon he weyvith milk, and flessche, and al,
> And every deyntee that is in that house,
> Swich appetyt hath he to ete a mous.

Scores of passages in praise of felines and their natures flowed from the pens of nineteenth-century

French writers and poets. Hippolyte Taine (1828-93) wrote twelve sonnets to his cats Ébene, Puss, and Mitonne. Étienne (Stéphane) Mallarmé (1842-98) often mentioned his favorite felines, Lilith and Neige, in his letters. Théophile Gautier (1811-72) elegantly described his cats Seraphita, Don Pierrot de Navarre, Gavroche, and Eponine in *La Ménagerie Intime.*

The most dedicated French ailurophile, surely, was Charles Baudelaire (1821-67). He believed that cats personified a segment of the occult. Carl Van Vechten writes in *The Tiger in the House* (see "Bibliography of the Cat" in Chapter XVI) that "Cats abound in the verse of Baudelaire as dogs in the paintings of Paolo Veronese, and are a kind of signature." He adds that Baudelaire's "poems to cats are mystic masterpieces and no other poet has been able to create works to rival them." In one, "The Clock," time is told by watching the eyes of cats.

Émile Zola (1840-1902) was another cat lover and includes them in many of his works: the black and white cats of *Nouveaux Contes à Ninon;* the huge red theatrical cat of *Nana;* the country cats of *La Faute de L'Abbé Mouret;* Minouche, the elegant white puss of *La Joie de Vivre,* which was repelled by the sight of mud; and the luckless François of *Thérèse Raquin,* the cat with the demoniac stare.

Numerous cats appear in the works of Charles Dickens (1812-70): Mrs. Popchin's cat of *Dombey and Son,* and the three of *Bleak House*—Mr. Krook's hissing, green-eyed Lady Jane, the nameless cat of the barrister Vohles, and the milk-loving cat of the Jellybys, to name a few. Dickens not only created many fictional felines but owned a white cat named William, whose name was changed to Williamina after she gave birth to kittens. Dickens kept one of Williamina's kittens and gave it no name because it was deaf. His servants named the kitten "The Master's Cat" because the little fellow so adored Dickens that he followed him everywhere like a dog and sat on his desk while he worked.

Rudyard Kipling's (1865-1936) "Cat that Walked by Himself" of the *Just So Stories* is another literary favorite. The end of the tale conclusively fixes the cat's destiny:

> Then the man threw his two boots and his little stone axe . . . at the Cat, and the Cat ran out of the Cave and the Dog chased him up a tree; and from that day to this, Best Beloved, three proper men out of five will always throw things at a Cat whenever they meet him, and all proper Dogs will chase him up a tree. But the Cat keeps his side of the bargain too. He will kill mice, and he will be kind to babies when he is in the house, just as long as they do not pull his tail too hard. But when he has done that, and between times, and when the moon gets up and night comes, he is the Cat that walks by himself, and all places are alike to him.

The English short-story writer Saki (pen name of H. H. Munro, 1870-1916) created the extraordinarily intelligent Tobermory, the English cat of *The Chronicles of Clovis*. The story takes place at Lady Blemley's houseparty, where Mr. Cornelius Appins reveals to the astonished guests that he has taught his cat to speak the English language with perfect correctness.

"Hadn't we better have the cat in and judge for ourselves?" suggested Lady Blemley.

Sir Wilfrid went in search of the animal, and the company settled themselves down to the languid expectation of witnessing some more or less adroit drawing-room ventriloquism. In a minute, Sir Wilfrid was back in the room, his face white beneath its tan and his eyes dilated with excitement. "By Gad, it's true!" . . .

Collapsing into an armchair he continued breathlessly: "I found him dozing in the smoking room and called out to him to come for tea. He blinked at me in his usual way, and I said 'Come on, Toby; don't keep us waiting'; and by Gad! he drawled out in a most horribly natural voice that he'd come when he dashed well pleased! I nearly jumped out of my skin!"

Mark Twain (pen name of Samuel Langhorne Clemens, 1835-1910) alluded to cats in *The Adventures of Huckleberry Finn, More Tramps Abroad,* and *The Tragedy of Pudd'nhead Wilson,* and created Tom Quartz, the large gray mining cat "with more hard natchral sense than any man in this camp," of *Roughing It,* a collection of sketches based on Twain's early experiences in the mining camps of California. The Clemens home was never without cats.

English poet and critic Algernon Swinburne (1837-1909) dedicated a touching poem to his cat:

> Stately, kindly, lordly friend
>   Condescend
> Here to sit by me, and turn
> Glorious eyes that smile and burn,

Golden eyes, love's lustrous mead,
On the golden pages I read.

T. S. Eliot (1888-1965), the poet, critic, and play-wright, adored cats. He wrote several amusing poems about them and made many references to cats in other nonfeline works. Eliot's *Old Possum's Book of Practical Cats* is a series of poems about the most delightful creatures. There is Gus, the Theatrical Cat, and Rum Tum Tugger, the curious cat and terrible bore, and the roly-poly, black and white Jellicle Cats, who know how to dance a gavotte and a jig.

Literature has a few nonsensical cats, too, such as the one in Edward Lear's "The Owl and the Pussy Cat," and Don Marquis's alley cat mehitabel, to whome archy (a cockroach) writes free verse on an office typewriter.

Among the modern writers who have loved cats, the names of Colette and Paul Gallico stand out. Colette (pen name of Sidonie Gabrielle Claudine Colette, 1873-1954) is considered one of the greatest writers of modern times, although her books shocked the French bourgeoisie. She surrounded herself with animals, particularly cats, and many were immortalized in her works, in particular Kiki-la-Doucette, the orange and white Persian, one of two main characters in *Dialogues des Bêtes*, and La Chatte, a Chartreux that Colette bought at a cat show. La Chatte was the model for the feline character, Saha, in Colette's novel *La Chatte*, the story of a love triangle between a man, a woman, and a cat. Paul Gallico once owned twenty-three cats when he lived in France, and he wrote many cat books including *Thomasina*, *The Silent Miaow*, *Honorable Cat*, and *Jennie*.

Poets and writers have presented touching remembrances, too, of the death of cats. Thomas Gray (1716-71) composed "Ode on the Death of a Favourite Cat Drowned in a Tub of Gold Fishes," upon hearing of the demise of Selima, Horace Walpole's cat. Christina Rossetti (1830-94) wrote a poem entitled "On the Death of a Cat, a Friend of Mine Age Ten Years and a Half." Thomas Hardy (1840-1928) mournfully remembers his cat in "Last Words to a Dumb Friend," which closes:

> Housemate, I can think you still
> Bounding to the window sill,
> Over which I vaguely see
> Your small mound beneath the tree,
> Showing in the autumn shade
> That you moulder where you played.

The Cat in Children's Literature

Of all the domestic animals that have become closely associated with man, probably the cat has received the most attention in children's literature. Lewis Carroll (pen name of Charles L. Dodgson, 1832-98) created the inscrutable Cheshire Cat of *Alice's Adventures in Wonderland,* a creature so celebrated that the phrase "to grin like a Cheshire cat" is included in most dictionaries.

> The only ones who remained calm were the cook and a big cat sitting beside the fire. The cat was grinning from ear to ear. "Excuse me, my Lady," said Alice a little timidly to the Duchess, "Why is your cat like that?" "Because he's a Cheshire cat," replied the Duchess simply.

Carroll's feline had the ability to "vanish quite slowly, beginning with the end of the tail and ending with the grin, which remained for some time after the rest of it had gone." For his charming illustrations of Carroll's work, Sir John Tenniel (1820-1914) possibly was inspired by the cheeses from the Cheshire section of England, which were molded into the shapes of grinning cats.

"Puss in Boots" is another beloved children's classic. The origins of the tale of a roguish feline that kills an ogre and wins fortune and a princess for his master are obscure, but one version, entitled "Eleventh Night," appears in Giovanni Francesco Straparola's book of fairy tales, *Tredici Piacevoli Notti*, published in Italy, and similar accounts are found in Scandinavian nursery tales. The story was immortalized in 1695 under the title "Le Maître Chat" or "Le Chat Botté" by French poet and critic Charles Perrault (who was the first to write and publish other charming folk tales such as "The Sleeping Beauty," "Little Red Riding Hood," and "Cinderella") in his book *Contes du temps passé*, which was prepared for the niece of Louis XIV. The famous French illustrator Gustave Doré (1833-83) furnished the drawings for an 1862 edition of Perrault's version of the story, in which he depicted a swashbuckling Puss, wearing a flowing cape, broad-brimmed hat with great plume, and large Cavalier boots. A wide leather belt encircles Puss in Boots's waist, from which hang two mice, one enclosed in a pouch.

Then there was the wise cat of "The Cat and the Fox," one of the *Fables of La Fontaine* (Jean de La Fontaine, 1621-95), based on an Aesop tale. Each animal is very cunning and believes he is cleverer than the other. The fox boasts that he knows many artful tricks, while the cat answers that he always has one good plan for any situation. Their conversation is interrupted when three dogs suddenly appear and charge at them. The cat scrambles up the nearest tree and quickly hides in its branches. But the panic-stricken fox runs from hole to hole in the ground, changing hiding places a hundred times, until the dogs pounce on and destroy him. At the end of the fable, the wise cat prescribes: "Poor fox, he had one hundred ideas, one hundred cunning tricks. And what use were they to him? None at all. One single, well-thought-out plan is better than a hundred different untried tricks."

Nursery-rhyme cats are loved by children throughout the world, and the tender verses frequently offer humane advice:

> I love little Pussy
> Her coat is so warm.
> And if I don't hurt her
> She'll do me no harm.
> So I'll not pull her tail
> Nor drive her away
> But pussy and I
> Very gently will play.

The hostility between cat and mouse is often the subject of rhyme:

> Pussy cat, pussy cat
> Where have you been?
> I've been to London
> To look at the Queen.

Pussy cat, pussy cat
What did you there?
I frightened a little mouse
Under her chair.

A verse from *Popular Rhymes of Scotland*, published in *Chamber's Journal* (1870), delightfully reveals a mouse's distress:

There was a wee bit mousikie
That lived in Gilberaty, O.
It couldna get a bite of cheese
For cheety-poussie-cattie, O.
It said unto the cheesikie:
O fain wad I be at ye O,
It 'twere na for the cruel paws
O' cheety-poussie-cattie, O.

The Cat in Painting and Illustration

Many of the world's great artists from the old masters to the modernists put cats into their works—as principal subjects, as conversation pieces, in portraits (where they sometimes are accorded prominence almost equal to the subject), or as incidental interest to a main subject. The appearance of cats in paintings and illustrations through the centuries often tells us much about the preferences of the times as well as traces cats' own development.

Italy

Italian art abounds with cats, beginning with the early religious and allegorical painters who included them in frescoes or on canvases. A fine early example is Benozzo Gozzoli's (1421-97) fresco cycle of scenes from the Old Testament in the Campo Santo at Pisa.

A splendid large cat appears in a scene showing animals leaving Noah's Ark.

The prolific artist Pinturicchio (Bernardino di Betto, 1454-1513) painted a majestic cat in *The Return of Odysseus* (National Gallery, London). Half a century later Jacopo Robusti (1518-94), known as Tintoretto, a name derived from his father's profession as a dyer, tucked saturnine cats into the dark backgrounds of his religious scenes. Federico Barocci (1526-1612) also inserts cats into many religious paintings. *Holy Family with a Cat* depicts John the Baptist as a child tormenting a cat with a bird (a symbol of the soul). By keeping the bird at arm's length, the young John symbolically guards the soul from danger. In Barocci's *Annunciation* (Vatican Gallery), a handsome gray cat sleeps on a chair beside the kneeling Virgin.

Paolo Cagliari (1528-88), called Veronese, surely was an animal lover, for he inserted cats and dogs as often as possible in his paintings. One of Veronese's most beautiful paintings is the immense religious-feast scene *Marriage at Cana* (Louvre, Paris). The entire canvas is alive with people and animals, including a cat scratching a wine vessel in the foreground. Bartolommeo Guidobono (1654-1709) was another ailurophile. In his *Sorceress* (Metropolitan Museum of Art, New York) a child points to a seated witch who is casting an incantation. The sorceress is surrounded by a number of animals including a glaring gray tabby.

Perhaps no painter is more celebrated in the world than the Renaissance master Leonardo da Vinci (1452-1519). Leonardo had a passion for animals, and he kept and trained many cats, dogs, and horses. One of his masterpieces, *Madonna of the Cat* (Noya

Collection, Savona, Italy), completed about 1476, shows Mary caressing the baby Jesus, who fondles a cat in his arms. Leonardo made a number of sketches of cats for a treatise on animal locomotion. His drawings illustrate the whole range of feline habits and movements: napping, cat play, self-cleaning, falling, predatory stalking, and fighting. These are now in the Victoria and Albert Museum and British Museum in London, the Royal Collection at Windsor Castle, and the Biblioteca Ambrosiana in Milan.

Spain

Spanish artists are not noted for painting animals. Most of the great Spanish masters concentrated on portraits of royalty and aristocracy, or scenes of religious and allegorical events. Few painted cats or even introduced them into paintings as conversation pieces.

Cats are seen most often in the works of Diego Rodriguez de Silva y Velázquez (1599-1660) and Francisco Goya (1746-1828). Along with his many royal portraits and religious canvases, Velázquez painted a series of *bodegónes,* or scenes of everyday life, influenced perhaps by the animated genre paintings from the Low Countries that were popular in Spain at the time. In one of Velázquez's most brilliant works, *The Spinners* or *The Fable of Aracne* (Prado Museum, Madrid), a group a peasant women diligently spin and card wool for tapestries while a large tortoiseshell-and-white cat sleeps nearby.

Francisco Goya, court painter to Spanish King Charles IV, painted the most "feline" cats in Spanish art in his portrait of the young *Don Manuel Osorio Manrique de Zuniga* (Metropolitan Museum of Art, New York). It depicts a child fashionably dressed in a brilliant red velvet and silk outfit trimmed with lace. The animals, rather than the splendidly dressed boy, however, dominate the painting. Don Manuel holds a magpie on a string, a favorite child's pet since the Middle Ages. A cage filled with birds sits at his left, while on the right, three cats (a tabby, a tortoiseshell, and a black) stare menacingly at the birds.

The Low Countries: Germany, Holland, and Belgium

Early artists of the Low Countries of northern Europe placed more emphasis on domestic and natural scenes, rather than on biblical or mythological themes. Cats appear most often in genre paintings—landscapes and interior scenes.

Some of the finest examples of the cat in German art appear in the works of Albrecht Dürer (1471-1538), the painter, engraver, and woodcutter. He uses a serene gray cat as a symbol of conjugal unity in *Adam and Eve*. Dürer's pupil Hans von Kulmbach (c.1480-1522) painted *Girl Fashioning a Garland* (Metropolitan Museum), in which a demure young woman sits near a window making a garland of flowers while her white cat regally occupies the sill.

Flemish artist Pieter Brueghel (c.1525-69) painted a study of several cats gathered around a music stand examining the *Solfege d'Italie*. A close look at the music reveals that the notes are really rats, with their tails forming the eighth and sixteenth notes.

An early Dutch artist, Jeroen Anthoniszoon van Aken (1450-1516), better known by the pseudonym Hieronymus Bosch, painted cats in his dreamlike allegorical fantasies. Bosch, often called the "ancestor of surrealism," was essentially a religious painter, and his complex symbolic and often bizarre works are psychological enigmas even today. Examples of Bosch's early work include *The Adoration of the Magi* (Metropolitan Museum), where a fierce cat frightens the people trying to catch it, and *The Creation of Eve* (Prado Museum, Madrid), in which a cat is greedily downing a tadpole. Perhaps Bosch's best-known painting is *The Garden of Earthly Delights* (Prado), a strangely modern tryptich populated with hundreds of grotesque humans, cats, dogs, and other bizarre creatures.

Another Dutch artist, Jan Steen (1626-79), delighted in painting scenes of merrymaking, especially of ordinary people enjoying life. His charming *The Cat's Reading Lesson* shows three children patiently trying to teach a cat how to read. Beautiful cats appear in *After the Drinking Bout* and *The Effects of Intemperance* (National Gallery, London), other lively Steen works. Gabriel Metsu's (c.1629-67) *Kitten Scene* shows one of the loveliest tabbies of Dutch art reaching toward its mistress for some of her food.

The Dutch artist most famous for painting cats is Henriette Ronner (1821-1909). Though Henriette was born in Amsterdam, Henriette's father was fond of traveling and moved the family from Holland to Belgium, then to Italy and France. After marriage Henriette and her husband settled in Brussels, where she painted the most precious and appealing cats in the world of art. Madame Ronner's biographer remarked, "She produced a cat world as impressive as the cattle world of Potter, and as beautiful and touching as the stag and dog worlds of Landseer."

Switzerland

Another famous artist who specialized in painting cats was Gottfried Mind (1768-1814) of Berne, Switzerland. He was called the "Raphael of Cats," a title bestowed on Mind by Madame Elisabeth Vigée-Lebrun, the famous French painter and confidante of Marie Antoinette. Mind had a passion for cats, and his studio teemed with them. He produced many outstanding sketches and watercolors of cats. One magnificent study, *Mother Cat with Kittens* (Kunstmuseum, Basel), shows a doting mother licking her kitten's stomach while two other babies snuggle beneath her body.

France

The French, of all the artists throughout the world, are renowned for painting cats. They appear in many paintings by Louis Le Nain (1593-1648), most notably the black-and-white cat of *The Peasant Family* (Louvre) and the relaxed cat in *The Dairywoman's Fantasy* (The Hermitage, Leningrad).

Jean Baptiste Chardin (1699-1779) added cats to many still life and genre paintings. In *The Silver Tureen* (Metropolitan Museum) a tortoiseshell-and-white cat stares hungrily at a dead partridge and hare lying near a tureen. A hungry cat is tempted by game in *The Dead Hare* (Musée des Beaux-Arts, Lyons). Chardin was accepted into the Académie des Beaux-Arts on the strength of *La Raie* (Louvre), a still life of a cat lustily eyeing some oysters and fish. Art critics of the day extravagantly praised *La Raie* for its realism.

Jean Antoine Watteau (1684-1721) painted winsome cats. His *Sick Cat* portrays a veterinarian treating an ailing feline being restrained by its concerned mistress. Another anecdotal genre painter, Jean Baptiste Greuze (1725-1805), created a beguiling scene of a cat playing with its mistress as she winds yarn in *The Wool Winder* (Frick Collection, New York). Jean

Honoré Fragonard (1732-1806), famous for his small, sensuous paintings immortalizing the frivolity of the court of Louis XV, inserted many cats into his scenes.

Théodore Géricault (1791-1824) was one of the founders of the French Romantic school. His naturalistic treatment of animals is evident in *Le Chat Blanc*, a sensitive portrayal of a serene white cat. Louis Eugène Lambert (1825-1900) was another great cat painter. His *Les Chats du Cardinal* is a portrait of Cardinal Richelieu and his kittens. One of Lambert's best-known works, *La Chatte et Le Perroquet,* is based on Théophile Gautier's story of his pet cat and a parrot. Lambert's anatomical knowledge of cats was so admired that he was selected as one of the judges of the first cat show held in Paris.

Cats are very prevalent in the works of the Impressionist and Post-Impressionist painters. Édouard Manet (1832-83) gives us many cats. Manet's famous *Rendezvous des Chats,* created for Champfleury's book *Les Chats,* published in Paris in 1870, was very risqué in its day. A splendid black tomcat arches its back in the picture near a white queen on a rooftop as their tails undulate in the moonlight. Pierre Auguste Renoir (1841-1919) put sensuous and gossamery cats in *La Petite Fille au Chat, Portrait of Madame Manet,* and *Woman with a Cat.* Henri Rousseau (1844-1910) painted a colorful portrait of the French writer Pierre Loti and his vividly-striped tabby (Kunstmuseum, Zurich). Mary Cassatt (1845-1926), an American who painted mainly in France, created the tender *Children Playing with a Cat,* in which an infant on its mother's lap reaches out to touch a sleeping cat sitting with a girl nearby. Paul Gauguin (1848-1903) inserted a tranquil cat in *Te Rerioa*. In Gauguin's *Still Life with Cats* a cat glares directly at the viewer while another sleeps. Henri de Toulouse-Lautrec (1864-1901), portrayed the chanteuse *May Belfort* (Cabinet des Estampes, Paris) as she sang "Daddy Wouldn't Buy Me a Bow-Wow," dressed as a little girl in brilliant red, holding a black kitten with an enormous yellow ribbon around its neck. During the same period Théophile Alexandre Steinlen (1859-1923) was obsessed with cats and portrayed them with great charm and realism in an array of advertisements, illustrations, and posters. Steinlen's favorite subjects were the cats owned by artists and concierges of the Butte de Montmartre.

England

While English painters are known for their unsurpassed style of portraying dogs, none specialized in painting cats, and few artists even included them in scenes as conversation pieces. The celebrated animal artist Sir Edwin Landseer (1802-73) was so annoyed with two of his early paintings of domestic cats that he seldom sketched them again. One of Landseer's most violent and controversial paintings, however, was *The Cat's Paw*, created in 1824. In the picture a monkey holds a terrified cat on a chair in a fiendish grip as it forces the cat's paw onto a burning stove to remove chestnuts, while the poor creature's frightened kittens in their wicker basket look on.

William Hogarth (1697-1764), who tucked many scrawny-looking cats into his engravings, produced the best-known feline in English art in *The Graham Children* (Tate Gallery, London). The painting shows a lifelike, glaring tabby slinking her way up the back of a chair to attack a goldfinch in a nearby cage. Sir Kenneth Clark comments in *A Hundred Details from*

Pictures in the National Gallery (printed for the trustees in 1938): "Hogarth enjoyed painting this cat so much that the Graham children look hollow and lifeless beside her. She is the embodiment of Cockney vitality, alert and adventurous—a sort of Nell Gwyn among cats."

China, Korea, and Japan

The cat was one of the favorite subjects of oriental artists, who had a genius for portraying feline subtleties in their delicately shaded scrolls, watercolors, paintings on silk, woodblock prints, and pen and ink drawings.

Cats first appeared in Chinese art during the Sung Dynasty (A.D. 960-1279), where they are seen with children of high rank. They appear alone in later centuries in almost ethereal natural surroundings. An eighteenth-century Chinese scroll, *Spring Frolic in a T'ang Garden* (Metropolitan Museum), executed in the style of the Chinese emperor Hsüan Tsung (1398-1435), shows five beautiful and delicate wide-eyed cats playing or napping among flowers and foliage. One cat is cleaning his paw, another naps near bamboo plants, while a third rolls on its back and tries to taste some flowers. A fourth cat, sitting behind hollyhocks, rivets its eyes on a bird in a tree, as the fifth carries a bird in its mouth.

The great Korean painter Li-Shizuo (active around 1750) studied under the landscape master Wang Hui and the famous finger-painter Gao Qipei. Both influences are visible in his exquisite *Landscape, Flowers and Birds* (British Museum), where an almost gossamery cat chases a butterfly.

Two of the most renowned masters of the Japanese colorprint, Katsushika Hokusai (1760-1849) and An-

do Hiroshige (1797-1858) painted elegant and sinewy
cats. They both seemed so sensitive to feline moods
and movements that there is an almost mysterious
quality to their works. Another delicate scene on silk,
Pet Cat (Metropolitan Museum), was painted by
Kawabata Gyokusho (1842-1913). Two modern Japanese artists who understood and perceptively portrayed cats are Yasuo Kuniyoshi (1893-1953) and
Tsugouhara Foujita (1886-1968). Foujita, born in
Japan of a Samurai family, lived and worked in Paris
from 1913 to 1940, where he earned worldwide
renown for his sketches, watercolors, and oil paintings of cats.

The United States

One of the earliest American paintings with a cat is
Lady with Her Pets (Metropolitan Museum) by the
primitive painter Rufus Hathaway (1770?-1822),
showing an elegantly dressed woman holding a fan.
She is surrounded by a black cat with yellow eyes
sitting at her side, a robin perched on the back of her
chair, and a parrot and two butterflies above her
head. The woman is believed to be a member of the
Leonard family, a prominent Colonial group of
Marshfield, Massachusetts.

During the nineteenth century, portraits of children (especially demure little girls, fastidiously
groomed and attired in their best dresses) posing with
their cats were popular. The pictures were frequently
painted by itinerant folk artists, as were scenes of cats
and kittens doing all the mischievous things that cats
normally do, such as playing with yarn or spools of
thread, knocking things off tables, and romping with
their littermates. The American folk painter John
Bradley (who painted c. 1832-47) gives us many de-

lightful cats, notably the gray tabby in his portrait of *Emma Brown* (Metropolitan Museum), in which a beautifully dressed, rosy-cheeked little girl moves a pink rose on a small tree to reach her cat; and the wide-eyed tabby in his portrait *Little Girl in Lavender* (National Gallery of Art, Washington, D.C.).

The nineteenth century was also the heyday of the colored lithograph, and the firm of Currier & Ives became a national institution. They gave the public inexpensive pictures that were within the tastes and understanding of the average American. Irresistible scenes of cats and kittens produced by Currier & Ives adorned the walls of many an American parlor.

One of the few nineteenth-century scenes inside an American home is *Just Moved* (Metropolitan Museum) by Henry Mosler (1841-1920). A young couple have obviously just arrived in a new home with all their possessions. The black-and-white family cat is tied to a boiler and sits on a trunk to observe the proceedings.

Edward Penfield (1866-1926), one of America's best-known graphic artists, created many captivating and magesterial cats for the covers of *Harper's Magazine,* and for posters and calendars.

A modern artist whose cats are unusually delightful is Morris Hirshfield (1872-1946). His *Angora Cat* (Museum of Modern Art, New York) pictures a round-eyed, fluffy creature lounging on a blue and gold settee, and similar furry felines abound in Hirshfield's *Cat and Kittens on Grass* (Sidney Janis Gallery collection, New York). Many modern American artists and graphic designers have portrayed the cat, including Andrew Wyeth (1917-   ), Norman Rockwell (1894-1978), and Will Barnet (1911-   ).

And the subject would not be complete without a brief mention of Mimi Vang Olsen, a contemporary artist who specializes in portraits of cats, done in an enchanting style.

Caricatures, Satire, and Cartoon Cats

No discussion of the illustrated cat would be complete without a brief mention of caricatures, satire, and cartoon cats. Amusing portrayals of felines date back to the New Kingdom of Egypt (1580-1085 B.C.) and among the British Museum's extensive Egyptian collection there is a strip of satirical drawings inspired by tomb paintings, showing cats performing human-like activities. Over two thousand years later Russian caricaturists satirized their tzar, Peter the Great, as a fat tabby surrounded by corrupt rat courtiers.

Grandville (Jean Ignace Isidore Gérard, 1803-47), the famous French illustrator, portrayed human pretensions with anthropomorphic mockery. Grandville specialized in ridiculing society by using animals in human situations and clothing to condemn man's affectations. No one escaped his satire, he knocked the rich and the poor, the stylish and the shabby, the educated and the illiterate, the liberals and the conservatives. Grandville became famous in the middle of the nineteenth century when his illustrations appeared in *Scenes from the Public and Private Lives of Animals, or Les Animaux*. The work consisted of short stories by some of the most renowned writers of the day with Grandville's illustrations. Two delightful tales involve cats: "Heartaches of an English Cat" by Honoré de Balzac and "Heartaches of a French Cat" by P. J. Stahl. The latter tells the story of two poor sister cats, Minette and Bébé. Minette goes to Paris to better herself, becomes terribly vain, and marries a handsome tom named Brisquet. After a short honeymoon the philandering Brisquet deserts Minette for an exotic Chinese cat. "This gay intriguer had been imported by the manager of a theater who wisely foresaw that a Chinese cat would create a tremendous sensation among the Parisians." Minette returns to live with Bébé and for the rest of her life gives the cold shoulder to toms that come courting. Brisquet joins a gang of nocturnal caterwaulers and meets death by falling from a rooftop into the street.

Another famous anthropomorphic artist is Louis Wain (1860-1939), who at his peak was said to have completed over 1,500 drawings a year. A lover of cats and a judge of the cat fancy, Wain dreamed of being a landscape painter. But after his first cat illustration appeared in the *Illustrated and Dramatic News* in 1883, he became famous as "the man who drew cats." Wain's frolicking, grinning, and dancing cats of all breeds appeared everywhere in Victorian and Edwardian England: newspapers, magazines, children's books, calendars, and picture postcards. He dressed cats in human clothing and placed them in charming settings, imitating the activities and characteristics of humans. Among his drawings is one involving 150 cats that took eleven days to complete. Unfortunately, Wain's last years were clouded by mental illness. His psychological decline is documented in his illustrations, and in Wain's last years the cats become increasingly maniacal, gradually changing from charming, happy creatures into grotesque, wild-eyed monsters.

Satire was the speciality of English painter and

engraver William Hogarth. Cats appear in *Industry and Idleness; A Rake's Progress; A Harlot's Progress;* Hogarth's illustrations for Samuel Butler's *Hudibras;* and the *Four Stages of Cruelty.* The *First Stage of Cruelty* is a particularly grisly scene. It shows a group of cheering children watching two cats hanging upside down claw each other in fright; a dog attacking a cat; and two people throwing a cat with artificial wings out of an attic window. Hogarth, a true animal lover, produced the series "to prevent in some degree the cruel treatment of animals which makes the streets of London more disagreeable to the human mind than anything whatever, the very describing of which gives me pain."

Cats often assume a comic role. Who can forget such feline cartoon stars as Krazy Kat and Felix the Cat? In his time Felix was a worldwide favorite and king of the animated movies through the silent and early sound era. Ironically it was a mouse named Mickey who dislodged him from his throne. Today we are entertained by Sylvester; Tom, of Tom and Jerry; the whimsical cats of Ronald Searle; the zany wacka-wacka cats of B. Kliban; and Garfield, Jim Davis's irresistible gluttonous feline with a passion for Italian food. And for years fans of Ted Key's "Hazel" cartoons have followed the escapades of Mostly and Two Ton, Hazel's adorable cats.

The Cat in Sculpture and Related Art Forms

Early examples of sculpture, wall decorations, and related forms not only depict the domestic cat in artistic motifs but, more importantly, they trace its history. One of the earliest reproductions of a domestic cat comes from ancient Egypt, carved on the

Tomb of Ti or Ty at Saqqara, dating from the Fifth Dynasty (2560-2300 B.C.). Cats also appear in several forms on tombs from Thebes (on one a cat acts as a retriever) from 1600 B.C. Wall paintings from different periods indicate that cats were house pets as well as sacred in ancient Egypt, for different striped and spotted cats are pictured inside residences, lying under their masters' chairs, playing with children, and nursing kittens.

The cat sculptures of ancient Egypt are unsurpassed even to this day, for they are modeled with such finesse that one can almost identify the precise breed. Sculptures of the goddess Bastet or Bast, one of the most important divinities of Egyptian religion, are extremely prevalent. She usually appears with the body of a woman (clad in a robe) and the head of a cat. In one hand Bastet holds a sistrum, an ancient percussion instrument, adorned with the heads or figures of cats, and in the other hand, a shield in the shape of a sacred cat's head. A sacred kitten or group of kittens often sit at her feet. Bastet, the goddess of love and joy, sometimes appears with a gold ring in one ear. A fine example is the bronze sculpture of Bastet with gold earring from Egypt's Late Period (c. 900-300 B.C.) in the Metropolitan Museum of Art, New York.

Excavations on the island of Crete yielded wall tiles from the palace at Knossos, c. 1600 B.C., showing cats hunting beside wild sheep, and at Hagia Triada cats were carved on stone palace facades.

Animals were represented in the sculptures and art of ancient Greece and Rome, but they were overshadowed by the glorification of the human form. An enchanting bas-relief in the Capitoline Museum pictures a girl trying to show her cat how to dance. The cat is not paying any attention to his mistress and instead is spitting at a duck nearby. A cat also appears in a statue at the feet of the Goddess of Liberty in a temple built by Tiberius Gracchus. Cats are portrayed on Greek and Roman coins in hunting scenes or playing with children, and they are engraved on war shields and targets of Roman soldiers. Mosaics from Pompeii and Herculaneum show cats demonstrating their feline ways, devouring partridges or menacing parrots perched at the edge of a bird bath.

In the Middle Ages cats appear in stone scenes and designs on facades of European cathedrals and large estates, burial vaults, and other statuary. One particularly beautiful stone scene is located in the fifteenth-century French cathedral of Saint-Omer, where the seated Virgin Mary nurses the baby Jesus while a cat lies at her feet. During the same period cats were carved on wooden fonts, misericords, and at the end of church pews. A group of amusing carvings in the Bristol cathedral portrays the adventures of Tybart, a cat owned by the parish priest. In one scene Tybart has scratched his master in a delicate area of his body; the priest's startled housekeeper is forcibly pulling Tybart's tail, and the instigator of this plot laughs fiendishly in the corner.

At the beginning of the nineteenth century, when people began to believe that animals possessed emotions, the art of bronze sculpture reached its pinnacle with the establishment of the Animalier school. The height of Animalier sculptures dates from around 1830 to the turn of the century, with the best pieces fashioned in France and others made in Germany or Austria. Suddenly, bronzes became alive and exciting.

Instead of portraying animals in passive positions, the Animaliers gave them spirit. Foremost of the sculptors who produced beautiful cat bronzes were Antoine Louis Barye (1795-1875), considered the supreme Animalier, Emmanuel Frémiet (1824-1910), and Pierre Jules Mene (1810-77). The heads on Barye's cats were exquisite. And one art critic commented that no artist before or since Barye "has ever rendered quite so well the expressions that cats register by the sinuous movements of their tails." While Barye was primarily concerned with animals in action, Frémiet concentrated on animals at play and at rest, and on mothers nursing their young; he produced some of the most captivating of cat bronzes.

Traveling ailurophiles can today visit two impressive monuments to cats: the statue of the swashbuckling fairy-tale character Puss in Boots, a monument to Charles Perrault in the Jardin des Tuileries in Paris, and the statue of Dick Whittington's cat on Highgate Hill in London. The story of Dick Whittington is probably the most famous English cat tale.

There are several versions of the legend of Dick Whittington, a poor orphan boy employed by Mr. Hugh Fitzwarren, a rich shipping merchant. Dick's garret bedroom was infested with rats, so he bought a cat for a penny to remedy the situation. Soon after, one of Mr. Fitzwarren's ships was about to set sail, and all the servants were asked to venture a small sum and perhaps win good fortune. The penniless Dick, having no possessions, "invested" his cat. During a storm the ship stopped at an unknown port off the Barbary coast, where the captain found the royal palace overrun with rats and mice. The captain brought Dick's cat to the palace, and in no time she killed all the rodents, making the king and queen so ecstatic that they exchanged a fortune in gold for her. Meanwhile, on All Hallows' Day (the first of November), Dick was unhappy and decided to run away from his master. He reached the top of Highgate Hill in London when he heard the Bow Bells ringing out: "Turn back, Dick Whittington, Lord Mayor of London." Dick returned home and discovered his good fortune. Of course, Dick married Mr. Fitzwarren's daughter and eventually became one of the wealthiest merchants in London. Actually, Sir Richard Whittington (1358?-1423), not an orphan but the son of Sir William of Pauntley, was a three-time Lord Mayor of London but there is little hard evidence to prove the truth of the cat story.

The Cat in Philately

Beautifully illustrated postage stamps showing cat portraits, fairy-tale, fable, or nursery-rhyme cats, cartoon cats, children and cats, and cats in the paintings of world-famous artists, have been issued by nearly one hundred countries of the world. It is interesting to note that although dogs have appeared on more than fifteen United States postage stamps since 1848, the cat appears only once, on an eight-cents stamp issued in 1972. Entitled Mail Order Issue, the stamp shows an old country store cum post office with a black cat on a flour sack in the foreground.

Fairy-tale, fable, and nursery-rhyme cats are popular stamp themes. Puss in Boots occurs most frequently on stamps from Hungary (1965), Poland (1968), the German Democratic Republic (1968), West Germany (1971), Mali (1972), Manama (1972), and Monaco (1978). Cats are also portrayed in scenes from

"Hansel and Gretel" (Hungary, 1959, and West Germany, 1961); "Sleeping Beauty" (Hungary, 1959, and West Germany, 1964); "The Big Turnip" (Bulgaria, 1964); "The Quarreling Cat" (Burundi, 1977); "The Spellbound Castle" (Czechoslovakia, 1968); "The Cat, the Weasel and the Rabbit" (Dahomey, 1972); "The Cat's Journey" (Sweden, 1969); "King Drosselbart" (German Democratic Republic, 1967); and a delightful 1971 Mongolian stamp (based on a local fairy tale) of a large cat wearing a kimono, licking his lips, surrounded by a semicircle of mice. For Christmas 1980, Tristan da Cunha issued a miniature sheet of nine charming nursery rhyme stamps executed by the artist G. Vasarhelyi. Cats appear in scenes from "Hey Diddle Diddle" and "The Owl and the Pussy Cat."

Cartoon cats appear on several stamp sets. Fujairah released a set of twenty stamps with scenes from *The Aristocats*, a Walt Disney film. Fujairah also issued a 1972 stamp featuring Gepetto the carpenter and Figaro the cat from the children's classic *Pinocchio*. Sharjah released four stamps in 1972 with cartoon scenes of Tom and Jerry.

Touching illustrations of cats and children are frequently displayed, among them, a cat curled up in a child's lap (Andorra, 1967); children playing with a cat (Belgium, 1966); a girl with a tennis racket and a kitten (Colombia, 1974); a winter scene with a child and sleeping cat (France, 1974); a girl pushing a carriage with kittens, and a little boy fishing alongside his cat (both Grenada, 1970); a girl spinning wool and her cat (Iran, 1974); children playing with cats and dogs (New Zealand, 1974); and a boy writing with his cat nearby (Netherlands Antilles, 1968). Children's drawings of cats decorate the stamps of India (1974,

1977), Malaysia (1971), Bulgaria (1969), and The German Democratic Republic (1967).

Reproductions of the works of famous painters frequently appear on stamps, and many of these include cats as a part of the work. To name a few: Gabriel Metsu's *Lady Doing Lacework* (German Democratic Republic, 1959); Francisco Goya's *Don Manuel Osorio Manrique de Zuniga* (Panama, 1967); Pierre Auguste Renoir's *Woman with a Cat* (Burundi, 1968); Jean Baptiste Perronneau's *Girl with a Cat* (Dubai, 1968); Jan Steen's *The Feast* (Hungary, 1969); Jean Honoré Fragonard's *The Music Lesson* (Rwanda, 1969); William Hogarth's *The Graham Children* (Dubai, 1970); Louis Le Nain's *Peasant Family* (People's Republic of the Congo, 1976); François Boucher's *The Milliner* (Sharjah, 1972); and Gustave Courbet's *The Painter's Studio* (Senegal, 1977). France honored her famous writer Colette in 1973 with a stamp showing a portrait of the author of *Gigi, Cheri,* and other classics with her cats.

The most popular cat stamps, though, are illustrations of head studies or full body portraits of the various breeds. The Tabby unquestionably is the most popular, followed by the Persian, Siamese, Burmese, and the Angora. Sharjah issued one of the most colorful sets in 1972, which included individual stamps of the Siamese, White Persian, Blue Persian, Odd-eyed White Persian, and Tabby, and six others showing scenes of Tabby, Persian, and Siamese kittens. A magnificent 1971 set from Ras al-Khaimah features the Persian, Siamese, Tabby, Tabby kitten, Himalayan, and Domestic Shorthair. Hungary issued a colorful set in 1968 showing the head of a domestic cat, a Cream Angora, a Smoke Angora, another domestic, a White Angora, a Brown-striped Angora, a Siamese, and a Blue Angora. The Isle of Man honored its tailless Manx on a stamp in 1973, and Thailand (formerly Siam) issued a set of four stamps in 1971 honoring the Siamese.

Collecting cat stamps can be a fascinating and educational hobby. Readers wishing more information should consult *Cat Mews* (a publication for collectors of stamps), 607 South Hamline Avenue, St. Paul, Minnesota 55116, and *The Gaines Basic Guide to Collecting Dog and Cat Stamps,* by Harry L. Tankoos (see "Free and Low Cost Literature" in Chapter XVI). Included in the Tankoos book are chapters on how to start a collection, where to get stamps (both by mail and at retail stamp stores), and how to arrange and mount them, plus illustrations and descriptions of the various breeds of cats.

The Cat in Music, Dance, and the Theater

Sixteenth-century engravings indicate that unprincipled show producers used cats in cruel and inhumane ways to entertain the public. At least a dozen cats were confined in a long and narrow box perforated with many holes. The tails of the cats passed through the holes and were fastened to organ keys, causing the poor creatures to howl when the keys were depressed. "Cat organs" were a popular diversion from the sixteenth to the eighteenth centuries.

On the brighter side, cats have been the companions of many of the world's greatest composers and an influence on their works as well. Most cat compositions imitate cat meows, caterwauls, and spits, or mimic feline movements. The sounds made by Domenico Scarlatti's (1685-1757) cat as she ran softly over the keyboard inspired him to compose *Fuga del Gatto,* or *The Cat's Fugue,* a collection of sonatas for the harpsichord. In Gioacchino Rossini's (1792-1868) delightful "Duetto Buffo di Due Gatti" ("Comic Duet for Two Cats"), feline sounds are imitated by female voices. Frédéric Chopin's (1810-49) "Cat Waltz" and Gabriel Fauré's (1845-1924) "Kitty Waltz" bring to mind the litheness of felines playing on the keyboard. Maurice Ravel's (1875-1937) opera *L'Enfant et les Sortilèges,* based on a story by Colette (herself a cat lover), contains a charming duel for male and female cats. Aaron Copland's (1900-   ) "The Cat and the Mouse" emulates a cat's furtive stalking and playing with his prey.

Then there is a story that the renowned Polish composer and pianist Ignace Jan Paderewski (1860-1941) credited the success of his London concert debut to the resident cat of the St. James's Theatre. When the very nervous Paderewski walked on stage, he noticed the cat curled up near the piano, in the presence of the audience. Paderewski whispered a few words to the cat, then seated himself at the piano. Soon after he began to play, the cat sprang onto the piano bench, curled up in his lap, and stayed there "purring in concert pitch," according to Paderewski, until the conclusion of the piece. The composed virtuoso honored the cat at the end of the brilliant concert by playing Scarlatti's *Cat's Fugue.*

Musicians used the violin to represent feline sounds at one time, but modern composers have turned to the woodwind instruments to imitate the cat. Igor Stravinsky chose a clarinet to denote cat voices in *Berceuses du Chat* (*Lullabies of the Cat*) in 1917, and

Sergei Prokofiev used the same instrument in 1936 to play the cat's role in *Peter and the Wolf*.

In the world of dance, the pas de chat, or "cat's step," in classical ballet suggests a lithe cat jumping over a cushion. The most famous feline music and dancing in ballet is the pas de deux for Puss in Boots and the White Cat in Peter Ilyich Tchaikovsky's *The Sleeping Beauty*. Two dancers perform the classical steps, but they let down their hair occasionally to claw at each other while the orchestra meows. The choreography and the music produce a great feline intensity.

Modern choreographers have been inspired by cats too. George Balanchine choreographed *La Chatte*, a contemporary ballet based on an Aesop fable about a cat who was changed into a woman. The ballet was first performed by Sergei Diaghilev's Ballets Russes in Monte Carlo and starred Olga Spessivtseva as the cat. Henri Sauguet composed the music for *La Chatte*, and it is said that when his own cat, Cody, heard his master playing the score, he would jump on the piano and roll over or lick Sauguet's fingers.

In Roland Petit's masterpiece *Les Demoiselles de la Nuit*, based on a story by Jean Anouilh, the leading role of a white cat named Agathe was danced by Dame Margot Fonteyn. The famous ballerina vividly describes the orchestra and costume rehearsals in her autobiography. Leonor Fini, the designer, was obsessed with cats and had created ravishing costumes and elaborate cat masks with pink noses and whiskers. Dame Margot refused to wear her mask because she "could not imagine expressing emotion with her head shut in a cat box." So the mask was cut down to a more comfortable size. The 1948 premiere of *Les Demoiselles de la Nuit* was a smashing success, but not without its momentous occurrences. Dame Margot recalls: "The ballet went surprisingly well in the last scene, when the poet follows Agathe and her cat friends across the rooftops. Leonor had designed a sensationally realistic roof setting, and as we all pounded about chasing each other over the tiles, the structure collapsed. We brought the ballet to a close, amid a mass of splinters on stage, and to cheers from the public."*

Pyewacket, the Siamese in John Van Druten's symbolic comedy *Bell, Book and Candle,* is surely the most famous cat of the legitimate theater. Rex Harrison and Lilli Palmer starred in the original Broadway production, and there is a delightful passage in Miss Palmer's autobiography *Change Lobsters and Dance* describing Pyewacket's escapades in the first act.† As the curtain went up, Miss Palmer sat in front of a fireplace with the cat on her knee. She describes how she had to forcefully hold the cat in her lap every night to make her stay in place. The frustrated Pyewacket would raise her head and meow so loudly that the audience was sure she was doing it on cue!

Early in 1980 the play *Heartaches of a Pussycat* opened on Broadway after a brilliant season in both London and Paris, and an enthusiastic tour of Italy, Germany, Belgium, Luxembourg, and Switzerland. The production was adapted from Honoré de Balzac's story about Beauty, a white cat raised by a prim, old-maid crow, from the nineteenth-century *Scenes From The Public and Private Lives of The Animals.*

---

*Margot Fonteyn, *Autobiography* (New York: Alfred A. Knopf, 1971).

†Lilli Palmer, *Change Lobsters and Dance* (New York: Macmillan Publishing Co., 1975).

Unfortunately the New York production ran for only a few performances, but the play was favorably reviewed by some critics. One of the most prized tickets of the 1980-81 London theatrical season was to *Cats,* musical adaptation of T. S. Eliot's *Old Possum's Book of Practical Cats. The New York Times,* announcing the arrival of the Broadway production, commented that "Cats has no story line but it is a catalog of feline virtues and peccadilloes, anthropomorphizing household pets into a cavalcade of pusillanimous freebooters, streetwalkers and waggish philosophers." *Cats* opened October 7, 1982, at the Winter Garden Theater to rave reviews and a $7.5-million-dollar advance ticket sale, the largest in the history of Broadway.

XIV Feline Myths, Proverbs, and Sayings

The bad luck in meeting a black cat really depends on whether you're a man or a mouse.

—Anonymous

Feline Myths: Fact or Fiction?

Beliefs about cats have existed through the centuries. Their sources are mostly unknown, but undoubtedly they are based on superstition and coincidence as well as common sense. Some are factual to a degree, but others are totally incorrect and often affect our attitudes or knowledge about cats. The following are some of the most common feline beliefs. How many have you heard?

Cats have a very keen sense of taste.
Fact. Cats do have a discriminating sense of taste. They are able to discern differences at thresholds far below that of a man or dog.

Cats are smarter than dogs.
Fiction. There is no proof of supremacy in either animal. Each cat or dog is an individual, and intelli-

gence, abilities, and temperament can vary considerably.

Spaying or castrating makes a cat obese.
Fiction. Thousands and thousands of unwanted kittens are born every year because of this myth. Obesity generally is the result of overeating, metabolic problems, and/or inadequate exercise, and has little to do with neutering.

All white cats are deaf.
Fiction. All white cats are not deaf, but *some* may be. Deafness is a hereditary factor associated with the color white.

Cats can suffocate babies by sucking the breath out of them.
Fiction. This preposterous ancient belief still prevails in many parts of the world. And uninformed friends or relatives still frighten expectant parents with this old wives' tale, begging them to give up their cats.

Cats kept indoors do not need vaccinations.
Fiction. Every cat needs to be immunized against certain infectious diseases, especially those that stay indoors. Animals that go outdoors and come into contact with others may develop a sort of "natural" immunity to diseases they are exposed to. Cats that remain indoors exclusively have little chance to develop "natural" immunity. They need more protection because they are more susceptible to diseases that can be carried inside.

Vaccination during kittenhood against certain infectious diseases guarantees lifetime immunity.

Fiction. Kittens should be vaccinated at an early age against five infectious diseases: panleukopenia (also called feline infectious enteritis), rhinotracheitis, calivicirus, pneumonitis, and rabies, and these should be supplemented by boosters. The frequency of boosters depends on the type of protective vaccine, but generally they are given yearly.

Calico cats are worth thousands of dollars.

Fiction. The Calico might be called a "female only" variety. Few males appear, and these are born infertile. A fine quality female Calico has the same value as any other choice pure-breed cat. The same rule applies to the occasional sterile male. But if a fertile male ever appeared, he might be worth thousands!

White cats bring good luck; black cats bring bad luck.

Fiction. Old wives' tales involving black and white cats and luck trace back to ancient times and are extremely complicated. In most countries (including the United States) a black cat is a symbol of bad luck while a white cat represents good luck. The roles are reversed in United Kingdom countries, where it is considered unlucky to have a white cat cross your path. The wives of English sailors used to keep black cats as good luck charms when their husbands went to sea.

Cats have nine lives.

Fiction. Cats do not have nine lives. But the frequent occurrence of the numeral nine in sacred and occult literature concerning cats signifies something more than a random number. M. Oldfield Howey reveals in *The Cat in the Mysteries of Religion and Magic*: "In the Egyptian pantheon, three companies of nine Gods each were fully developed by the period of the Fifth Dynasty, and because of their protecting love of the cat, may have originated the thought that she had nine lives. Probably this idea that all divinities could be enumerated in nines was the reason why nine was dedicated to both sun and moon and the cat that had symbolized them, by nations that had contacted Egyptian thought." Another belief concerning the number nine comes from the Middle Ages and involved witches who could transform themselves into cats by black magic. An association with the Devil permitted them to do this nine times.

Cat bites are not as harmful as dog bites.
Fiction. Humans are frequently bitten by cats and dogs. While a dog bite may cause more tissue damage (depending on the animal's size), a bite from a cat can be even more dangerous because of the presence of certain bacteria in the cat's mouth. The deep and narrow punctures made by feline teeth are troublesome to clean, and they often heal on the surface and trap the bacteria inside to cause infection. Seek medical advice immediately if you are bitten by a cat.

A falling cat always lands on its feet.
Fiction. Many cats are severely injured or killed because people believe that they can fall from excessive altitudes and survive. Most cats possess a "body righting reflex," a series of turns accomplished in about an eighth of a second, in which they will land on all four feet with their backs arched to buffer the

impact. This reflex is activated from signals from (1) the feet losing contact with a solid surface, (2) a reaction from the balancing mechanism inside the ears, (3) the picturing of an unnatural body position by the eyes, and (4) the body muscles becoming aware of the same unnatural position. Blindness or deafness will not inhibit the righting reflex unless the cat suffers from both handicaps at the same time. Then it will come down in any position.

A cat's whiskers should never be trimmed.
Fact. A cat's whiskers, or vibrissae, are antennalike sensory organs that relay their slightest contact with an object to roots rich in nerves and blood vessels implanted in the skin. The whiskers fan out sideways and help a cat to determine whether a particular opening will contain him or signal objects ahead. Claire Necker, in *The Natural History of Cats* (see "Bibliography of the Cat," in Chapter XVI), explains that "whiskers supplement a cat's vision at all times and all but replace it in darkness. Normal cats evade objects skillfully at night; a cat deprived of its whiskers will frequently collide with objects or clumsily evade them if its head has made a slight contact. A dewhiskered cat is less precise in all its movements and under experimental conditions, at least, was found to be very slow in discovering exits to barriers impeding its progress."

Cats are color-blind.
Fiction. Scientists believed for many years that cats could see only shades of black and white, but now they know that cats can distinguish color (particularly red and green), although not as effectively as humans

can. Cats also recognize dimensions of limited size and can distinguish accurately between circles, squares, and triangles.

Cats can see in total darkness.
Fiction. Although cats can see objects in dim light that cannot be observed by human eyes, they cannot see in *total* darkness.

Cats and dogs are natural enemies and can never live peacefully together.
Fiction. Although cats and dogs are natural adversaries, most will eventually develop a mutual respect for one another when they live together in the same household.

Humans can get toxoplasmosis from cats.
Fact. Toxoplasmosis is a parasitic disease that can infect animals and humans. It is spread by eating raw meat or through contact with cat fecal material. Infected domestic cats shed oocysts or egg spores in their feces. When flies or cockroaches eat the infested fecal material, they become the intermediate hosts and spread the disease to birds and rodents. Healthy cats become infected when they consume diseased birds and rodents. Toxoplasmosis is most dangerous to women in their first three months of pregnancy. (This disease is discussed in detail in Chapter VI, "Keeping Your Cat Healthy.")

Cat Proverbs

American Folk
Never was a drowned cat or dog that could see the shore.

A cat has nine lives.
As curious as a cat.
Never let a cat watch your chickens.
The tongue of a dog cures; the tongue of the cat is poison.

English
The dog for the man; the cat for the woman.
A woman hath nine lives like a cat.
Curiosity killed the cat; satisfaction brought it back.
The cat would eat fish but would not wet its feet.
Don't let the cat out of the bag.

French
A cat with little ones never has a good mouthful.
For a good cat, a good rat.
Every black cat is not a witch.
Whoever cares for cats well will marry as happily as he or she wishes.
He that denies the cat milk must give the mouse cream.

Irish
Beware of people who dislike cats.
An old cat never burned itself.
To fight like Kilkenny cats.
The more you stroke a cat, the more it lifts its tail.
A cat pent up becomes a lion.

Italian
A cat in gloves never catches a mouse.
All cats have claws.
The best cat can lose a mouse.

Beware the cat in May.
An old cat sports not with his prey.

Middle Eastern
God gave man the cat so that he might have the pleasure of caressing the tiger.
If you want to know what a tiger is like, look at a cat.
The cat does not catch mice for God.
A cat is a lion in a jungle of small bushes.
Beware the tiger that lurks in every cat.

Oriental
When the cat has gone, the rats come out to stretch themselves.
A lame cat is better than a swift horse when rats infest the palace.
The cat is a tiger to the mouse; but only a mouse to the tiger.
If the dog goes when the cat comes, there will be no fight.
A rat who gnaws at a cat's tail invites destruction.

Russian
The cat is a lion to the mouse.
The day is young, said the cat, remembering that he could wait.
A cat is hungry when a crust of bread contents her.
There is no kitten too little to scratch.
After a time, even a dog makes a truce with a cat.

Spanish/Portuguese
In the dark, all cats look gray.
The cat always leaves a mark on her friends.

When the mice laugh at the cat, there you will find a hole.

A house with neither dog nor cat is the house of a scoundrel.

A gloved cat never was a good hunter.

Cat Words

Alley cat: (slang) A cat without a pedigree.

Bear cat: Difficult person to reason with.

Cat: A person who is spiteful; a gossip; (slang) a devotee of jazz.

Cat burglar: A burglar who breaks into houses from second-story windows.

Cat-eyed: Able to see well in the dark.

Cat-o'-nine-tails: Whip (usually made of nine knotted cords fastened to a handle) used for flogging.

Cat stane: Battle stone in Scotland.

Cat wash: A quick cleaning.

Catbird: North American songbird, having a call similar to the meow of a cat.

Catboat: A boat having one mast set well forward and one large sail.

Catbrier: Various species of *Smilax,* so named because it scratches.

Catcall: Cry of disapproval (like that of a cat) made by a human voice.

Caterwaul: To howl or screech like a cat.

Catfish: Various species of fish characterized by barbels around the mouth, possibly named from its spines resembling cat's claws.

Cathead: Nautical term for a projecting timber or metal beam to which an anchor is hoisted.

Cathouse: (slang) A brothel.

Catnap: A short nap.

Catnip: Plant of the mint family.

Cat's cradle: Child's game played with string or thread.

Cat's paw: A person used by another.

Cat's sleep: A sham sleep, like that of a cat watching a mouse.

Cat's whisker: Any wire for making contact with a semiconductor.

Cattails: Tall, reedlike marsh plants.

Catty: Feline; spiteful or malicious.

Catwalk: A narrow walkway.

Copycat: An unimaginative imitator.

Fat cat: (slang) A person who has everything.

Fraidy-cat: A fearful person.

Glamour puss: An attractive person.

Hellcat: A person who causes trouble.

Hepcat: (slang) A person familiar with the latest ideas.

Kitty: A pool or reserve of money.

Kitty-corner (or catty-corner; cater-corner): To set diagonally.

Pickle-puss: (slang) A person with a sour look.

Puss: (slang) The face.

Pussycat: (slang) A highly agreeable or well-liked person.

Pussyfoot: To walk or act cautiously.

Pussy willow: A small American willow with fuzzy flowers that feel like a cat's fur.

Scaredy-cat: A person who is easily frightened.

Tomcat: (slang) A man who chases women.

Cat Phrases

To live a cat and dog life: To quarrel constantly.

To play cat and mouse: To dally with someone.

Raining cats and dogs: Pouring rain.

To bell the cat: To struggle with hardship with a degree of success.

Let the cat out of the bag: To tell a secret.

The cat's got his tongue: When someone becomes suddenly speechless.

The cat did it: Putting the blame on someone else.

The cat's meow: Something or someone unique.

Grin like a Cheshire cat: To smile widely.

To see how the cat jumps: To see which way the wind is blowing.

To turn cat-in-pan: To turn traitor.

To have kittens: To become upset about something.

To live under the cat's foot: To be henpecked.

Be made a cat's paw: A person who does another's dirty work.

To rub one's fur the wrong way: To irritate someone.

To be catty: To gossip.

To look like the cat that has swallowed the canary: To look self-satisfied.

XV A Dictionary of Celebrated Cats, The Cats of Celebrated People, And a Few Legendary Fictional Felines

ABANAZAR. Cat owned by the British Office of Works that lived longer than several prime ministers at 10 Downing Street.

AGRIPPINA. Jet-black cat with white markings belonging to Agnes Repplier (1855-1950), author of several books about cats. When Agrippina, named for the Roman empress, gave birth to a kitten, he was appropriately named Nero Claudius after the son of her namesake. Agnes Repplier dedicated her authoritative work *The Fireside Sphinx* (1901) to Agrippina's memory.

ANDY. Cat belonging to Senator Ken Myer of Florida that is the world record holder for the longest fall by a living pet. Andy survived a fall from the sixteenth floor of an apartment building.

ARIEL. Orange Persian belonging to Carl Van Vechten (1880-1964), U. S. author of the now-classic *The Tiger in the House*.

The cat has been called a thief. . . . Ariel used to hide spools, keys, pens, pencils, and scissors under rugs. She saw no more reason why she should not make such booty her own than the early settlers of America saw any reason why they should not convert aboriginal property to their uses. These early settlers looked upon the Indians as inferiors who had no rights, and the cat looks upon man in the same way.

ATOSSA.   Persian belonging to English essayist and poet Matthew Arnold (1822-88). Atossa was named for a queen of Persia who was the wife of Cambyses and later of Darius. Arnold referred to "Toss" in many letters to his mother, describing her sweet voice; how she slept on the armchair before the drawing-room fire; how she stretched out on the floor to let the sunshine bathe all the deep, rich, tawny fur of her stomach; and how she made the servants let her go outside. Atossa was immortalized in Arnold's poem "Poor Matthias," about his pet canary.

BATHSHEBA.   Cat belonging to American poet John Greenleaf Whittier (1807-92), who composed the following tribute after her demise:

> Bathsheba
> To whom one never said scat
>   No worthier cat
>   Ever sat on a mat
>   Or caught a rat
>   Requies-Cat.

BÉBÉ, CREVETTE, IBLIS, LILITH, and SATAN.   Beloved pets of French poet, playwright, and novelist Judith

Gautier (1850-1917), daughter of Théophile Gautier.

BEELZEBUB and BLATHERSKITE. Cats belónging to Mark Twain, pen name of American author and humorist Samuel Langhorn Clemens. Twain was a passionate ailurophile and adored having lots of cats around him. Some others were called Apollinaris, Buffalo Bill, Cleveland, Frauline, Satan, Sin, Soapy Sall, and Sour Mash, names given them, according to Twain, "not in an unfriendly spirit, but merely to practice the children in large and difficult styles of pronunciation."

BIS. Pet, owned by a wealthy Parisienne, that was nicknamed "The Rothschild of Cats." When Bis's owner died, she willed her fortune and splendid mansion (complete with servants) to him. To prevent irate relatives from breaking the will, the clever owner named the city of Paris as coheir, which forced the city to act as watchdog over Bis for as long as he lived. For the next five years until Bis's death, trustees faithfully visited the mansion twice a month to make sure the cat was healthy and contented.

BLACK JACK. Cat that lived in the reading room of the British Museum in the early 1900s. It is said that Jack would languish on a table for hours, indifferent to the researchers working about him. When he wanted to go out, he expected the doors to be opened. One Sunday when he was accidentally locked in one of the newspaper rooms, Jack passed the time by sharpening his claws on some leather bindings. The museum officials banished Jack as punishment, but to everyone's delight he reappeared a few weeks later and was officially dubbed "The Reading Room Cat" (see MIKE).

BOB.   Black cat that lived at 10 Downing Street in London during World War II. The press often photographed Bob, a special favorite of Winston Churchill's, sitting on the steps of the prime minister's residence.

BOMBALURINA.   Fictional character in *Old Possum's Book of Practical Cats* by T. S. Eliot.

BROWNIE and HELLCAT.   Cats from San Diego, California, that inherited more than $400,000 when their owner, Dr. William Grier, died in 1963.

BULGARIAN BELLE.   Cat that became the mascot of the "Black Watch," or 42nd Royal Highland Infantry Brigade. She was found by one of the Highlanders near the Bulgarian town of Varna and adopted by the regiment. Belle traveled in the soldiers' knapsacks to the Crimea, where the armies of Britain and France waged devastating war against the tsar's troops, and where she became the first mascot cat to see battle.

CALVIN.   White Angora belonging to Charles Dudley Warner (1829-1900), American novelist and essayist. Dudley Warner received the cat from Harriet Beecher Stowe, author of *Uncle Tom's Cabin,* and named him after the Protestant reformer John Calvin "on account of his gravity, morality and uprightness." The handsome cat was immortalized in Dudley Warner's memoir *Calvin, A Study of Character.*

CAPTAIN JINKS OF THE HORSE MARINES.   Celebrated black Maine Coon owned by F. R. Pierce; mentioned in his work *The Book of the Cat* (1861).

CATARINA.   Tortoiseshell cat belonging to Edgar Allan Poe (1809-49), American poet and short-story writer. When Poe's young wife, Virginia, lay dying of consumption, an acquaintance described a poignant bedroom scene with Catarina:

> The weather was cold, and the sick lady had the dreadful chills that accompany the hectic fever of consumption. She lay on the straw-bed, wrapped in her husband's great coat, with a large tortoiseshell cat in her bosom. The wonderful cat seemed conscious of her great usefulness. The coat and the cat were the sufferer's only means of warmth.

CHANOINE.   Cherished Persian belonging to Victor Hugo (1802-85), French poet, novelist, and dramatist.

CHESHIRE CAT.   Fictional feline of the children's classic *Alice's Adventures in Wonderland,* created by Lewis Carroll, pen name of Charles L. Dodgson; most famous for its crafty grin and remarkable knack of appearing and disappearing on the spur of the moment (see "The Cat in Children's Literature," Chapter XIII).

CHESSIE.   Fictional symbol of the Chesapeake & Ohio Railway. The sleeping kitten first appeared in a portrait of a gray tabby by G. Gruenwald of Vienna, Austria. The picture was printed in the magazine section of the *New York Herald Tribune,* and seen by Mr. L. C. Probert, then C&O vice-president. Probert was so captivated by the little kitten peacefully resting its head on a pillow that the company purchased the exclusive rights, christened the kitten "Chessie," and made her the company spokes-cat.

CHILDEBRAND.   One of the many beloved cats of French poet, novelist, and critic Théophile Gautier. Gautier described Childebrand as "a splendid cat of common kind, tawny and striped with black . . . with his large green, almost almond-shaped eyes and his symmetrical stripes, there was something tiger-like about him that pleased me."

CHILDEBRAND.   Favorite companion of Vicomte François René de Chateaubriand (1768-1848), French author and statesman.

COBBY.   Gray persian with deep orange eyes belonging to English poet and novelist Thomas Hardy.

COLUMBINE.   Black cat belonging to Thomas Carlyle (1795-1881), Scottish essayist and historian. Columbine's presence disturbed Carlyle's wife, Jane, who was a dog lover. She once wrote to her maid: "As long as Columbine attends Mr. C. at meals, so long will Mr. C. continue to give her bits of meat and driblets of milk, to the ruination of the carpets and hearth rugs."

CRISTOBAL COLON.   Gray tabby mascot of the Spanish cruiser *Cristobal Colon*. When American warships *Oregon* and *Brooklyn* bombarded the cruiser off the coast of Cuba in 1898, its terrified little mascot was rescued from the sinking. The crew of the *Oregon* presented her to their captain, who named the cat after the sunken ship and sent her temporarily to his brother for safekeeping. A sign was attached to her travel-case that read:

To Good Americans
Treat me kindly and give me food, as I am a prisoner of war from the *Cristobal Colon*, being

forwarded by my captors, the crew of the *Oregon*, to their gallent commander, Captain Charles E. Clark, whose brave efforts forced the *Colon* to surrender July 3, 1898.

DESDEMONA, OPTELLO, and PANTALONE. Angora cats belonging to Monsignore Alfonso Capecelatro (1744-1836), the Archbishop of Taranto in Naples. In her *Book of the Boudoir* (1829), the Irish writer Lady Morgan describes a dinner party at the archbishop's palace: "Between the first and second courses, the door opened and several enormously large and beautiful cats were introduced by the names of Pantalone, Desdemona and Otello. They took their places on chairs near the table and were as silent, as quiet, as motionless, and as well behaved, as the most bon ton table in London could require."

DEUTERONOMY and GENESIS. Cats belonging to Mark Twain (see Beelzebub and Blatherskite.)

DINAH. A fictional feline belonging to Alice that appears in *Alice's Adventures in Wonderland* and *Through the Looking Glass,* classic children's stories written by Lewis Carroll (see Cheshire cat). Dinah was inspired by and named for a real cat owned by three sisters who influenced Carroll's writings.

DISRAELI, GLADSTONE, and BISMARCK. Persian cats belonging to English nurse Florence Nightingale (1820-1910), called the "Lady with the Lamp."

DON-PIERROT-DE-NAVARRE. White cat belonging to Théophile Gautier, French poet, novelist, and critic. Gautier wrote that "he was very fond of books, and when he found one open on a table he would lie down on it, turn over the edges of the leaves with his paws, and after a while fall asleep, for all the world as if he had been reading a fashionable novel."

DORA and DICK.   Companions of English novelist Frances Hodgson Burnett (1849-1924). Dora is described in *The One I Know Best of All,* Burnett's description of her childhood when her family was poverty-stricken. Dick, her pet after she settled in America, was entered at the first cat show held in New York City.

DOROTHÉE.   Beloved pet of Madame Récamier (Jeanne Françoise Julie Adélaide Bernard, 1777-1849), social leader in literary and political circles of Paris.

DUSTY.   Siamese cat from Bonham, Texas, that gave birth to a total of 420 kittens during her lifetime.

ENJOLRAS.   Cat belonging to Théophile Gautier, French poet, novelist, and critic. Gautier described Enjolras as "solemn, pretentious, aldermanic from his cradle, even theatrical at times in his vast assumption of dignity."

EPONINE.   Pet belonging to Théophile Gautier. She was a delicate, fastidious little cat whose "intelligence, fine disposition, and sociability led to her being elevated by common consent to the dignity of a person," wrote Gautier. "That dignity conferred upon her the right to eat at table, like a person, and not in a corner, from a saucer like an animal. Eponine had a chair by my side at breakfast and dinner, but in consideration of her size, she was privileged to place her forepaws on the table."

FAFNER, FASOLT, and MIME.   Pets belonging to Catulle Mendès (1841-1909), French poet and author. A devout ailurophile, Mendès served on the jury at the first cat show held in Paris, along with Théophile Steinlen, Eugène Lambert, Pierre Mégnin, François Coppée, and others.

FAITH.   Gray Tabby that lived in the Church of St. Augustine-with-St. Faith in London during World War II. Originally a stray, Faith was adopted by the rector and named after one of the patron saints of the church. She produced a black and white kitten in 1940, called "Panda" by the rector because he so resembled the Tibetan bear. Faith's extraordinary perception caused her to move her kitten to a recessed area one night during the German bombing of London, and as a result both survived a direct hit on the rectory. The brave little feline was presented with a silver medal from the People's Dispensary for Sick Animals, which read: "From the P.D.S.A. to Faith of St. Augustine's, Watling Street, E.C. For steadfast courage in the Battle of London, September 9, 1940."

FAT OLIVE.   Tomcat that survived a fall from a 160-foot-high penthouse, according to his owner, Pat Lazaroff of Toronto, Canada. Fat Olive landed on grass and broke two legs.

FEATHERS.   Tortoiseshell and white smoke Tabby Persian belonging to Carl Van Vechten, American author.

FELIX-MENDELSSOHN-BARTHOLDY-SHEDLOCK-RUNCIMAN-FELINIS.   The companion of John Runciman (1866-1916), English writer and critic. Felix was musically inclined and it is written that he attempted to play the viola alta by trailing the bow across the floor.

FELIX THE CAT.   Famous cartoon cat created in 1917 by Pat Sullivan (1887-1933).

FIGARO. Fictional cat belonging to Gepetto, the woodcarver in *The Adventures of Pinocchio*—a boy puppet who wants to be human and whose nose grows every time he tells a lie—by Carlo Collodi (1826-90). The children's classic was made into a full-length animated cartoon by the Walt Disney studios.

FISHERMAN and LONGY. Cats belonging to Aleksandr Borodin (1834-87), Russian composer and chemist. They are described in Nikolai Rimski-Korsakov's biography, *Ma Vie Musicale* (1941).

FOSS. Cherished companion of Edward Lear (1812-88), English landscape painter, writer, and poet. Lear's humorous poems, such as "The Owl and the Pussycat," have captivated children and adults for more than a century. He wrote charming letters about Foss to friends and relatives, and decorated them with amusing renditions of himself and the cat as well. Lear immortalized his faithful companion in many humorous sketches, most notably a series of drawings for Foss's heraldic blazon, showing the cat in rampant, regardant, couchant, and delightfully dansant poses. One can assume from Lear's merry sketches that Foss was a strapping Tabby, for he always appears with rounded belly, tiger stripes, and a funny stump of a tail. When Foss died at the ripe old age of seventeen, Lear buried the cat in the garden of his villa at San Remo on the Italian Riviera and erected a monument over the gravesite.

FRANCES and CATHERINE. The companions of Émile Zola (1840-1902), French novelist.

GARFIELD. A gluttonous orange tiger cartoon cat with a passion for Italian food ("I never met a

lasagna I didn't like"), created by Jim Davis
(1945-   ) and named after the artist's grandfather. Garfield made his first appearance in 1978
and quickly became the most popular cartoon cat in
America. His antics entertain millions of newspaper readers, who glance at "Garfield" even before
turning to the stock market quotations. He has
been the subject of many best-selling books, including *Garfield at Large, Garfield Gains Weight, Garfield
Weighs In,* and *Garfield Bigger Than Life,* and he was
the star of his own TV extravaganza.

GAVROCHE.   Companion of Théophile Gautier,
French poet, novelist, and critic. Gavroche loved to
tumble and twirl, and he would lead home all the
bedraggled street cats, who would gobble up all the
food prepared for him. Gautier wrote: "Gavroche
was born of Bohemian temperament and en-
amored of low company and of careless comedies
of life."

GAZETTE.   Cat belonging to Armand Jean du Plessis,
Duc de Richelieu (1585-1642), French cardinal and
statesman. Gazette was "an outrageously indiscreet
little cat who was embarrassed at nothing."

GIPSY.   Fictional cat, "half bronco and half Malay
pirate, of *Penrod and Sam,* created by Booth Tar-
kington (1869-1946), American novelist and play-
wright.

GRI-GRI.   Siamese belonging to Raymond Poincaré
(1860-1934), French statesman and President of
France, 1913-1920. Poincaré described Gri-Gri as
"intelligent as any man."

GRIMALKIN.   Cat belonging to Christina Rossetti, English poet. When Grimalkin died, Rossetti com-

posed a poem entitled "On the Death of a Cat, A Friend of Mine Age Ten Years and a Half."

GRISETTE.   The favorite cat of Madame Antoinette Deshoulières (1638-1694), French poet, and celebrity at the court of Louis XIV. Madame Deshoulières wrote a play, *La Mort de Cochon,* in which all the characters are cats.

GRIZABELLA.   A character in the musical *Cats,* with music by Andrew Lloyd Webber (1948-   ), based on T. S. Eliot's *Old Possum's Book of Practical Cats,* which premiered in London in May 1981 and on Broadway in October 1982. Although the character Grizabella does not actually appear in Eliot's charming book of verses, her story was discovered in his unpublished writings and incorporated into the lyrics of the musical.

GUS.   The fictional "theatre" cat in *Old Possum's Book of Practical Cats* by T. S. Eliot.

HAMILCAR and PASCAL.   The feline companions of Anatole France (pen name of Jacques Anatole François Thibault, 1844-1924), French novelist and essayist. Hamilcar appears as a character in Anatole France's first successful novel *Le Crime de Sylvestre Bonnard.*

HAMLET.   Gray and white resident cat of the Algonquin Hotel in New York City, the famed meeting place of literary and theatrical personalities for half a century. Hamlet succeeded Rusty, a tortoiseshell tomcat, and inherited Rusty's cat-sized door installed into the hotel wall, allowing him to enter or exit when he pleased, under the careful surveillance of the doorman. Hamlet was the subject of the book *Algonquin Cat* (1980), written by Val Schaffner and illustrated by Hilary Knight. When

Hamlet died, his obituary appeared in *Variety* and in *The Times* of London. (See: RUSTY; HAMLET II.)

HAMLET II. Resident cat of the Algonquin Hotel in New York City, and successor to Hamlet. Donated by Jane Boutwell, a staff writer at *The New Yorker* and Algonquin regular, Hamlet II enjoys all the pleasures and privileges of his predecessors.

HEATHCLIFF. Comic-strip cat created in 1973 by George Gately (1929–   ) and named after the moody and virile character Heathcliff of Emily Brontë's *Wuthering Heights*.

HINOKO. Cat belonging to Lafcadio Hearn (1850-1904), American (born in Greece) journalist, novelist, and essayist. As a newspaper correspondent, Hearn was assigned to the Orient and became obsessed with all things Japanese. He became a citizen of Japan, converted to Buddhism, and married a Japanese woman of samurai rank. One day while Hearn's wife was walking along the seashore, she spied some naughty boys trying to drown a black cat. She grabbed the bedraggled little victim and ran home and presented it to her husband. Hearn named it Hinoko—the Japanese word for spark—because its eyes sparkled like glowing coals.

HINSE OF HINSEFIELD. Black tomcat belonging to Sir Walter Scott (1771-1832), Scottish novelist and poet. Scott owned many dogs during his lifetime but never a cat until he dined with Archbishop Capecelatro in Naples. After he saw the archbishop's beautifully mannered Angoras—Desdemona, Otello, and Pantelone, eating at the dinner table, he introduced Hinse to his Abbotsford estate, where the cat quickly held sway over the dogs. Even Scott's huge Deerhound, Maida, deferred to the black tom. "Hinse keeps Maida in the best possible order," wrote Scott, "and insists on all rights of precedence and scratches with impunity the nose of an animal who would make no bones of a wolf and pull down a red deer without fear or difficulty."

HODGE.   Black cat belonging to Samuel Johnson (1709-84), English lexicographer, poet, and critic. When Hodge began to age, Dr. Johnson would go to market every morning to buy the cat's favorite food, fresh oysters, then clean them and feed them to him one by one. James Boswell (1740-95), Johnson's friend and "one of those who have an antipathy to a cat," immortalized Hodge when he described the practice in his famous biography *The Life of Samuel Johnson, LL.D.*

JAKE.   Fictional feline character in the Walt Disney Productions film *The Cat From Outer Space* (1978).

JAMES and PIPPA.   Cats belonging to Oswald Barron (1868-1939), English journalist, genealogist, and herald. "James was the sort of cat to whom adventure calls," wrote Barron. "He would sidle out of the house at dusk, not to come home again until the morning brought him to the door, a weary cat with the signs of battle upon him. Pretty it was to see the sleek Pippa welcome back James from his battles, mewing about him, asking him how he came by his scratches."

JELLICLE CATS.   Black and white fictional cats with bright black eyes and merry faces, characters in *Old Possum's Book of Practical Cats* by T. S. Eliot.

JELLYLORUM and JENNYANYDOTS.   Fictional characters from *Old Possum's Book of Practical Cats* by T. S. Eliot.

JEOFFRY. Cat belonging to Christopher Smart (1722-71), English poet, and faithful companion during Smart's four-year term in Bedlam prison for the insane. During confinement Smart composed a long mystical and contemplative poem on bits of paper, entitled *Jubilate Agno,* in which he praises Jeoffry's many virtues.

JOCK. Marmalade cat belonging to Sir Winston Churchill (1874-1965), British statesman; prime minister 1940-45 and 1951-55. Churchill's private secretary found the tiny kitten in a home for strays and presented him to the prime minister on his eightieth birthday. Jock and Churchill became inseparable, and the little cat commuted regularly with his master between London and Chartwell, the family estate in Kent. After Sir Winston's death Jock remained at Chartwell, where he lived peacefully for eleven more years. He died in 1976 and was buried in the gardens of the family estate, where a memorial marks his gravesite. Chartwell is maintained by the British National Trust, and that organization concluded that a marmalade cat should always be in residence to preserve the cozy Churchillian flavor. Another marmalade kitten was adopted from a home for strays, christened Jock II, and installed at Chartwell.

JOEY. Cat belonging to Neville Chamberlain (1869-1940), British prime minister, 1937-40.

JOSEPH. English striped tabby belonging to Miss Agatha Frazer Higgins. Joseph (who tipped the scales at forty-eight pounds) became England's richest cat in 1969 when his owner died and bequeathed him her fortune.

KAROUN. Cat belonging to Jean Cocteau (1889-1963), French writer, dramatist, and painter. Cocteau once said that he did not start as a "cat maniac" but had "one by chance, then two, four, five, and more."

KIKI-LA-DOUCETTE. Dappled white and orange Persian belonging to French novelist Colette. The cat was given to Colette in 1893 by her first husband, Henry Gauthier-Villars (popularly known as Monsieur Willy). Colette wrote that Kiki knew the difference between tap and bottled water and ate peas one by one.

KRAZY KAT. Comic-strip cat created by George Herriman (1880-1944).

LA CHATTE. Chartreux cat belonging to French novelist Colette. In 1933 Colette wrote a risqué novel, *La Chatte,* about a strange love triangle involving a husband and wife and the husband's cat, and she selected her beloved La Chatte as the model for Saha, the feline character in the story.

LANGBOURNE. Formally known as The Reverend Sir John Langbourne, D.D., the beloved companion of Jeremy Bentham (1748-1832), English philosopher, economist, and writer on jurisprudence.

LEO. Tabby Maine Coon that was named "Best Cat" at the first professional American cat show, held in 1895 at Madison Square Garden in New York City.

LILITH. Cat belonging to Prosper Mérimée (1803-70), French novelist and poet. Mérimée wrote that Lilith "has such spirit, but what a pity she's so sensitive."

LILITH and NEIGE. Cherished companions of Étienne (Stéphane) Mallarmé, French poet. Lilith was sketched by Whistler.

LUCIFER, LUDOVIC LE CRUEL, and LUDOVISKA. Cats belonging to Armand Jean du Plessis, Duc de Richelieu, French cardinal and statesman. Lucifer was jet-black. Ludovic "was named, as it were, by his cruelty to rats." Ludoviska came from Poland.

MACAVITY. Fictional character in *Old Possum's Book of Practical Cats* by T. S. Eliot.

MADAME THÉOPHILE. The favorite companion of Théophile Gautier, French novelist and critic. Gautier described her as "a reddish cat with a white breast, a pink nose and blue eyes, so named because she lived with us in an intimacy which was quite conjugal, sleeping at the foot of our bed, dreaming on the arm of our chair while we write, going down to the garden to follow us in our walks, assisting at our meals, and sometimes ever intercepting a tid-bit from our plate to our mouths."

MADAME VANITÉ. Cat belonging to Michel Eyquem de Montaigne (1533-92), French essayist. "When I play with my cat who knows whether she diverts herself with me, or I with her!" wrote Montaigne.

MARLAMAIN. Cat belonging to Louise Benedicte de Bourbon, Duchesse du Maine (1676-1753).

MEHITABEL. Fictional cat of *archy and mehitabel*, created by Don Marquis (1878-1937) in 1927.

MICETTO. Beloved companion of Vicomte François René de Chateaubriand, French author and statesman; presented by Pope Leo XII when the Pontiff learned he was dying. Chateaubriand wrote: "My companion is a large gray and red cat, striped with black. He was born in the Vatican, in the loggia of Raphael. Leo the Twelfth reared him on a fold of his white robe, where I used to look at him with envy when, as ambassador, I received my audience."

MICKEY.   British tabby that is the greatest mouser on record. Mickey was owned by Shepherd & Sons Ltd. of Burscough, England, and according to *The Guinness Book of World Records,* he killed more than 22,000 mice during his twenty-three-year affiliation with the company. He died in 1968.

MIGNONNE and PALÉMON.   Cats belonging to Charles Augustin Sainte-Beuve (1804-69), French poet, writer, and literary critic. Palémon, a tabby, once brought home a female that gave birth to six kittens shortly thereafter. Sainte-Beuve placed the following notice on the front door of his house on the rue du Montparnasse in Paris: "Small cats here to be given to people who really love them."

MIKE.   Celebrated British tabby that guarded the main gate of London's British Museum from 1909 to 1929, when he died of old age. Mike made his first appearance in 1908 as a stray kitten carried to the venerable institution by Black Jack, the museum's resident "Reading Room Cat" (see Black Jack). The kitten was fed and permitted to stay, and eventually made his home in the gatekeeper's quarters. Mike took his duties seriously, and no visitors dared to touch him, for he would growl or bite like a fierce watchdog. He maintained a warm friendship only with the gatekeeper and Sir Ernest A. Wallis Budge, the famous Egyptologist. After Mike died, Sir Ernest composed a tribute to his memory, and F.C.W. Hiley, M.A., an assistant in the museum's Department of Printed Books, composed a long epitaph, which ended:

Old Mike! Farewell! We all regret you,
Although you would not let us pet you;
Of cats, the wisest, oldest, best cat
This be your motto—Requiescat.

MIN. "Maltese" cat belonging to Henry David Thoreau (1817-62), American naturalist and author. Thoreau seemed fascinated with all cats, and referred to them often in his works.

MINETTE. Cherished companion and favorite model of Gottfried Mind, artist of Hungarian extraction who lived and painted in Switzerland and was called the "Raphael of Cats." In 1809 a virulent epidemic of rabies swept through Berne, and some eight hundred cats were taken into custody and destroyed by the police. Mind managed to hide and save most of his own cats, including Minette, but the fate of the others obsessed him for the rest of his life.

MINNA MINNA MOWBRAY. Short-haired tortoiseshell tabby belonging to Michael Joseph (1897-   ), English writer and publisher. Minna always wore a green collar decorated with two brass bells. Her vocal cords were partially paralyzed, and, Joseph notes, "she put the bells to practical use, whenever she wanted to be admitted to a room, by shaking her head outside the closed doors. She never worried if she were late for breakfast, knowing that the tinkle of her bell would cause the door to be opened. Sometimes when she rang outside the door I delayed, for the satisfaction of hearing her tinkle imperiously repeated. And with what an air of affronted majesty she stalked into the room if she had been thus kept waiting."

MINNALOUSHE.   Black fictional feline created by Irish poet William Butler Yeats (1865-1939), which first appeared in 1919 in the poem "The Cat and the Moon."

MISTIGRIS, PETIT-LOULOU, and BOURGET.   Cats belonging to François Coppée (1842-1908), French poet and dramatist. Coppée composed the preface to Paul Mégnin's classic work *Notre Ami le Chat,* composed a sonnet for a book of cat drawings by Henriette Ronner, and was one of the judges of the first cat show held in Paris.

MISTY MALARKY YING YANG.   Siamese belonging to Amy Carter, daughter of James Earl Carter, President of the United States, 1977-81. Misty lived in the White House during the Carter administration.

MORRIS.   Celebrated orange tabby television personality that appeared in the 9-Lives cat food commercials. Morris was found in 1968 at the Hinsdale, Illinois, Humane Society by trainer Bob Martwick. The cat was scheduled for euthanasia, but Martwick distinguished a "certain something" and bought him for five dollars. Shortly thereafter Lucky, as he was called at the time, competed with hundreds of felines to play a part in the 9-Lives advertising program. The patient and unflappable cat literally astonished the advertising agency, and they refashioned the campaign to place the emphasis on him. Lucky was renamed Morris and became a television superstar. Morris won the Patsy Award in 1973 for his outstanding performance in TV commercials. He is the subject of the book *Morris: An Intimate Biography,* by Mary Daniels (New York: William Morrow & Co.), and costar (with Burt Reynolds and Dyan Cannon) of the film *Shamus.*

MORRIS II.   Orange tabby cat, successor to Morris, as the television spokes-cat for 9-Lives cat food. Like his predecessor, Morris II was discovered at an animal shelter. When the original Morris died in 1978, 9-Lives contacted humane shelters throughout the United States, searching for a cat to replace the world's No. 1 feline celebrity. After a fourteen-month search a cat that resembled the original Morris turned up at a Cape Cod shelter. He lives with trainer Bob Martwick in Lombard, Illinois, and works, according to *Time* magazine, "about 20 days a year and grosses $5,000 to $10,000."

MOUCHE.   Cat belonging to Victor Hugo, French poet, novelist, and dramatist, that he described as "a magisterial cat, defiant and reserved."

MOUMOUTTE BLANCHE and MOUMOUTTE CHINOISE.   The beloved pets of Pierre Loti, pen name of Louis Marie Julien Viaud (1850-1923), French novelist. The cats are the subjects of Loti's book *Vies de Deux Chattes,* in which he described how he obtained Chinoise. Loti was a lieutenant in the French navy and serving on a ship stationed in the China Sea in 1890. When Chinese pirates tried to capture the ship and were defeated, a starveling cat vaulted from the sinking junk onto the deck of the warship. Loti carried the terrified creature to his cabin and fed and cared for her. He called her Chinoise and decided to keep her. When Loti returned home, he introduced Chinoise to the regal Angora, Blanche, who had held sway over the household for five years without a competitor. She was the proud possessor of calling cards that read: *Madame Moumoutte Blanche. Première chatte. Chez M. Pierre Loti.* The two cats waged a furious battle at first, but gradually they became close friends, washing each other's fur, sleeping together, and sharing the same food, sitting at Loti's right and left at the dinner table.

MOUNARD LE FOUGUEUX and MIMI-PAILLON. Cats belonging to Armand Jean du Plessis, Duc de Richelieu, French cardinal and statesman. Mimi-Paillon was an Angora, and Mounard le Fougueux was a "well-known quarreller, capricious, worldly, especially in the month of March."

MOURKA. Russian cat that was commended for bravery during World War II. During the bombardment of Stalingrad in the winter of 1942, Mourka carried dispatches about enemy gun installations from a group of Russian soldiers through gunfire to headquarters.

MOUSCHI. Cat belonging to Anne Frank (1929-45), that lived with the Frank family and others in an attic in Holland, hiding from the Nazis. Mouschi is the subject of several entries in *The Diary of a Young Girl*.

MR. MISTOFFELES. Literary character that appears in *Old Possum's Book of Practical Cats* by T. S. Eliot.

MR. THOMAS and THE GREAT MR. THOMAS. Cats belonging to P. Wilson Steer (1860-1942), English painter.

MUEZZA. The companion of Mohammed (A.D. 570-632), the founder of Islam. Legend has it that Mohammed so loved his cat that he cut off the hem of his robe with scissors, for fear of disturbing the little creature which had fallen asleep thereon.

MUNGOJERRIE and RUMPLETEASER. Literary characters, a "very notorious couple of cats," that appear in *Old Possum's Book of Practical Cats* by T. S. Eliot.

MURR. Beloved companion of Ernst Theodor Amadeus Wilhelm Hoffmann (1776-1822), German author, composer, and illustrator. Murr appears in many of Hoffmann's stories and was coauthor, Hoffmann confides, of *Lebensansichten des Katers Murr* (Murr the Cat and His Views on Life).

MYSOUFF I, MYSOUFF II, and LE DOCTEUR. Cats belonging to Alexandre Dumas (1802-70), French novelist and dramatist. Both Mysouffs are described in Dumas's *Histoire de mes Bêtes.*

NAPOLEON. White Persian belonging to Mrs. Fannie de Shields of Baltimore, Maryland, that became famous when it was reported he could forecast the weather. When Napoleon would rest on his side, the weather would not change, but when he put himself in his "predicting position"—lying flat on the ground with head resting between his front paws—one could be reasonably sure that the weather would change within twenty-four hours. Napoleon was seldom wrong, and his forecasts often ran counter to those of the official meteorologist, generally to the embarrassment of the Weather Bureau. When the celebrated prophet died at the ripe old age of nineteen, *The Baltimore Sun* declared, NAPOLEON, THE WEATHER CAT, HAS FORECAST LAST STORM.

NAPOLEON THE GREAT. Persian bred by a French nobleman, born at the Château Fontainebleau near Paris in 1888. Described as a "magnificent fellow with bushy orange fur and lion-like head," Napoleon was sold to an American and won many prizes in this country at cat shows. He was so highly prized that his owner reportedly turned down an offer of $4,000 for him.

NELSON.   Large black cat belonging to Sir Winston Churchill. Nelson lived at Admiralty House, and then moved to 10 Downing Street when Churchill became prime minister. Sir Winston called Nelson "My Dear," and he insisted that a chair be reserved for the cat in the Cabinet Room as well as at the dining-room table. There is a well-documented story that one day in 1943, while recuperating from influenza acquired in Casablanca, Sir Winston was visited at Chequers (the prime minister's country estate in Buckinghamshire) by one of his ministers. The devoted Nelson was reclining at his master's feet. "This cat," Churchill stated emphatically, "does more for the war effort than you do. He acts as a hot water bottle and saves fuel and power!"

NEMO.   Siamese belonging to Harold Wilson (1916-   ), British statesman; prime minister 1964-70, 1974-76.

NEW and BOY.   Siamese cats belonging to actress Vivien Leigh (1913-67).

OLD DEUTERONOMY.   Fictional feline "who has lived many lives in succession," and buried nine wives or more, that appears in *Old Possum's Book of Practical Cats* by T. S. Eliot.

OLLIE.   British comic-strip orange cat with huge feet, created by Harry Hargreaves (1922-   ).

ORANGEY.   Orange tabby film and television personality that appeared in the motion picture *Breakfast at Tiffany's* with Audrey Hepburn and George Peppard, and in the TV series *Our Miss Brooks*. Orangey won Patsy Awards in 1952 and 1962.

PATROCLE.   The cherished pet of Jean Auguste Dominique Ingres (1780-1867), French painter. One New Year's Day, according to Fernand Mery in

The Life, History and Magic of the Cat, while Ingres was Director of the French School in Rome, he was preparing for an audience with Prince Borghese when a servant announced that Patrocle had suddenly died. Ingres was so upset that he shut himself into his bedroom for the rest of the day.

PÉRONNELLA. Cat belonging to French novelist Colette. She described her beloved companion in *Chance Acquaintances.* "Péronnella," she said, "has her meals in the bistro, rides in taxis . . . showing off a splendid . . . classically striped face and two green eyes filled with supernatural radiance."

PERSIAN SNOW. Cat belonging to Dr. Erasmus Darwin (1731-1802), English physician, scientist, and writer, and grandfather of Charles Darwin.

PESTILENCE and FAMINE. Cats belonging to Mark Twain (see BEELZEBUB and BLATHERSKITE).

PETER. Black and white cat belonging to English artist Louis Wain. He trained Peter to perform many tricks, the most outstanding being to say his prayers while sitting erect on his hindquarters, with his paws encircling his face.

PETER. Legendary rat-killing tabby that lived in the Stonehouse railway station in Gloucestershire, England. According to Gerald Wood's *Animal Facts and Feats,* Peter killed more than four hundred large rats during a four-week period in June and July of 1938.

PETER WELLS. Cat belonging to H. G. Wells (1866-1946), English novelist and historian.

PLUTO. Fictional feline character created by Edgar Allan Poe, American poet, short-story writer, and critic, in his classic horror tale *The Black Cat.*

PRINCESS SIX TOES.   Cat belonging to Ernest Hemingway (1899-1961), American novelist, short-story
writer, and journalist. Hemingway was a true
ailurophile, and in the last half of his lifetime he
kept nearly sixty cats of various breeds, most of
which were strays that had followed him home.
Princess Six Toes became one of the best-known
felines in this country when her photograph appeared in *The New York Times* and various national
periodicals. Some of Hemingway's other cats were
named Alice B. Toklas, Gertrude Stein, F. Scott
Fitzgerald, Zelda Fitzgerald, Miss Frances, Agatha
Christie, Robin Hood, and Jeanette MacDonald.

PRROU.   Ginger cat belonging to French novelist
Colette, whom she immortalized in *Retreat from
Love,* published in 1907. Prrou is described as
having "a ferocious face, sandy and leonine, with
green-amber eyes . . . a broad nose, a prominent
chin and cheeks muscular as those of a wild beast.
She kills hens, attacks tomcats, eats birds, and
scratches the cook."

PRUDENCE.   Blue Persian belonging to Georges
Clemenceau (1841-1929), French statesman and
journalist; premier of France 1906-09 and 1917-20.
Clemenceau bought Prudence in London when he
traveled there to attend a conference of heads of
state.

PUFF.   Fictional feline character that appeared in the
Dick and Jane series of children's stories first published in 1917.

PUSS.   Tabby belonging to Mrs. T. Holway of North
Devon, England. Puss holds the record for feline
longevity, reaching the ripe old age of thirty-six

years on November 28, 1939, according to *The Guinness Book of World Records*.

PUSS, EBÈNE, and MITONNE.   Cherished pets of Hippolyte Adolphe Taine (1828-93), French historian, critic, and philosopher.

PUSS IN BOOTS.   Fictional feline character made famous by Charles Perrault (1628-1703), French poet, critic, and author of fairy tales (see "The Cat in Children's Literature").

PYEWACKET.   Present-day witch's Siamese cat character in the play *Bell, Book and Candle,* written by John Van Druten. The 1951 Broadway production co-starred Lilli Palmer and Rex Harrison. A movie version appeared in 1959, costarring James Stewart and Kim Novak, and the film Pyewacket won the Patsy Award as the "Outstanding Animal Actor of the Year."

PYRAME and THISBÉ.   Cats belonging to Armand Jean du Plessis, Duc de Richelieu, French cardinal and statesman. The cats were named after the two lovers of Babylon of classical mythology because "they continually slept in each other's paws."

RACAN and PERRUQUE.   Cats belonging to the Duc de Richelieu, and named because they were born in a wig (*perruque*) owned by the French academician Racan.

RHUBARB.   Siamese cat that served as a seeing-eye helper to her blind owner, Elsie Schneider of San Diego, California, for seventeen years. Mrs. Schneider trained Rhubarb as a kitten to help with household duties and shopping, and the cat learned to respond as proficiently as a Seeing Eye dog. Rhubarb posthumously received the first "Hero

Cat of the Decade" award from the Carnation Company's Friskies Cat Council in 1980.

ROGER and GEOFFREY.   Cats belonging to John D. MacDonald (1916-   ), American suspense novelist. MacDonald wrote a charming book about his cats, entitled *The House Guests*.

RUFUS.   Huge, sandy British tomcat that made the rounds of the Treasury Building on Whitehall Street in London in the 1930s. Rufus and several other Treasury cats guarded the packets of banknotes from the bites of mice and rats, and for this service each was paid a wage of fourpence per day.

RUM TUM TUGGER.   Fictional "curious cat" character in *Old Possum's Book of Practical Cats* by T. S. Eliot.

RUMPLESTILZCHEN.   Cherished companion of Robert Southey (1774-1843), English poet and writer; Poet Laureate 1813-43. Notifying a friend of the cat's death, Southey wrote: "Alas Grosvenor, this day poor Rumpel was found dead, after as long and happy a life as a cat could wish for, if cats form wishes on that subject."

RUSTY.   Tortoiseshell tom that lived at the Algonquin Hotel in New York City. Rusty was the hotel's resident cat during the 1930s when the glittering group of writers, actors, and socialites assembled at the Algonquin Round Table and became celebrated as the smart set. Rusty was given his own private entrance, a cat-sized door, built into the wall of the hotel, to allow him to enter or exit when he pleased. Rusty was succeeded by Hamlet (see HAMLET; HAMLET II).

SCOOPY.   Cat columnist in the 1940s for *The Villager*, a weekly newspaper published in New York City.

Scoopy originally was the office mouser, a job he performed with cunning and flair, and he was soon elevated to journalist, where he recounted the goings-on of neighborhood felines and endorsed meritorious local and national occasions. His copy was prepared by two clever newspaper women, Clara Bell Woolworth and subsequently Emmeline Page. When Scoopy died shortly after reaching the age of fourteen, *Time* magazine declared "Death has taken Scoopy the cat, the most celebrated literary feline since Don Marquis discovered Mehitabel."

SELIMA, HAROLD, and ZARA. Cats belonging to Horace Walpole, fourth earl of Oxford (1717-97), English novelist and essayist. When Walpole informed his close friend, the poet Thomas Gray, that his beloved Selima had died, Gray composed the famous "Ode on the Death of a Favourite Cat Drowned in a Tub of Gold Fishes" in the cat's honor.

SERAPHITA. White cat belonging to Théophile Gautier, French novelist and critic.

SHAN. Siamese belonging to Susan Ford, daughter of Gerald Ford (1913-   ), President of the United States, 1974-77. Shan lived in the White House during the Ford administration.

SHEILA. Siamese belonging to Ethel Barrymore (1879-1959), American actress.

SHERRY. Siamese that was lost in the cargo section of a 747 jetliner while her owners were en route from Guam to San Francisco in 1979. Sherry was finally located inside the plane thirty-two days later, but after she had traveled to twelve countries and covered more than 200,000 miles.

SHIMBLESHANKS.   Fictional "Cat of the Railway Train" in *Old Possum's Book of Practical Cats* by T. S. Eliot.

SHUANG-MEI.   Cherished pet of Chu Hou-Tsung (1507-66), eleventh emperor of the Ming Dynasty of China. The *Ku-chin T'u-shu Chi-ch'eng*, a monumental Chinese encyclopedia with ten thousand chapters, describes the Emperor's favorite: "she was of faintly blue color but her two eyebrows were clearly jade-white and she was called Shuang-mei [frost eyebrows]. She surmised the Emperor's intentions very well. Whomever His Majesty summoned and wherever her Imperial master went, she always led."

SIMON.   Famous ship's cat of the British gunboat HMS *Amethyst*. When the ship was stranded after a fierce battle in the Yangtze River, huge rats overran its decks. Simon valiantly defended the precious food supplies for three months until repairs could be completed. He was posthumously awarded the Dickin Medal, known as the "Animal Victoria Cross." Simon was the first cat to win England's highest award for animal bravery.

SLIPPERS.   Gray six-toed cat belonging to Theodore Roosevelt (1858-1919), President of the United States, 1901-09. Slippers lived in the White House during the Roosevelt administration, and it is said he frequently disappeared for days at a time but always turned up for important occasions. Jacob Riis remarks in *Slippers: The White House Cat* that one evening after a glittering diplomatic dinner, Roosevelt, escorting the wife of an ambassador, led a procession of ambassadors, plenipotentiaries, and ministers from the state dining room to the East Room, when suddenly the group came to a halt:

> There on the rug, in the exact middle of the corridor, lay Slippers, stretched out at full length and blinking lazily at the fine show which no doubt he thought got up especially to do him honor. . . . With an amused bow, as if in apology to the Ambassadress, he [Roosevelt] escorted her round Slippers . . . whereupon the representatives of Great Britain, and of France, of Germany and Italy . . . followed suit.

SOUMISE and SERPOLET. Cats belonging to Armand Jean du Plessis, Duc de Richelieu, French cardinal and statesman.

SUGAR. Tomcat from Anderson, California, that became famous when he traveled more than fifteen hundred miles to reach Gage, Oklahoma, to be reunited with his owners. The determined cat took more than fourteen months to make the trip.

SYLVESTER. Character created by I. "Friz" Freleng (1906-   ) that appears in animated film and television cartoons. His voice is usually expressed by actor Mel Blanc.

TABBY. Cat belonging to Tad Lincoln, son of Abraham Lincoln (1809-65), President of the United States, 1861-65.

TABITHA LONGCLAWS TIDDLEYWINK. Cat belonging to Thomas Hood (1799-1845), English poet and humorist. Tabitha gave birth to three kittens, which were named Pepperpot, Scratchaway, and Sootikins.

TAMA. Tortoiseshell cat belonging to Lafcadio Hearn, American journalist, novelist, and essayist (see HINOKO).

TARAWOOD ANTIGONE. Brown Burmese owned by Mrs. Valerie Grane of Oxfordshire, England, that produced the largest recorded litter of kittens— one female, fourteen males, and four incompletely formed, on August 7, 1970.

THOMASINA. Fictional feline created by Paul Gallico (1897-1976) that first appeared in *Thomasina: The Cat Who Thought She Was God* (1957).

THUMPER. Record-holding Tabby owned by Mrs. R. Buckett of London. According to *The Guinness Book of World Records,* Thumper was trapped in an elevator shaft without food or water for fifty-two days in 1964.

TIBERIUS. Cat belonging to Giles Lytton Strachey (1880-1932), English biographer and literary critic. Tiberius was named after lines in Matthew Arnold's poem "Poor Matthias."

TIGER. Longhair belonging to Mrs. Phyllis Dacey of England. Tiger holds the record as the heaviest domestic cat of record, tipping the scales at forty-three pounds.

TIGER and BLACKY. Cats belonging to Calvin Coolidge (1872-1933), President of the United States, 1925-29. Margaret Truman mentions in *White House Pets* (New York: David McKay Co., 1969) that Tiger, a gray tabby, wandered onto the White House grounds through the iron fence. He lived in the White House for a while but eventually wandered off as abruptly as he had arrived. Blacky was an unwanted pet that was shipped to the President by a woman in Massachusetts.

TOBERMORY.   Fictional feline created by Saki (pen name of Hector Hugh Munro), Scottish short-story writer and novelist (see "The Cat in Literature," Chapter XIII).

TOKI.   Beloved companion of Raymond Chandler (1888-1959), American mystery writer; creator of the Philip Marlowe stories.

TOM.   Comic-book and animated cartoon cat of the Tom and Jerry adventures, created by Fred Quimby, William Hanna, and Joseph Barbera in 1939.

TOM KITTEN.   Cat belonging to Caroline Kennedy, daughter of John F. Kennedy (1917-63), President of the United States, 1961-63. Tom Kitten was raised in the Kennedy's Georgetown home and then moved to the White House after President Kennedy's inauguration.

TOM KITTEN.   Fictional character created by Beatrix Potter (1866-1943). The son of Mrs. Tabitha Twitchet, Tom Kitten made his first appearance in 1907 in *The Tale of Tom Kitten*.

TOMMY POST OFFICE.   Black and white resident cat of the Hartford, Connecticut, post office. Tommy's mother lived in a post office in New York City in the early 1900s. One night she tucked him into a mail pouch for safekeeping, and while she went to retrieve his four littermates, the sack was closed and shipped to Connecticut. When the pouch arrived at its destination twelve hours later, Tommy was miraculously still alive. Tommy spent his entire lifetime as an employee of the Hartford post office, catching mice and overseeing the handling of the mail.

TOM QUARTZ.   Cat belonging to Theodore Roosevelt. Tom Quartz, the successor to Slippers, was named after the large gray mining cat in Mark Twain's 1872 novel *Roughing It* (see SLIPPERS).

TONTO.   Fictional ginger tabby of *Harry and Tonto*, created by Josh Greenfield and Paul Mazursky. The story was made into a motion picture starring Art Carney, for which role Mr. Carney won the Academy Award as Best Actor in 1974.

WEBSTER.   Fictional cat created by P. G. Wodehouse (1881-1975), English writer.

WHITE HEATHER.   Persian belonging to Queen Victoria of England (1819-1901). White Heather lived at Buckingham Palace, and after Victoria's death was cared for by the surviving Royal Family. She was truly loved by King Edward VII.

WILLIAMINA.   White cat belonging to Charles Dickens, English novelist. She was originally named William, but when she produced a litter of kittens, her name was changed to Williamina.

WINDY.   "Swimming and flying" cat belonging to British Wing Commander Guy Gibson, V.C., 1943, Royal Air Force hero. Commander Gibson recorded that Windy has chalked up more flying hours than any other cat on record.

WINNIE.   Famous London cat that once lived in St. Paul's Cathedral, and was affectionately called "Winnie the Pooh." Winnie gave birth to several litters of kittens in the cathedral, which she would occasionally deposit in the pews during services.

ZIZI, ZOBEIDE, and ZULEIKA.   Cats belonging to Théophile Gautier, French novelist and critic, and described in his *La Nature chez elle et le ménagerie intime*, a delightful book about cats. Zizi, a silver gray Angora, was fond of music, according to Gautier. She would listen carefully, he writes, and then walk up and down the piano keyboard, trying to produce the sounds she had heard.

ZOROASTER.   Cat belonging to Mark Twain (see BEEL-ZEBUB and BLATHERSKITE).

XVI   Reference Material

Glossary of Feline Terms

ACA: American Cat Association (USA).

ACC: American Cat Council (USA).

ACFA: American Cat Fanciers Association (USA).

Ailurophile: A lover of cats.

Ailurophobe: One who dislikes or fears cats. Some famous ailurophobes include Alexander the Great, Julius Caesar, Napoleon, King Henry III of England, James Boswell, Oliver Goldsmith, and Voltaire.

Albino: Lack of pigmentation.

Almond: A term describing the eye shape in some breeds, especially the Siamese, Abyssinian, and Oriental Shorthairs.

Alter: To castrate a male or to spay a female cat; to neuter.

Anatomy: The structure of the cat's body.

Angora: One of the original varieties of long-haired cats found in Turkey. A name once used synonymously with Persian.

Balance: Overall symmetry of proportion.

Barring: The bracelet-like bands of color around the legs and tail of the Tabby coat pattern. A fault in self-colored cats.

Bi-color: A term describing a coat with patches of white and any other solid color.

Bite: The position of the upper and lower teeth when a cat's mouth is closed.

Blaze: A contrasting mark running from the forehead to the nose on a cat's face.

Blue: A coat color in many breeds of cats. It may range from pale gray to dark slate.

Break: A change in direction of the nose profile.

Breeder: One who breeds cats.

Brindling: An effect produced when hairs of incorrect color are scattered among those of correct color.

Brush: A term describing the full tail of a long-haired cat.

Butterfly: The shape of the pattern of markings on the shoulders of some Tabby cats.

Button: A patch of white or contrasting-colored hair anywhere on the body.

Calling: A term describing the cry of a female cat in heat.

Castrate: To remove the testicles of a male cat.

Cat fancy: A term describing persons interested in some phase of pure-breed cats.

Caterwauling: The mournful night cry of a cat.

Catnip: Catmint or *Nepeta cataria*. A plant of the mint family with strongly scented leaves that attract and excite cats.

Cattery: A place where cats are bred and housed.

CC: An abbreviation for Challenge Certificate. An award issued by the Governing Council of the Cat Fancy at United Kingdom shows.

CCA: Canadian Cat Association (Canada).

CCFF or *CROWN:* Crown Cat Fanciers Federation (USA).

CFA: Cat Fanciers' Association. The largest American association.

CFF: Cat Fanciers' Federation (USA).

Champion: A title used before the name of a cat designated as a Champion as a result of a certain number of wins under at least four different judges (*see also* Premier).

Classic: A term describing a Tabby coat pattern.

Cobby: A term used to describe short-coupled, deep-chested cats with short, sturdy legs that are square in appearance.

Condition: The general health as reflected in the cat's appearance and coat.

Conformation: The manner of formation; the arrangements of the cat's parts in accordance with its breed standard specifications.

Crossbreeding: The mating of two pure-breed cats of different varieties.

Cryptorchid: A male cat with neither testicle descended into the scrotum (*see also* Monorchid).

Dam: The female parent.

Declawing: A surgical procedure to remove a cat's claws.

Dentition: The number and arrangement of the teeth.

Dewclaw: The extra toe on the inside of the leg.

Dilute: A paler version of a standard feline color.

Disqualification: A condition that eliminates a cat's further competition in showing because of a defect specified under the standard for its breed.

Double coat: Two layers of hair: a soft, dense undercoat with a slightly longer and coarser outercoat.

Ear leather: The earflap or *pinna.*

Entire: A term describing a male cat with both testicles descended into the scrotum.

Estrus: The period of heat when the female accepts the male.

Exhibitor: One who shows cats.

Expression: The overall appearance of the features of the head when viewed from the front.

FCV: Feline calicivirus.

Felidae: The cat family.

Feline: Of or pertaining to the cat family; catlike.

Felis catus: The domestic cat.

FeLV: Feline leukemia virus.

FIA: Feline infectious anemia.

FIE: Feline infectious enteritis, also known as feline panleukopenia (FPL).

FIFE: Fédération Internationale Féline de l'Europe. An association of Austrian, Belgian, Danish, Dutch, Finnish, French, German, Italian, Norwegian, Swedish, and Swiss cat societies.

Foreign type: A term describing a distinct body type —a cat with long, svelte lines, a long, tapering tail, and a refined head, such as in the Siamese.

FPL: Feline panleukopenia (*see also* FIE).

Frill: The hair around the neck of long-haired cats that stands out and frames the face. Also called the "ruff."

Fur: The cat's hair covering.

FUS: Feline urological syndrome.

Gait: The way a cat moves.

GCCF: Governing Council of the Cat Fancy (UK).

Genetics: The study of heredity.

Gestation: The period of pregnancy; in the cat, generally about nine weeks.

Gloves: White paws of the Birman cat.

Grand Champion: A title attained by a Champion cat after it has won a number of Grand Ribbons by accumulating the required number of points in Best Champion competition.

Grand Premier: A title earned by neutered cats that is the equivalent of the title of Grand Champion for entire cats.

Grooming: Combing, brushing, or otherwise making a cat's coat neat.

Growling/Hissing: Vocal warning sounds made when a cat is angry or feels challenged by another cat or dogs. These are often accompanied by wailing, spitting, back arching, and fur standing on end.

Guard hair: The longer, coarser hairs that grow through the undercoat.

Hairball: An accumulation of hair swallowed by cats (especially longhairs) during self-grooming, which forms into a ball in the stomach or intestines.

Haw: The nictating membrane or third eyelid. This thin membrane unfolds from the inner corner and spreads horizontally across the cat's eye. It helps protect the eye and also to distribute tears to lubricate the cornea.

Heat: The female's season; the estrus.

Hot: A term describing too much red in the coat of a cream-colored cat.

Hybrid: The offspring of a cross between two different species or breeds.

Inbreeding: The breeding of two closely related cats, such as brother to sister or parent to offspring.

Infertile: Unable to breed.

Jowls: Well-developed cheeks.

Judge: A person qualified to give an opinion at a cat show.

Kink: A bend in the cat's tail caused by a malformation of several vertebrae.

Kitten: A cat eight months of age or younger in the United States; nine months or younger in the United Kingdom.

Kneading: The fluid up-and-down action of a cat's front paws against its mother's breast, a person, or a soft object. An expression of contentment.

Lactation: The production of milk in the female cat.

Level bite: The teeth of the upper and lower jaws meeting edge-to-edge when the mouth is closed.

Line breeding: The breeding of cats within a close family or line of descent to keep the progeny as closely related as possible to an exceptional ancestor. True line breeding, according to geneticists, involves matings no closer than first cousins.

Litter: (1) The kittens born to a queen after pregnancy; (2) shredded paper, sand, or commercial litter spread in a tray and used as a cat's toilet.

Locket: A white or contrasting-colored spot under the neck.

Mackerel: A term describing a Tabby coat pattern.

Mask: Darker facial coloring as seen in some cats, such as Siamese and Himalayans.

Monorchid: A male cat with one testicle descended into the scrotum and the other retained in the abdominal cavity (*see also* Cryptorchid).

Molt/moult: The periodic shedding of a cat's hair.

Mutation: A sudden departure from the parental type in one or more heritable characteristics caused by a change in a gene or chromosome.

Muzzle: The cat's nose and jaws.

Necklace: The chainlike markings on the neck and chest of Tabby cats.

Neuter: To castrate a male cat or to spay a female cat.

Nictating membrane: The haw or third eyelid (*see* Haw).

Nose leather: The skin at the end of a cat's nose.

Odd-eyed: Having one blue eye and one gold eye, ideally of equal color depth.

Ovario-hysterectomy: The surgical removal of the uterus and ovaries.

Overshot: The front teeth of the upper jaw extending beyond the front teeth of the lower jaw, when the mouth is closed.

Outcross: The mating of unrelated cats of the same breed.

Parti-color: Having a coat of two distinct colors.

Patched: A coat with patches of different coloring.

Paw pads: The cushiony underpart of the cat's paws.

Paws: The cat's feet.

Pedigree: A written record of the cat's ancestry.

Peke-faced: A cat with a head resembling a Pekingese dog: large round eyes, very short nose, indented between the eyes, and a broad and decidedly wrinkled muzzle.

Penciling: The delicate facial markings on Tabby cats.

Placenta: The membrane covering an unborn kitten, attached to the lining of its mother's uterus, through which it receives nourishment and eliminates waste.

Points: Darker coloring on the cat's extremities—mask, ears, paws, and tail. Also, a term used for the marks given in the standards of the various breeds.

Polydactylism: A condition in which a cat has six or more toes on the front feet and five or more toes on the hind feet.

Prefix: A registered cattery name used before the name of each cat bred by such establishment.

Premier: A title earned by neutered cats that is the equivalent of the title of Champion for entire cats.

Progeny: The offspring of a particular cat.

Purring: Rhythmic vibrations produced by the cat when it is contented and happy.

Queen: An unneutered female cat, especially one used for breeding purposes.

Register: To record a cat's name, date of birth, sex, and pedigree with an official registry association.

Ringed: Bands of darker color on the legs or tails of Tabby cats.

Ruff: *See* Frill.

Rumpy: A Manx cat with a well-rounded rump and no discernible tail.

Scruff: The loose skin at the back of a cat's neck.

Self-colored: The same color hair all over.

Sexing: Determining the sex of a kitten.

Shedding: *See* Molt/Moult.

Sire: The male parent.

Snub: A term describing the short noses seen on many long-haired varieties.

Spay: To neuter a female cat (*see also* Ovario-hysterectomy).

Spraying: A male cat's urination to mark his territory and possibly to attract females. This is a natural way of claiming territorial rights and can be compared to a dog lifting his leg in places where other dogs go.

Squint: When the eyes seem to look toward the nose and make the cat appear cross-eyed.

Standard: An enumeration of the essential qualities of the ideal of each recognized breed of cat, which serves as a written description by which cats are judged at shows.

Stripes: Markings on Tabby cats.

Stud: A male cat used for breeding purposes.

Stumpy: A Manx cat with a short tail stump, instead of being completely tailless.

Tangles: Mats that form in the hair (especially on longhairs), caused by neglect in brushing and combing.

TICA: The International Cat Association (USA).

Ticking: The bands of contrasting color seen on each hair shaft, especially on the Abyssinian.

Tipping: Contrasting color, usually darker, on the tips of the coats of certain breeds.

Tom: An unaltered male cat.

Tortie: Tortoiseshell.

Tri-color: Having a coat with three distinct colors.

Tufts: The wisps of hair growing from the ears or between the toes.

Type: The characteristics that distinguish and identify each breed; the embodiment of a standard's essentials.

UCF: United Cat Fanciers (USA).

Undercoat: The soft dense hair layer under the outercoat of a double-coated cat.

Undershot: The front teeth of the lower jaw extending beyond the front teeth of the upper jaw when the mouth is closed.

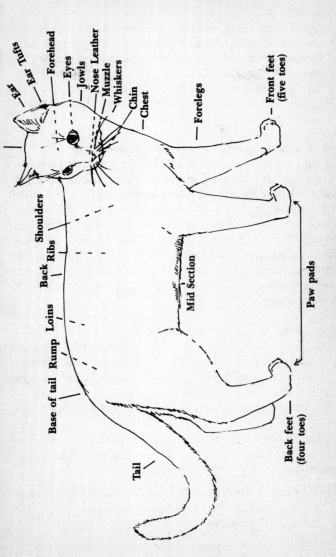

ANATOMY OF A CAT

Vibrissae: See Whiskers.

Wedge: A term describing the head shape of certain breeds, especially the Siamese.

Whiskers: The long, sensitive bristles growing out of the cat's muzzle.

Whip: A long, thin, and tapering tail.

Wrinkle: The loose folds of skin on the face of some varieties.

Free and Low-cost Literature About Cats

The following is a list of free or low-cost publications available to cat owners. Some of the material is offered by commercial companies, and readers may find those slightly promotional in nature. All materials are free unless otherwise indicated. Readers should keep in mind that the following organizations and companies are constantly revising, deleting, or adding publications to their list. Because prices are also subject to change, it is suggested that you inquire before ordering.

American Humane Association

Care of Cats. GI-1005	15 cents plus postage
Cat bookmark. HE-703b	3 cents plus postage
Cat care poster. HE-708b	25 cents plus postage
"It's Raining Cats and Dogs" color poster	40 cents plus postage

Request brochure listing special publications, operational guide, posters, flyers, bookmarks, and calendars.

Order from: American Humane Association
5351 South Roslyn Street
Englewood, CO 80111

American Humane Education Society/ Massachusetts Society for the Prevention of Cruelty to Animals

Cat Care book	50 cents
Angell Memorial Guide to Animal First Aid	60 cents
Animals and You: Handbook of Animal Activities for People	50 cents
AHES Guide to Animal-Related Career Resources	$1.25
Overpopulation—Causes, cures, and controversies associated with the millions of unwanted dogs and cats in the United States	25 cents

Request list of booklets, posters, teaching aids, calendars, and cards.

Order from: A.H.E.S Headquarters
450 Salem End Road
Framingham, MA 01701

American Society for the Prevention of Cruelty to Animals

ASPCA Guide to Pet Care	50 cents
Coloring Book	$1.50
Animals and Their Legal Rights	$2.25
Traveling with your Pet	$3.50
Thinking of Adopting a Cat?	English/Spanish
Your Cat, The Litter Bug— Housebreaking	English/Spanish
10 Easy Steps to Remember When Traveling with Your Pet	English/Spanish
Cold Weather Tips for your Pet	English/Spanish

Hot Weather Tips for your Pet　　English/Spanish
First Aid for Pets　　　　　　　English/Spanish
Humane Euthanasia—Why?
It's Raining Cats and Dogs—
　　Overpopulation

Request "Educational Resources Booklet" for a more extensive list of publications, films, T-shirts, and so forth. Include self-addressed stamped envelope.

Order from:　　ASPCA Education Department
　　　　　　　　441 East 92nd Street
　　　　　　　　New York, NY 10028

American Veterinary Medical Association

What You Should
　Know About:　　External Parasites
　　　　　　　　Feline Panleukopenia
　　　　　　　　Rabies
　　　　　　　　Traveling with Your Pet
Choose Your Pet:　Pethood or Parenthood
Today's Veterinarian
Your Career in Animal Technology

Single copies are free of charge when request is accompanied by a long, self-addressed stamped envelope. Request order form for multiple copies.

Order from:　　AVMA
　　　　　　　　930 North Meacham Road
　　　　　　　　Schaumburg, IL 60196

Animal Protection Institute of America

Cat Care Bookmarks	one free/100 for $1.00
How to Care for your Pets—chart covering basic care for 10 popular pets	1-24 copies $1.00 each
First Aid for Dogs and Cats	25 cents

Order from: Animal Protection Institute
P.O. Box 22505
Sacramento, CA 95822

Borden

The Borden Guide to the Care and Feeding of Orphan and Rejected Kittens	25 cents
Borden Kitten Weaning Formula (brochure)	
KMR Milk Replacer (brochure)	

Order from: Borden Inc.
Pet/Vet Products
R.R. #1, Box 127
Elgin, IL 60120

Boy Scouts of America

Pet Merit Badge pamphlet #3281	55 cents

Order from: Boy Scouts of America
Supply Division
North Brunswick, NJ 08902

California Veterinary Medical Association
  Infectious Disease in
    Dogs and Cats   English/Spanish
  Intestinal Worms
  Spay Me, Spay Me Not

Order from: CVMA
         1024 Country Club Drive
         Moraga, CA 94556

Calo Pet Foods
  "Love Your Cat" booklet

Order from: Calo Pet Foods
         Borden Foods, Inc.
         P.O. Box 388
         Allentown, PA 18105

Carnation/Friskies
  The Cat You Care For—Manual
    of cat care by Felicia Ames
    with 60 color photos by Walter
    Chandoha $1.50
  Care and Feeding of Your Cat
  My Cat's Health Record

Order from: Friskies Publications
         Carnation Company
         5045 Wilshire Blvd.
         Los Angeles, CA 90036

Fort Dodge Laboratories
Rabies Can Be Prevented

Order from: Fort Dodge Laboratories
800 Fifth Street, N.W.
Box 518
Fort Dodge, IA 50501

Gaines
Gaines Guide to America's Cats—25" x 38" color chart, folded copy $1.25

Dog and Cat Stamps Chart—rolled in a tube $2.50

Gaines Basic Guide to Collecting Dog and Cat Stamps $4.95

Order from: Gaines Booklets
P.O. Box 1007
Kankakee, IL 60902

Humane Society of the United States
Companion Animals—What it means to be a responsible pet owner. GR-3024. 10 cents

Unwanted Animals—How we can all help curb the pet population explosion. GR-3025 10 cents

Caring for Your Cat. HE-1011 20 cents
You and Your Pet. HE-1009 10 cents
Pet Care. HE-1010 20 cents

Minimum order $1.00. Request publications list of teaching aids, films, promotional materials, coloring books, and general reading.

Order from: Humane Society of the United States
                2100 L Street, N.W.
                Washington, DC 20037

ICN
  Hairballs! The instinct for good grooming can have
  some serious side effects.

Order from: ICN Pharmaceuticals
                Pet Care Products
                222 North Vincent Avenue
                Covina, CA 91722

Kal Kan
  Feeding Your Cat—A Matter of Nutrition
  The Nutrition Story (for cats)

Order from: Kal Kan Foods Inc.
                3386 East 44th Street
                Vernon, CA 90058

Missouri Veterinary Medical Association
  A Guide to the Care and
    Feeding of Your Cat   10 cents
  A Guide to the Care and
    Feeding of Your Aging Pet   10 cents

Order from: MVMA
                1221 Jefferson Street
                Jefferson City, MO 65101

North Carolina Veterinary Medical Association
Care of Your Feline Friend   20 cents

Order from: NCVMA
112 Johnston Street
Smithfield, NC 27577

Pet Food Institute
Basics of Cat and Kitten Care
How to Choose Your Four Footed Friends

Order from: Pet Food Institute
111 East Wacker Drive
Chicago, IL 60601

Ralston Purina
Handbook of Cat Care—76 page
booklet   50 cents

Order from: Ralston Purina Company
P.O. Box 552
Checkerboard Square
St. Louis, MO 63164

Tree House Animal Foundation
Allergic? You Can Have a Pet   25 cents
Help Me . . . I Found a Stray   25 cents
Household Dangers to Pets   25 cents
Cat Tales—A Beginner's Guide to
Feline Health, Care and Behavior   25 cents
Only You Can Prevent Pet
Overpopulation   25 cents

Charges cover printing and postage.

Order from: Tree House Animal Foundation
                P.O. Box 11174
                Chicago, IL 60611

Upjohn Veterinary Products
  Upjohn Pet Book

Order from: Upjohn Veterinary Products
                7171 Portage Road
                Kalamazoo, MI 49001

**Magazines, Periodicals, and Yearbooks of Interest to
  Cat Owners**
All-Cats
Suite 7
15113 Sunset Boulevard
Pacific Palisades, CA 90272

Abyssinian Cat Magazine
Donna Cross, Publisher
21106 River Road
Marengo, IL 60152

Animal News
2002 Fourth Avenue
Santa Rosa, CA 95404

Birman Cat Quarterly
Box 76297
Los Angeles, CA 90076

Cat Fanciers Association Yearbook
Marna Fogarty
Deer Lane
South Londonderry, VT 05155

Cat Fancy
Subscription Department
P.O. Box 2431
Boulder, CO 80322
(Excellent reading from Charlene Beane, Margaret Reister, DVM, and other feline experts.)

The Cat Lover
Box 889
Midtown Station
New York, NY 10018

Cat-Tab Newspaper
7700 Old Dominion Drive
McLean, VA 22101

Cat World
P.O. Box 127
Golden, CO 80401

Cats
Watmoughs Limited
Idle,
Bradford, West Yorkshire BD10 8NL, England

CATS Magazine
Subscription Department
P.O. Box 83048
Lincoln, NB 68501

(Expert advice from Susie Page, Donald Caslow, DVM, and other cat authorities.)

Feline Practice
Journal of Feline Medicine and Surgery for the Practitioner
Veterinary Practice Publishing Company
P.O. Box 4457
Santa Barbara, CA 93103

Himalayan World
Donna Andrews, Editor
1459 Cortez Lane, N.E.
Atlanta, GA 30319

Kind Magazine
Humane Society of the United States
2100 L Street, N.W.
Washington, DC 20037

The Manx Cat
Leslie Falteisek
623½ La Bore Road
Little Canada, MN 55117

The Persian Quarterly
Holfin Publishing Ltd.
5766 Old Wadsworth Blvd.
Arvada, CO 80002

Purrrrr!
The Newsletter for Cat Lovers
118 Massachusetts Avenue
Suite 187
Boston, MA 02115

The Siamese Quarterly
Holfin Publishing Ltd.
5766 Old Wadsworth Blvd.
Arvada, CO 80002

Cat Fancy Organizations

AMERICAN CAT ASSOCIATION
Susie Page, Secretary
10065 Foothill Blvd.
Lake View Terrace, CA 91342

AMERICAN CAT COUNCIL
Althea A. Frahm, Secretary
P.O. Box 662
Pasadena, CA 91102

AMERICAN CAT FANCIERS ASSOCIATION
Ed Rugenstein, Secretary
P.O. Box 203
Point Lookout, MO 65726

CANADIAN CAT ASSOCIATION
14 Nelson Street W., Suite 5
Brampton, Ontario, Canada L6X 1B7

CAT FANCIERS' ASSOCIATION
Walter A. Friend, Jr., President
1309 Allaire Avenue
Ocean, NJ 07712

CAT FANCIERS' FEDERATION
Barbara Haley, Recorder
9509 Montgomery Road
Cincinnati, OH 45242

CROWN CAT FANCIERS FEDERATION
Sister Vincent, Recorder
P.O. Box 34
Nazereth, KY 40048

THE INTERNATIONAL CAT ASSOCIATION
211 East Olive, Suite 208
Burbank, CA 91502

UNITED CAT FEDERATION
Davis Young, Secretary
6621 Thornwood Street
San Diego, CA 92111

FÉDÉRATION INTERNATIONALE FÉKUBE DE L'EUROPE
Friedrichstrasse 48
6200 Wiesbaden, West Germany

GOVERNING COUNCIL OF THE CAT FANCY
Dovefields
Petworth Road
Witley, Surrey GU8 5QU, England

FELINE ASSOCIATION OF SOUTH AUSTRALIA
P.O. Box 104
Stirling, South Australia 5152

NEW ZEALAND CAT FANCY INC.
P.O. Box 3167
Richmond, Nelson, New Zealand

Useful Addresses
American Animal Hospital Association
3612 East Jefferson
South Bend, Indiana 46615

American Anti-Vivisection Society
1903 Chestnut Street
Philadelphia, Pennsylvania 19103

American Boarding Kennels Association
311 North Union Boulevard
Colorado Springs, Colorado 80909

American Humane Association
5351 South Roslyn Street
Englewood, Colorado 80111

American Humane Education Society
450 Salem End Road
Framingham Center, Massachusetts 01701

American Society for the Prevention of Cruelty to
Animals
441 East 92nd Street
New York, New York 10028

American Veterinary Medical Association
930 North Meacham Road
Schaumburg, Illinois 60196

Animal Protection Institute
P.O. Box 22505
Sacramento, California 95822

Animal Welfare Institute
P.O. Box 3650
Washington, D. C. 20007

Bide-A-Wee Home Association
410 East 38th Street
New York, New York 10016

The Fund for Animals
140 West 57th Street
New York, New York 10019

Humane Society of the United States
2100 L Street, N.W.
Washington, D.C. 20037

International Association of Pet Cemeteries
27 West 150 North Avenue
West Chicago, Illinois 60185

Morris Animal Foundation
45 Inverness Drive East
Englewood, Colorado 80112

National Anti-Vivisection Society
100 East Ohio Street
Chicago, Illinois 60611

Pet Food Institute
1101 Connecticut Avenue, N.W.
Washington, D.C. 20035

Pet Pride
15113 Sunset Boulevard
Pacific Palisades, California 90272

Tree House Animal Foundation, Inc.
P.O. Box 11174
Chicago, Illinois 60611

Foreign:

Cats Protection League
29 Church Street
Slough, Berks. SL1 1PW, England

Feline Advisory Bureau
6 Woodthorpe Road
London SW15 6UQ, England

Petcare Information/Advisory Service
254 George Street
Sydney, New South Wales, Australia

Pet Health Council
418-422 The Strand
London, WC2R 0PL, England

Royal Society for the Prevention of Cruelty to Animals
The Manor House
Horsham, Sussex RH12 1HG, England

Society for the Prevention of Cruelty to Animals
Wellington, New Zealand.

Bibliography of the Cat
Behavior and Training

Beadle, Muriel. *The Cat*. New York: Simon and Schuster, 1977.

Beaver, Bonnie, DVM, M.S. *Veterinary Aspects of Feline Behavior*. St. Louis: The C. V. Mosby Company, 1980.

Fox, Michael, Dr. *Understanding Your Cat*. New York: Coward, McCann & Geoghegan, 1974.

Hafez, E. S. E. *The Behavior of Domestic Animals*. Third Edition. London: Bailliere Tindall; Philadelphia: Lea & Febiger, 1975.

Leyhausen, Paul. *Cat Behavior: The Predatory and Social Behavior of Domestic and Wild Cats*. New York: Garland STPM Press, 1979.

Loeb, Jo, and Loeb, Paul. *You Can Train Your Cat*. New York: Simon and Schuster, 1977.

Lorenz, Konrad, and Leyhausen, Paul. *Motivation of Human and Animal Behavior*. New York: Van Nostrand Reinhold, 1973.

Manolson, Dr. Frank, and Hardy, David. *Living With Your Cat*. New York: The Viking Press, 1978.

Mellen, Ida M. *The Science and the Mystery of the Cat*. New York: Charles Scribner's Sons, 1940.

Moyes, Patricia. *How to Talk to Your Cat*. New York: Holt, Rinehart & Winston, 1978.

Pond, Grace, and Sayer, Angela. *The Intelligent Cat*. New York: Dial Press/James Wade, 1978.

Thomas, Bernice. *The Truth About Cats*. New York: E. P. Dutton, 1979.

Wilbourn, Carole C. *Cats on the Couch*. New York: Macmillan, 1982. (Behavior/training plus a complete guide for caring for a cat.)

Wilbourn, Carole C. *Cat Talk: What Your Cat Is Trying to Tell You*. New York: Macmillan, 1979.

Wilbourn, Carole C. *The Inner Cat: A New Approach to Cat Behavior*. New York: Stein & Day, 1978.

Breeding and Reproduction

Manolson, Frank, DVM. *My Cat's in Love*. New York: St. Martin's Press, 1970.

Folklore/Religion/Myths/Occult

Dale-Green, Patricia. *Cult of the Cat*. New York: Barre Publishing Co., Weathervane Books, 1963.

Howey, M. Oldfield. *The Cat in the Mysteries of Religion and Magic*. New York: Castle Books, 1950.

Leach, Maria. *The Lion Sneezed (Folktales and Myths of the Cat)*. New York: Thomas Y. Crowell Company, 1977.

Grooming and Showing

Meins, Betty, and Floyd, Wanita. *How To Groom Your Cat*. Neptune City, N.J.: TFH Publications, 1972.

Meins, Betty, and Floyd, Wanita. *How to Show Your Cat*. Neptune City, N.J.: TFH Publications, 1972.

Wilson, Meredith D. *Showing Your Cat*. Cranbury, N.J.: A. S. Barnes & Co., 1974.

Health Care/Nutrition/First Aid

Burden, Jean. *The Woman's Day Book of Hints for Cat Owners*. New York: Fawcett Columbine, 1980.

Catcott, E. J., DVM. *Feline Medicine and Surgery*. Second Edition. Santa Barbara, Calif.: American Veterinary Publications, Inc., 1975.

Curtis, Patricia. *The Indoor Cat*. Garden City, N.Y.: Doubleday and Co. 1981.

Frazier, Anitra, and Eckroate, Norma. *The Natural Cat*. San Francisco: Harbor Publishing, 1981. (Also contains excellent grooming advice.)

Gerstenfeld, Sheldon L., DVM. *Taking Care of Your Cat*. Reading, Mass.: Addison-Wesley Publishing Co., 1979.

Green, Martin I. *The Home Pet Vet Guide—Cats*. New York: Ballantine Books, 1980.

Harper, Joan. *The Healthy Cat and Dog Cook Book*. New York: E. P. Dutton, 1979.

Johnson, Norman H., DVM, with Galin, Saul. *The Complete Kitten and Cat Book*. New York: Harper & Row, 1979.

Joshua, Joan O. *Cat Owner's Encyclopedia of Veterinary Medicine*. Neptune City, N.J.: TFH Publications, 1977.

Kirk, Robert W., DVM. *First Aid for Pets*. New York: E. P. Dutton, A Sunrise Book, 1978.

Kirk, Robert W., DVM, Editor. *Current Veterinary Therapy (VI)*. Philadelphia: W. B. Saunders Company, 1977.

Kirk, Robert W., DVM, and Bistner, Stephen, DVM. *Handbook of Veterinary Procedures and Emergency Treatment*. Second Edition. Philadelphia: W. B. Saunders Company, 1975.

Lewis, Lon D., DVM, Ph.D. *F.U.S. A Commentary on the Nutritional Management of Small Animals*. Topeka, Kans.: Mark Morris Associates, 1981.

Loeb, Jo, and Loeb, Paul. *Cathletics: Ways to Amuse and Exercise Your Cat*. Englewood Cliffs, N.J.: Prentice-Hall, 1981.

McDonough, Dr. Susan, with Lawson, Bryna. *The Complete Book of Questions Cat Owners Ask Their Vet, and Answers*. Philadelphia: Running Press, 1980.

McGinnis, Terri, DVM. *Dog and Cat Good Food Book*. San Francisco: Taylor & Ng, 1977.

McGinnis, Terri, DVM. *The Well Cat Book*. San Francisco: The Bookworks; New York: Random House, 1975.

Morris, Mark L., Jr., DVM, Ph.D. *Feline Dietetics. Nutritional Management in Health and Disease*. Topeka, Kans.: Mark Morris Associates, 1977.

Morris, Mark L., Jr., DVM, Teeter, Stanley M., DVM, and Doering, George C., DVM. *The Guide to Nutri-

tional Management of Small Animals. Topeka, Kans.: Mark Morris Associates, 1980.

Page, Susie. *Let's Talk Cats*. Brattleboro, Vt: The Stephen Greene Press, 1980.

Powell, Jean. *Good Food for Your Cat*. Secaucus, N.J.: Citadel Press, 1981.

Randolph, Elizabeth. *How to Be Your Cat's Best Friend*. Boston: Little, Brown and Company, 1981.

Rubin, Sheldon, DVM, and the editors of *Consumer Guide*. *Emergency First Aid for Cats*. New York: Crown Publishers, Beekman House, 1981.

Siegal, Mordecai. *The Good Cat Book*. New York: Simon and Schuster, 1981.

Siegmund, O. H. *The Merck Veterinary Manual*. Fourth Edition. Rahway, N.J.: Merck & Company, 1973.

Tottenham, Katharine. *Looking After Your Cat*. New York: Arco Publishing, 1981.

Vine, Louis L. *Common Sense Book of Complete Cat Care*. New York: William Morrow & Co., 1978.

Wright, Michael, and Walters, Sally, Editors. *The Book of the Cat*. New York: Summit Books, 1980. (Also contains a superbly illustrated section on the breeds.)

History (Early)

Clutton-Brock, Juliet. *Domesticated Animals from Early Times*. London: British Museum (Natural History). Austin: University of Texas Press, 1981.

Ewer, R. F. *The Carnivores*. Ithaca, N.Y.: Cornell University Press, 1973.

History/Literature/Art

Artley, Alexandra. *The Great All-Picture Cat Show*. London: Astragal Books, 1977.

Currah, Ann. *The Cat Compendium*. New York: Meredith Press, 1969.

De Lys, Claudia, and Rhudy, Frances. *Centuries of Cats*. Norwalk, Conn.: Silvermine Publishers, 1971.

Grilhé, Gillette. *The Cat and Man*. New York: G. P. Putnam's Sons, 1974.

Hamilton, Elizabeth. *Cats: A Celebration*. New York: Charles Scribner's Sons, 1979.

Kirk, Mildred. *The Everlasting Cat*. Woodstock, N.Y.: The Overlook Press, 1977.

MacBeth, George, and Booth, Martin, Editors. *The Book of Cats*. New York: William Morrow & Co., 1977.

Marks, Anne. *The Cat in History, Legend, and Art*. London: Eliot Stock, 1909.

Mery, Fernand. *The Life, History and Magic of the Cat*. New York: Grosset & Dunlap, 1975.

Necker, Claire. *The Natural History of Cats*. New York: Dell Publishing Company, 1977. (Contains fascinating chapters on behavior.)

Suarès, J. C., and Chwast, Seymour. *The Literary Cat*. New York: Push Pin Press/Berkley Wendover Books, 1977.

Suarès, Jean-Claude, and Chwast, Seymour. *The Illustrated Cat*. New York: Push Pin Press/Harmony Books, 1976.

Van Vechten, Carl. *The Tiger in the House*. New York: Alfred A. Knopf, 1920. (A classic work, containing an extensive bibliography of cat books published before 1920.)

Miscellaneous: Breed Guides, Yearbooks, Encyclopedias

Brearley, Joan McDonald. *All About Himalayan Cats*. Neptune City, N.J.: TFH Publications, 1976.

Cat Fanciers' Association, Inc. *Show Standards—May*

1982 to April 1983. Ocean, N.J.: Cat Fanciers' Association, Inc.

Cat Fanciers' Association, Inc. *Show Rules, May 1980*. Red Bank, N.J.: Cat Fanciers' Association, Inc.

Eustace, May. *100 Years of Siamese Cats*. New York: Charles Scribner's Sons, 1978.

Firestone, Judy, Editor. *Cat Catalog*. New York: Workman Publishing Company, 1976.

Fogarty, Marna. *The Cat Fanciers' Association Annual Yearbook*, 1976, 1977, 1978, 1979, 1980, 1981. Red Bank, N.J.: Cat Fanciers' Association, Inc.

Gebhart, Richard H., Pond, Grace, and Raleigh, Dr. Ivor. *A Standard Guide to Cat Breeds*. New York: McGraw-Hill Book Company, 1979.

Ing, Catherine, and Pond, Grace. *Champion Cats of the World*. New York: St. Martin's Press, 1972.

Lauder, Phyllis. *The Siamese Cat*. New York: Charles Scribner's Sons, 1971.

Loxton, Howard. *Guide to the Cats of the World*. Oxford, England: Elsevier Phaidon/Phaidon Press Ltd., 1975.

Naples, Marge. *This Is the Siamese Cat*. Second Edition. Neptune City, N.J.: TFH Publications, 1978.

Pond, Grace. *The Complete Cat Encyclopedia*. New York: Crown Publishers, 1972.

Ramsdale, Jeanne. *Persian Cats and Other Longhairs*. Neptune City, N.J.: TFH Publications, 1976.

Richards, Dorothy Silkstone. *A Cat of Your Own*. Tucson, Ariz.: HP Books, 1982.

Sayer, Angela. *The Encyclopedia of the Cat*. London: Octopus Books, 1979.

Steeh, Judith A. *The Complete Book of Cats*. New York: A & W Publishers, Galahad Books, 1978.

Wilson, Meredith. *An Encyclopedia of American Cat Breeds*. Neptune City, N.J.: TFH Publications, 1978.

Wolfgang, Harriet. *Shorthaired Cats*. Neptune City, N.J.: TFH Publications, 1976.

A dealer who specializes in out-of-print and antiquarian cat books is:

> The Cat Book Center
> Box 112, Wykagyl Station
> New Rochelle, New York 10804

Things Some People Know and Some Things They Don't

Cats are different breeds accordin to their dispositions. Cats thats made for little boys and girls to maul and tease is called Maltease Cats. Some Cats is known by their queer purs, - these is called Pursian Cats. Though most Cats is kind unles molested, some ain't - Cats with very bad tempers is called Angorrie Cats. Sometimes a very fine Cat is called a Magnificat. In tropic lands the Cat is called a Popocatapelt. Cats with deep feelins is called Feline Cats.

Oh yes, I almost forgot. What is it that walks like a Cat and has a tail like a Cat and makes noise like a Cat and looks jest like a Cat but it ain't a Cat? It's a kitten.

Uncle Ben's Great Grandfather used to tell him one every once in a while, - why is Cats like poor surgeons? Cause they mew-til-late and destroy patience. Then there wuz another that Uncle Ben says he wuz brought up on, - why are Cats' tails like eternity? Cause they're fur to the end.

—Anthony H. Euwer,
Christopher Cricket on Cats (1909)

Index

Italics indicate pages with illustrations.